Urban Growth and Spatial Transition in Nepal

DIRECTIONS IN DEVELOPMENT
Countries and Regions

Urban Growth and Spatial Transition in Nepal

An Initial Assessment

Elisa Muzzini and Gabriela Aparicio

THE WORLD BANK
Washington, D.C.

Contents

Boxes

Figures

Maps

Tables

Foreword

Nepal is undergoing two momentous transformations—from a rural to an urbanizing economy and from a unitary to a federal state. This book aims at understanding the first of these two transitions: Nepal's journey toward becoming a predominantly urban economy. Nepal is urbanizing rapidly—the Kathmandu Valley is one of the fastest-growing metropolitan regions in South Asia, and small towns are mushrooming in proximity to highways and on the border with India. At this critical juncture of Nepal's economic development, managing rapid urbanization is essential to improving the competitiveness of the urban economy, creating jobs, and accelerating economic growth. This growth will ultimately lead to reduced poverty.

The study carries out an initial assessment of Nepal's transition from a predominantly rural to an urbanizing economy. This assessment aims at strengthening our understanding of the demographic and economic dimensions of the transition, and exploring the links between urbanization and economic growth in the context of Nepal.

This book has five chapters. Chapter 1 presents an overview of the urban and economic transition in Nepal. Chapter 2 discusses the spatial patterns of Nepal's rapid urbanization and internal migration—a driving force of urban change—from both a demographic and an economic perspective. Chapter 3 presents an initial assessment of the challenges facing Nepal's cities in urban planning and the delivery of infrastructure and services. And it discusses the spatial distribution of public expenditure for local infrastructure based on the results of a public expenditure survey carried out as part of the study. Chapter 4 presents a scoping assessment of the growth drivers of Nepal's urban economies and the main constraints to turning these comparative advantages into competitive advantages. And chapter 5 draws the main conclusions and proposes strategic directions and actions to accelerate urban-based economic growth and foster sustainable urban development.

This initial assessment relies primarily on existing data sources and stakeholder consultations. The demographic analysis of the spatial transition is based on the population census statistics, including the 2011 Population and Housing Census data. The migration analysis relies on the latest data from Labor Force Surveys. The spatial economy analysis largely draws on the last two rounds of the Census of Manufacturing data made available for the study by the Nepal Central

Bureau of Statistics. This initial assessment of the status of infrastructure and service delivery is based on data from population censuses, Nepal Living Standard Surveys, and Labor Force Surveys. A public expenditure survey of central agencies and local governments has been undertaken to collect data on municipal infrastructure capital expenditure. The book also reflects the priorities that emerged during the consultations with central-government agencies, municipalities, and development partners as part of the study.

We hope this book will encourage and stimulate evidence-based dialogue on Nepal's urban transition and assist those working on the country's economic development—the decision makers in government, the private sector, civil society, and development partners—in framing policies and interventions for seizing the benefits and addressing the challenges of rapid urbanization.

Tahseen Sayed,
Country Manager for Nepal

Acknowledgments

This report has been prepared by a team led by Elisa Muzzini, Senior Economist in the South Asia Urban and Water Unit of the World Bank, and that included Gabriela Aparicio, Ph.D. student at Georgetown University and former Junior Professional Associate at the World Bank; Katrinka Ebbe, consultant; Santiago Guerrero, consultant; Eric Hansen, consultant and President of the Economic Transformations Group; Edward Leman, consultant and President of Chreod Ltd.; Pawan Lohani, consultant; Viviana Mora, consultant; Geoffrey Read, consultant; Tanya Savrimootoo, consultant; and Silva Shrestha, Water Supply and Sanitation Specialist in the South Asia Urban and Water Unit of the World Bank; with contributions from Gianni Brizzi, John Bowers, Mario de Filippo, and Gyan Pradhan. Overall support to the team was provided by Kalyan Nemkul. The study was prepared under the direction of Ellen Goldstein, formerly the Country Director for Bangladesh and Nepal; Tahseen Sayed, Country Manager for Nepal; and Ming Zhang, Sector Manager for the South Asia Urban and Water Unit. The team benefited from the advice and comments of Gayatri Acharya, Roshan Bajracharya, Bill Kingdom, Bala Menon, Ceren Ozer, Anil Pokhrel, Hisanobu Shishido, Trishna Thapa, Rajib Upadhya, Laura Anne Watson, and Johannes Widmann. The team is grateful for the helpful comments from peer reviewers Gabi Afram, Tony Bigio, and Forhad Shilpi. The team would like to thank the Ministry of Urban Development and the Ministry of Federal Affairs and Local Development for their collaborative efforts and support to the study, and the Central Bureau of Statistics of Nepal for making data and information available for the study. The team benefited from the valuable comments from the participants of the Urban Dialogue consultations and workshop held in April 2012 in Kathmandu, especially from Dr. Mahendra Subba, Director General, and Mr. G.P. Gorkhaly, Deputy Director General of the Department of Urban Development and Building Construction at the Ministry of Urban Development. The team also thanks the following agencies for providing useful information and insights for the study: the Department of Archeology in the Ministry of Culture, Tourism and Civil Aviation; the Federation of Nepalese Chambers of Commerce and Industry; the Federation of Handicraft Associations of Nepal; the Kathmandu Valley Water Supply Management Board; the High Powered Committee for the Integrated Development of the Bagmati Civilization; the Solid Waste Management Technical Center; the Nepal Tourism Board;

UNESCO (United Nations Educational, Scientific, and Cultural Organization); GIZ, Nepal office; the Asian Development Bank; Habitat for Humanity, Nepal office; and the agencies and local authorities that participated in the infrastructure capital expenditure survey. The study benefited from financial support from the Australian Agency for International Development (AusAID) through the World Bank–AusAID Policy Facility for Decentralization and Service Delivery and the World Bank–AusAID South Asia Infrastructure for Growth Initiative.

Abbreviations

DoA	Department of Archeology
DUDBC	Department of Urban Development and Building Construction
DWSS	Department of Water Supply and Sewerage
EU	European Union
GDP	gross domestic product
HPCIDBC	High Powered Committee for the Integrated Development of the Bagmati Civilization
Nr	Nepalese rupee
NUP	National Urban Policy
PMZ	protected monument zone
SAARC	South Asian Association for Regional Cooperation
SEZ	special economic zone
TIA	Tribhuvan International Airport
UNESCO	United Nations Educational, Scientific, and Cultural Organization
US$	U.S. dollar
VDC	village development committee

Overview

Urbanization and Growth

Nepal is both the least urbanized country in South Asia, with about 17 percent of its population living in urban areas, and the fastest-urbanizing country, with an average urban population growth rate of about 6 percent per year since the 1970s (UNDESA 2012). The spatial demographic transition has been accompanied by an equally important spatial economic transformation. Urban areas now generate about 62 percent of gross domestic product (GDP), according to the latest available estimates, compared with only 28 percent of GDP in 1975 (World Bank 2011b). The urban economy is growing significantly faster than the rural economy, and the incidence of poverty has decreased in urban areas from 22 percent to 15 percent over the period from 1995/96 to 2010/11 (CBS 1996, 2011).

Yet urbanization has historically been less correlated with economic growth in Nepal than in other countries in South Asia. Economic growth has slowed down in the past decade: annual real GDP growth averaged 3.8 percent over the last 10 years, compared with 7.5 percent in India, Nepal's main trading partner, and is well below the government of Nepal's real GDP growth target of 5.5 percent per year (Government of Nepal 2010c). The pace of the structural transformation of the economy has also been relatively slow. Nepal is among the poorest countries in the world, with a per capita GDP of US$619 (2011 prices). Overall, agriculture still contributes more than one-third of Nepal's GDP (38 percent), compared with about 22 percent in Pakistan, 18 percent in Bangladesh, 17 percent in India, and 14 percent in Sri Lanka (World Bank 2011b).

Political instability, an unfavorable business climate for private sector development, and an internationally uncompetitive and remittance-dependent economy have suppressed economic growth. Urbanization has taken place amid a conflict-ridden environment, and the country is caught in a prolonged period of political instability, which, together with weak infrastructure and labor market failures, is still perceived as the main constraint for private sector development (Afram and Salvi Del Pero 2012). Local elections have not been held in Nepal since 1997.[1] The lack of economic stimuli, combined with political instability, has resulted in a mass exodus of the Nepalese productive workforce out of the country, and Nepal's growth is becoming increasingly reliant on highly volatile external remittance flows rather than internal competitiveness. High remittances have, in turn, exposed Nepal to the risks of Dutch Disease, thereby leading to a decline in international competitiveness (World Bank 2011a). The overwhelming majority of private enterprises in Nepal are nonexporters, and despite some positive signs of recovery in the years following the end of the conflict, private investments remain low (Afram and Salvi Del Pero 2012).

Nepal needs to break the cycle of economic stagnation and meet its GDP growth target. Achieving the government's GDP growth target of 5.5 percent per year would require broadening the base of economic activity and job creation in urban areas, which are the main contributors to GDP growth. This effort in turn calls for tapping into the potential of Nepal's cities to turn their comparative advantages into competitive advantages. Only vibrant and competitive cities can attract high-return investments and generate the higher-productivity jobs required to accelerate growth to meet the government of Nepal's target.

The Spatial Transition

Nepal's demographic transformation is characterized by fast-growing population density in the Kathmandu Valley, along the main highways, and close to the border with India. While overall population growth has slowed since 2001, urban population growth has kept its pace at 3.4 percent per year from 2001 to 2011, compared with 3.6 percent per year from 1991 to 2001 (reclassification—that is, the conversion of rural areas to urban areas—excluded). Kathmandu Metropolitan City (hereafter, Kathmandu)—the only urban center in Nepal with a population above 1 million—is growing at 4.0 percent per year, medium cities (100,000–300,000) at 3.5 percent, and small cities (50,000–100,000) at 3.6 percent.[2] Pokhara in the Central Hills is the largest and fastest-growing medium city, with growth above 5 percent per year. Three medium cities have also sustained population growth in excess of 4 percent per year: Bharatpur (148,000) in the Central Tarai, Butwal (120,000) in the Western Tarai, and Dhangadhi (104,000) in the Far Western Tarai. A number of small urban growth centers are emerging along the main highways of the country and close to the border with India. The fastest-growing urban settlements, with populations below 100,000 and growth in excess of 4 percent, include Damak and Itahari (Eastern Tarai); Banepa (Central Hills); Byas and Tansen (Western Hills); Gorahi and Tulsipur (Midwestern Tarai); and Birendranagar (Midwestern Hills) (see map O.1; CBS 2001, 2012).

Rapid urbanization has transformed the Kathmandu Valley into one of the fastest-growing metropolitan regions in South Asia. The Kathmandu Valley is an urban system anchored on a core city surrounded by suburban areas and satellite cities and towns whose economies are becoming highly integrated. The Kathmandu Valley accounts for about one-third of the country's urban population and continues to sustain a fast pace of population growth at about 4.3 percent per year. The valley is characterized by high and sustained population growth in the urban core and fast urban sprawling at the periphery.

Map O.1 Development Regions, Corridors, and Urban Centers, 2011 Population

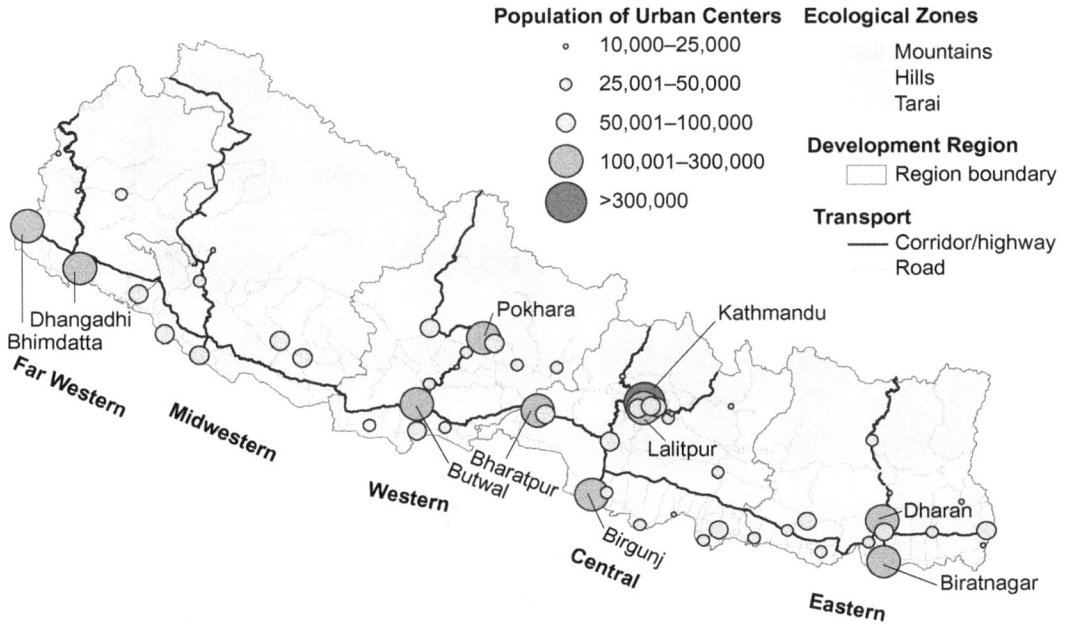

Population of Urban Centers
- ° 10,000–25,000
- ○ 25,001–50,000
- ○ 50,001–100,000
- ● 100,001–300,000
- ● >300,000

Ecological Zones
- Mountains
- Hills
- Tarai

Development Region
- Region boundary

Transport
- —— Corridor/highway
- Road

Source: Based on 2011 population census data (CBS 2012).
Note: Kathmandu refers to Kathmandu Metropolitan City; Biratnagar, Birgunj, Lalitpur, and Pokhara refer to the submetropolitan cities; and all other urban local governments are referred to as municipalities.

Kathmandu—the largest urban settlement in the valley, comprising 40 percent of the valley's population—has recorded a population growth rate of over 4 percent since the late 1970s (see figure O.1). The boundaries of the Kathmandu Valley's urban agglomeration are also rapidly expanding as a result of urban sprawl. Population growth is very high in the peripheral municipalities of Kirtipur (5.0 percent per year) and Madhyapur Thimi (5.7 percent per year) and in the peri-urban areas officially classified as rural space, where population growth reached 4.8 percent per year from 2001 to 2011. The Kathmandu Valley is one of the fastest-growing urban agglomerations in South Asia. The urban population in the Kathmandu Valley continues to grow at an annual rate of about 3.9 percent per year. By comparison, the Dhaka City Corporation, the urban core of the Dhaka metropolitan area and one of the largest Asian megacities, is growing at about 3.0 to 3.5 percent per year, according to 2010 population survey data (World Bank, forthcoming).

The conversion of rural space into urban space is an important contributor to urban growth. Reclassification accounted for 50 percent of total urban growth from 1991 to 2001, and the urban population growth rate from 1991 to 2001 almost doubles from 3.6 percent to 6.5 percent when reclassification is included. Forty-one new municipalities have been proposed for conversion to urban local governments. The establishment of these new municipalities, when effective, will

Figure O.1 Population and Annual Population Growth Rate of Kathmandu Metropolitan City, 1950–2025

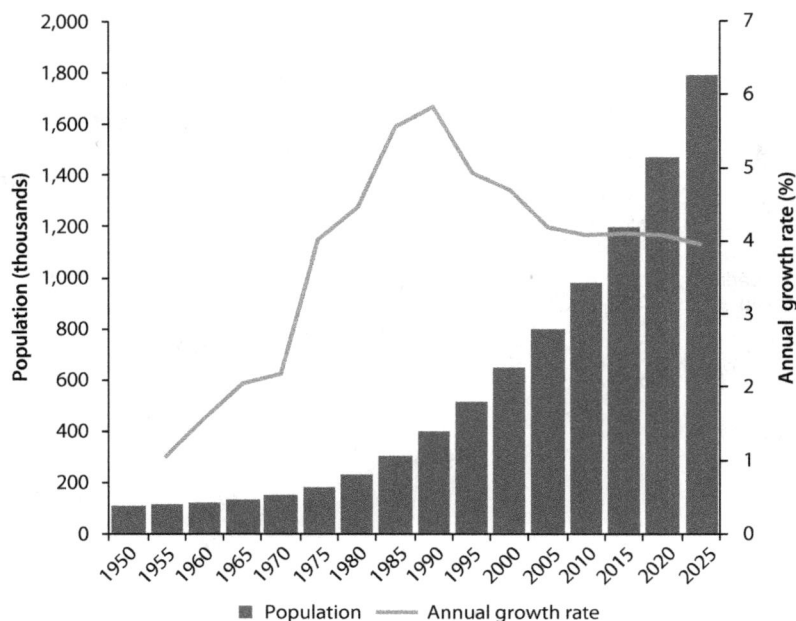

Source: Based on UNDESA 2012.

result in an increase in the proportion of population residing in urban areas by 4 percentage points, from 17 to 21 percent.

On the ground, the spatial transformation is not fully captured by the politico-administrative definition of urban areas. On one hand, a number of emerging towns with urbanlike characteristics continue to grow under the radar. On the other hand, a number of urban settlements contain large areas of land with rural characteristics. The disconnect between urban geography and the politico-administrative definition of urban areas is the result of Nepal's legal definition of urban settlements overemphasizing the role of population size, while assigning little weight to other urban criteria, such as population density and economic structure of urban areas.

The contribution of migration to urbanization is important and is increasing.[3] Migration is a powerful force for urban change: a net inflow of migrants to urban areas is balanced by a net outflow from rural areas, and urban areas are becoming more common migration destinations—34 percent of recent migrants[4] moved to urban areas, compared with 23 percent of lifetime migrants.

The number of migrants who move for economic reasons is growing; they are willing to travel longer distances and tend to settle in urban areas. Economic migration has gained importance as a livelihood strategy in recent years: pull factors (that is, the search for better employment and education opportunities) account for 43 percent of recent urban migration, compared with 32 percent of lifetime urban migration. Migration in search of job opportunities or for study and training purposes is more prevalent in urban areas; pull factors account for 32 percent of lifetime migration to urban areas but only 8 percent of lifetime migration to rural areas. Moreover, migrants who move for economic reasons are willing to travel longer distances. As many as 44 percent of nonlocal migrants to urban areas moved in search of jobs or for study purposes, compared with only 28 percent of local migrants to urban areas (CBS 1999, 2009).

The Central Region—where the Kathmandu Valley is located—is the largest gravity center for long-distance migration. Although physical distance is a barrier to internal mobility and constrains the majority of migrants to move locally, those who are able to afford long-distance migration move to the one location in Nepal where economic opportunities are greatest—the Central Region. About 20 percent of lifetime migrants in the Central Region are from a different region, compared with only 6 percent and 8 percent of lifetime migrants in the Eastern and Western Regions, respectively (see figure O.2). Kathmandu has the largest net inflow of migrants among urban areas (ADB 2010), and more and more migrants are pulled to the Kathmandu Valley by economic opportunities: about half the recent migrants to the valley moved for job-related reasons, compared with 25 percent of lifetime migrants.

Nonfarm economic production is clustered in the Kathmandu Valley and close to the border with India—the Eastern Tarai cluster surrounding Biratnagar and the Central Tarai cluster surrounding Birgunj. These clusters function as extended economic regions; they comprise a core urban center surrounded by a

Figure O.2 Regional Migration Patterns by Origin and Destination, Lifetime Migration, 2008

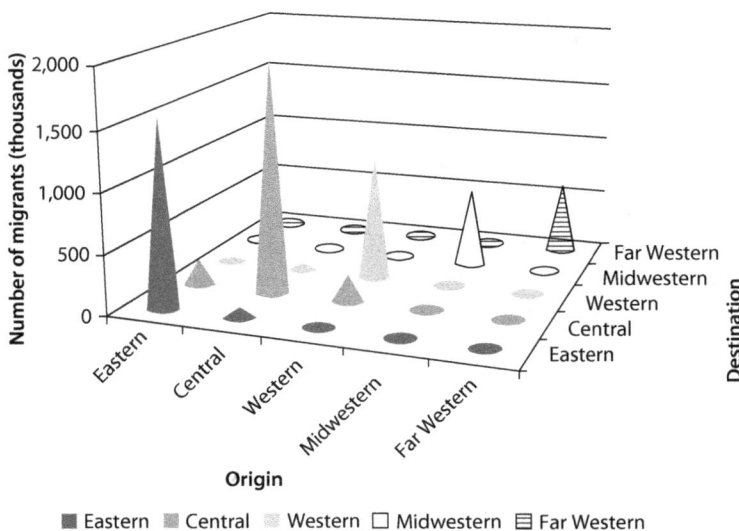

Source: Based on Labor Force Survey 2008 (CBS 2009).

Map O.2 Manufacturing Output Density, 2007

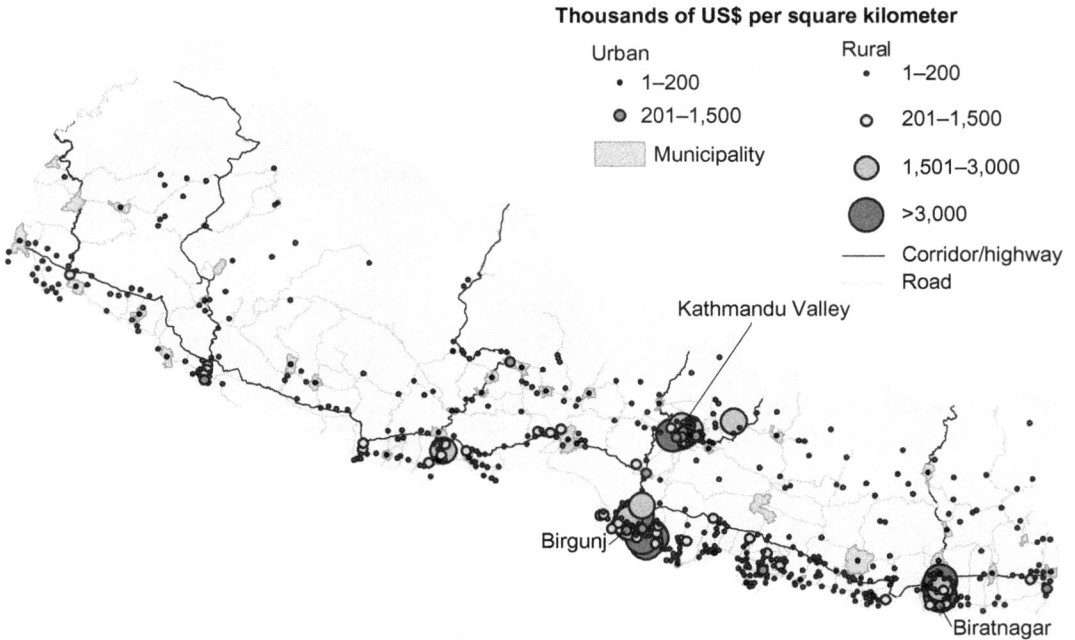

Thousands of US$ per square kilometer

Urban	Rural
• 1–200	• 1–200
◉ 201–1,500	○ 201–1,500
� Municipality	◎ 1,501–3,000
	⬤ >3,000
	—— Corridor/highway
	Road

Kathmandu Valley

Birgunj

Biratnagar

Source: Based on Census of Manufacturing 2007 (CBS 2007).
Note: Analysis includes firms with more than 10 employees. Biratnagar and Birgunj refer to the submetropolitan cities.

hinterland of small towns and rural areas. Within such extended regions, firms are able to reap the benefits from demand-and-supply links between rural and urban areas (see map O.2). The urban core of the extended economic region plays the role of service center for the rural hinterland, where manufacturing largely takes place, because services and manufacturing activities tend to locate near each other to benefit from agglomeration economies.

A new government industrial policy went into effect in 2010 with the objective of increasing employment opportunities while promoting industrial growth. The 2010 industrial policy provides fiscal incentives and facilitation measures for industrial development and serves as an important stepping stone toward implementation of special economic zones (SEZs). Among the fiscal incentives for industrial growth, the 2010 industrial policy includes tax incentives and government subsidies for infrastructure development in factory sites to firms that locate in lagging districts (Government of Nepal 2010a). Given that firms benefit from agglomeration economies and proximity to markets, fiscal incentives encouraging them to locate in districts with low population densities and far from major urban centers seldom yield the intended results, and may harm Nepal's industrialization process in the long term. Policy interventions to address the main constraints to industrial expansion—such as infrastructure—in strategic growth centers with the potential to drive economic growth in an extended region are likely to be more effective.

Urban Growth, Planning, and Infrastructure

Land patterns in urban areas are rapidly changing, and fast population growth is overtaking the capacities of existing institutions to manage urbanization in the Kathmandu Valley. The growth of the built-up areas in most urban settlements is haphazard and uncontrolled. Five-year development plans are required of all urban local bodies in Nepal, but because of inadequate funding, the plans are seldom implemented. The challenges of spatial planning are particularly complex in the Kathmandu Valley. In the absence of effective mechanisms for coordination at the metropolitan level, the Kathmandu Valley suffers from fragmentation and an overlap of institutional responsibilities between central and local authorities in the planning and delivery of infrastructure and services. This lack of coordination jeopardizes the efficient provision of transportation and infrastructure services spanning jurisdictions and the enforcement of development control tools at the metropolitan level. Institutional fragmentation and lack of cooperation on a territorial basis also create dysfunctional labor and housing markets and socioeconomic imbalances within the metropolitan area, which are manifested in low rates of innovation and job creation, social segregation, and deterioration of the urban fabric.

The urban development pattern in the Kathmandu Valley is environmentally unsustainable. Unplanned urban development and poor enforcement of regulation have led to rapid and uncontrolled urban sprawl and has contributed to dramatic changes in the urban footprint of the valley. If urban development continues through both infill in existing urban areas and outward expansion, the valley will face unprecedented stress on land resources. Unplanned growth has also led to irregular, substandard, and inaccessible housing patterns and significantly increased vulnerability to disasters. An earthquake striking the Kathmandu Valley would have devastating effects. Seismic hazard is very high in the Kathmandu Valley. Geologically, the Kathmandu Valley is as vulnerable as Haiti, which experienced a devastating 7.0 earthquake on January 13, 2010, that resulted in the loss of more than 200,000 lives and left 500,000 people homeless (Bhattarai and Conway 2010). Haphazard urban development has exposed an increasing percentage of the population to seismic hazards and decreased the capacity of emergency services to cope with the challenges associated with disasters. In most parts of the Kathmandu Valley, buildings stand side by side on narrow alleys, preventing fire brigades and ambulances from providing services. In the aftermath of a big earthquake, providing emergency services will be difficult because of the accumulation of debris on narrow roads (JICA and Ministry of Home Affairs 2002).

Nepal's connective infrastructure and power supply are a major constraint for leveraging the comparative advantages of Nepal's cities. In 2010–11, the *Global Competitiveness Report* ranked Nepal as the country with the least competitive infrastructure among the 139 countries covered by the Global

Competitiveness Index (World Economic Forum 2010). The ranking is driven mostly by the limitations of the country's connective infrastructure, also constrained by the country's geography, and the unreliability of the power supply. Nepal has the lowest road density in South Asia (Dudwick and others 2011). The limited internal and external connectivity is a constraint for the expansion of nonfarm activities, such as agroprocessing, and tourist development, whereas intermittent electricity supply is a major impediment to the expansion of Nepal's industrial base.

Rapid urbanization is intensifying the municipal infrastructure deficit. Access to piped water in urban areas declined from 68 percent to 58 percent from 2003 to 2010 as a result of inadequate service delivery and the sustained increase in urban populations. Solid waste management is one of the most pressing environmental problems in urban areas. Collection is low, and only two municipalities in Nepal dispose of waste in a sanitary landfill. In most cases, the main waste disposal sites are riverbanks, depressed land and dumps, open pits, or temporary open piles. Inadequate sanitation in urban areas is an obstacle not only for city livability but also for sustainable local economic development. The urban environment is becoming highly degraded because of discharge of untreated wastewater into water bodies and unmanaged solid waste. The important and growing economic role of the Kathmandu Valley, as well as the sustainability of its urbanization, is threatened by the valley's growing infrastructure deficits. The Kathmandu Valley has the worst water supply system in Nepal. The population in the valley has responded to the water shortfall by pumping out the balance of their daily water requirements themselves, through the extraction of groundwater. The lack of adequate sewerage and waste management infrastructure and the poor regulatory environment have turned the sacred Bagmati River system into an open sewer and garbage dump for nearby urban centers. The deteriorating condition of monuments and temples along the riverbanks undermines efforts to develop sustainable tourist activities along that river.

Public investment in municipal infrastructure is low given urban areas' infrastructure requirement. Public capital expenditure for municipal infrastructure, averaging US$11 per capita, is inadequate to meet the growing needs of urban areas and has declined in real terms (from US$14 per capita in fiscal year 2008). The decline in expenditure from an already very low base is particularly worrisome given the pressure on urban infrastructure from migration and urban growth. Moreover, the spatial distribution of capital expenditure for municipal infrastructure is biased against Kathmandu, where infrastructure needs are the greatest, and the submetropolitan cities (Biratnagar, Birgunj, Lalitpur and Pokhara) relative to the municipalities (see figure O.3).

The current expenditure bias against Kathmandu, if not timely reversed, will have high economic costs not only for the residents of the Kathmandu Valley but also for all Nepal's population that directly and indirectly benefits from the growth of the valley.

Figure O.3 Per Capita Public Expenditure for Municipal Infrastructure, by Urban Area and Funding Modality, Fiscal 2008 and 2010

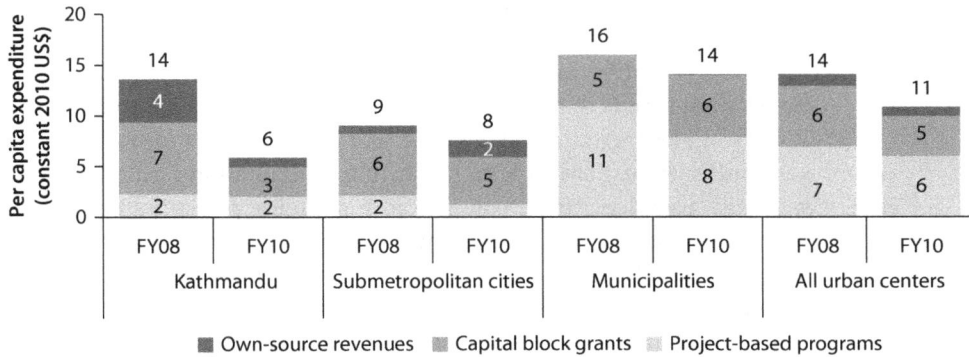

Source: Public infrastructure expenditure survey data.
Note: FY = fiscal year. A fiscal year is from July 1 through June 30 (for example, July 1, 2007, through June 30, 2008, constitutes fiscal 2008). Kathmandu refers to Kathmandu Metropolitan City; submetropolitan cities include Biratnagar, Birgunj, Lalitpur, and Pokhara.

The Comparative Advantages of Urban Areas

Urban areas have a comparative advantage in cultural tourism services, handicrafts, and agroprocessing. The challenge is to turn these comparative advantages into competitive advantages. These sectors are important from both an international perspective (export potential) and a regional perspective (contribution to regional job creation and local economic development). The *Nepal Trade Integration Strategy 2010* identifies tourism together with labor services (remittances) as the sector with the highest export potential and socioeconomic impact on the national economy, followed by agroproducts and handicrafts (Government of Nepal 2010b). An assessment of the economic growth drivers of Nepal's cities indicates that urban areas have a comparative advantage in the products and services that hold the largest potential for export. A common characteristic of Nepal's growth drivers is their links with the country's tangible and intangible cultural heritage—the effective management of Nepal's cultural heritage is vital for the competitiveness of cultural tourism, traditional handicraft production, and some agroproducts.

Nepal's urban areas are home to a vast array of tangible and intangible cultural heritage, which has evolved over many centuries, and maintains a considerable appeal and potential for tourism expansion. Tourism is an important source of income diversification and a contributor to poverty reduction through its economic, social, environmental, and cultural benefits. As Nepal's political situation stabilizes, tourist arrivals are steadily increasing. The number of international tourists has resumed at its pre-conflict level. Tourists from India are by far the largest group, and tourists from China are the fastest-growing segment. The Kathmandu Valley is Nepal's most important heritage destination and the gateway for tourism in the country. The UNESCO Kathmandu Valley World

Heritage site, which is composed of seven protected monument zones, is Nepal's most widely recognized cultural asset (ETG 2012).

The evolution of tourism in the Kathmandu Valley over the past 30 years, however, is of an increasing number of tourists but a decreasing quality of tourism experience. The public cultural and historic assets of the Kathmandu Valley have suffered considerable damage. Similar to the Kathmandu Valley at large, the UNESCO World Heritage site and areas surrounding the site's monuments and complexes (buffer zones) are suffering from the deterioration of infrastructure, lack of basic urban services, traffic congestion, and intense pressure from population growth and commercial development. Overlapping authority and responsibilities and insufficient monitoring capacity prevent central and local agencies from fulfilling their responsibilities in protecting the country's cultural heritage. In addition, community awareness and mobilization for the conservation of its heritage are weakening. The *guthis* of Nepal—one of the indigenous systems that traditionally played an important role in the conservation and perpetuation of cultural heritage—have been significantly weakened after the nationalization of *guthi* land in 1961.

Handicraft production has strong potential for growth given its ties to tourism. Nepal has a comparative advantage in the craft industry, which accounts for 6 percent of GDP. Handicrafts are labor intensive and draw on Nepal's artistic traditions dating back centuries. Many traditional and new products are known and reputed internationally. Urban local governments play a critical role in promoting the development of competitive handicraft clusters, because urban centers are not only the places where most artisans create and produce but also the natural location of wholesalers and retailers. Nepal's domestic handicraft market is led by sales to tourists, as many handicraft products share backward and forward links with tourism.[5]

In spite of the growth potential, handicraft exports are losing competitiveness because of the sector's inability to modernize to respond to international competition. One of the main reasons behind the decline in export competitiveness is the lack of effective marketing and branding. Individual artisans note that they lack working capital, access to microcredit, bargaining power with retailers and exporters, and dependable power and water.[6] The important decline in pashmina exports, for example, is mostly because of fierce competition from Indian and Chinese pashminas as a result of the lack of effective branding. Nepal's handicraft sector has, however, the potential to rebound by building on the availability of skilled artisans and the expected growth in tourism. The handicraft sector is well organized with multiple specialty associations and a Federation of Handicraft Associations. These associations are committed to improving the products of their associates and to promoting their sales on the export markets.

Agroprocessing has the potential to become an important driver of economic growth and poverty alleviation. Nepal has a comparative advantage in the production of horticultural products and specialty agroproducts. The country has a resource advantage in the production of fresh and processed horticultural products, fruits, orthodox tea, coffee, honey, pulses (lentils), instant noodles, vegetable

Figure O.4 Agroprocessing Output Density by Distance from Urban Centers, 2007

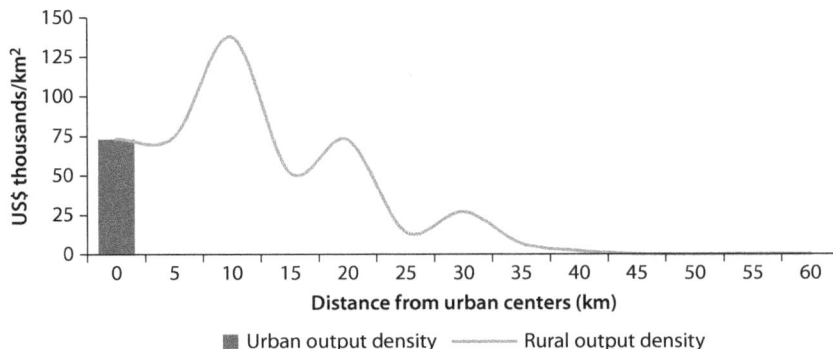

Source: Based on Census of Manufacturing 2007 (CBS 2007).

oils and fats (ghee), and medicinal and aromatic plants. Agroprocessing firms are clustered in the Tarai and Central Hills and benefit from proximity to urban centers, which play an important role in providing the necessary market infrastructure for trading agriculture commodities. Agroprocessing output density is highest at 10 kilometers from urban centers, with a second peak at 20 kilometers (see figure O.4).

Nepal has not been able to transform its natural resource advantages into profitable trade, however, because of inadequate infrastructure, lack of organized cluster support and market coordination, and low productivity from substandard production technologies. The agroprocessing industry remains a relatively small-scale operation in Nepal, with limited investments. Nepal's inadequate connective infrastructure is an important impediment to the expansion of agroprocessing operations because it limits access to markets. Market coordination is inadequate, and no organized cluster support and trading system exist for most agricultural commodities. Productivity is low because of substandard production technologies, partially as a result of inadequate cluster support in the area of farming technology, orchard management, and sustainable harvesting techniques.

Strategic Policy Directions

Nepal needs to foster the growth and sustainability of the urban regions, promote the development and regeneration of the Kathmandu Valley, and enhance the competitiveness of strategic urban clusters to unlock growth and make the spatial transformation sustainable. The study proposes broad policy directions and actions to achieve these objectives. The policy directions and actions are summarized in table O.1.

Pillar 1: Foster the Growth and Sustainability of the Urban Regions

Accelerating economic growth requires unlocking the economic potential of the urban regions by facilitating the clustering of economic activities and

Table O.1 Strategic Policy Directions and Actions for Fostering the Sustainable Growth of Nepal's Cities

Pillar 1: Foster the growth and sustainability of the urban regions	*Pillar 2: Promote the development and regeneration of the Kathmandu Valley metropolitan region*	*Pillar 3: Enhance the competitiveness of strategic urban clusters*
1.1 Prioritize the "where, what, and how" of public interventions in the urban regions based on development outcomes • Launch regional competitiveness strategies and develop action plans for the main urban clusters • Develop a countrywide infrastructure investment plan to prioritize investments • Design spatially targeted interventions, such as special economic zones, to unlock the economic potential of strategic manufacturing clusters	**2.1 Strengthen planning and its implementation in the valley** • Define the functional boundaries of the Kathmandu Valley metropolitan region • Develop customized institutional arrangements for metropolitan coordination • Promote integrated land-use and transport planning and mainstream the disaster risk management agenda at the metropolitan level	**3.1 Promote sustainable and responsible cultural tourism activities** • Improve and diversity tourism products in the Kathmandu Valley that respect local traditions • Develop tourism strategies and plans for heritage cities to enhance their market positioning • Improve human resources capacity in the tourism sector • Strengthen the municipal capacity to partner with the private sector to promote sustainable tourism activities
1.2 Improve internal and external connectivity • Prioritize strategic investments in transport corridors for improved market integration and trade facilitation • Upgrade and expand the international and domestic air transportation	**2.2 Develop an infrastructure financing policy and plan for the Kathmandu Valley** • Prioritize infrastructure investment needs at the metropolitan level • Develop a metropolitan infrastructure financing strategy and plan	**3.2 Support the modernization of the handicraft sector** • Promote market research for handicraft product innovation and commercialization • Develop a pilot public-private partnership program to support strategic handicraft products clusters • Promote initiatives in support of artisan communities to enhance their skills and facilitate access to the market
1.3 Create the enabling environment for sustainable and inclusive urban development • Strengthen municipalities' capacity to plan and provide basic services and connect all districts by all-season roads • Develop a coherent institutional framework for municipal capital financing • Facilitate the access of poor and disadvantaged local communities to markets	**2.3 Launch a regeneration program for the valley's historic city centers** • Realign the responsibilities for cultural heritage conservation among institutional actors • Promote integrated conservation and management of the built heritage • Raise community awareness and incentivize community mobilization for the sustainable conservation of cultural heritage	**3.3 Improve agroprocessing competitiveness** • Develop and upgrade market infrastructure in strategic locations • Strengthen agroprocessing cluster support through public-private partnership arrangements • Launch an action plan to improve production technology and commercialization to increase value addition

enhancing the competitiveness of existing clusters in the Central Region and along the border with India. In parallel, appropriate redistributive policies need to be undertaken for balanced and equitable development. Nepal needs to pursue the following strategic directions and actions to foster the growth and sustainability of the urban regions:

- *Prioritize the "where, what, and how" of public interventions in the urban regions based on development outcomes.* Given scarce financial resources, prioritizing strategic public investments based on economic returns would be a positive-sum game for the country. Economic dividends of sustained growth can be redistributed to ensure that the benefits are spread equally across the entire population. This effort would require launching regional competitiveness strategies and developing action plans for the main urban clusters based on a participatory approach. Nepal also needs a countrywide infrastructure investment plan to prioritize investments in order to maximize their socioeconomic impact. Cost-recovery mechanisms (such as user charges and land value capture instruments) need to be introduced to ensure the sustainability of the investments and contribute to the cost of infrastructure in the lagging regions. The government should also consider designing spatially targeted interventions, such as SEZs, to unlock the economic potential of strategic manufacturing clusters.

- *Improve internal and external connectivity.* The country's connective infrastructure has contributed to—and continues to affect—the shaping of the spatial transformation from both a demographic and economic perspective. Improving internal and external connectivity is therefore critical to reap the full benefits of urbanization. This effort would require prioritizing strategic investments to expand, rehabilitate, and maintain transport corridors for improved market integration and trade facilitation. In parallel, both international and domestic air transportation need to be upgraded and expanded, and the quality of airport services enhanced.

- *Create the enabling environment for sustainable and inclusive urban development.* In countries at an incipient level of urbanization, like Nepal, urban policy interventions should be directed at providing a minimum level of municipal services across urban areas, ensuring the sustainability of urban growth, and encouraging firms' efficient location decisions. This effort would require strengthening municipalities' capacity to plan and provide basic services and connecting all districts by all-season roads, while developing a coherent institutional framework for municipal capital financing. Improvements in local service delivery and capacity need to be supported by targeted programs to facilitate the access of poor and disadvantaged local communities to markets.

Pillar 2: Promote the Development and Regeneration of the Kathmandu Valley Metropolitan Region

The challenges of the Kathmandu Valley need to be addressed at the metropolitan scale. A Kathmandu Valley regeneration and development strategy needs to be formulated and implemented through a phased program of priority investments in infrastructure, environmental improvements, cultural heritage conservation, transport, and land development. The interventions need to be done at the spatial scale of the valley to maximize effectiveness and economies of scale and to minimize costs and inequities. Broad directions and actions to address the challenges of the Kathmandu Valley include the following:

- *Strengthen planning and its implementation in the valley.* To manage rapid urbanization in the valley and reduce vulnerability to disasters, strengthening planning and its implementation at the metropolitan level is urgently needed. Priority actions include defining the functional boundaries of the Kathmandu Valley metropolitan region and developing customized institutional arrangements for metropolitan coordination, building on the recent establishment of the Kathmandu Valley Development Authority and the new Ministry of Urban Development, and taking into account the valley's unique social, cultural, and political conditions. High priority should also be given to promoting integrated land-use and transport planning and mainstreaming the disaster risk management agenda at the metropolitan level, with a focus on improving accessibility; enforcing building codes and laws preventing land subdivisions and the building of substandard houses on open spaces; and improving community preparedness and retrofitting public buildings that are designated as evacuation centers or treatment centers.

- *Develop an infrastructure financing policy and plan for the Kathmandu Valley.* A strategy to raise capital for infrastructure financing is urgently needed to address the backlogs in infrastructure and the deficits in the provision of basic services in the Kathmandu Valley. A metropolitan infrastructure financing framework for the valley would comprise a series of policy initiatives and reforms to upgrade the financing instruments for infrastructure investments in the valley supported by a portfolio of related infrastructure investments. This task would require as a first step prioritizing infrastructure investment needs at the metropolitan level to remedy, in a phased manner, deficits in essential infrastructure and services. In parallel, a metropolitan infrastructure strategy and plan needs to be developed with a focus on improving cost recovery and sustainability in the provision of infrastructure and services, while strengthening the revenue generating capacity of the local governments in the valley.

- *Launch a regeneration program for the valley's historic city centers.* The urban fabric, not only the individual monuments, needs protection for all its historic, cultural, and architectural elements. The ideal development outcome is that the urban areas continue to change and evolve, but that change is managed to prevent the destruction of the historic environment, while improving the quality of life for the valley's citizens. Central and local agencies also have much to gain by reconsidering and strengthening the traditional role of local communities, such as the *guthis*, in the process of conserving cultural heritage. Priority actions include realigning the responsibilities for cultural heritage conservation among institutional actors, promoting integrated conservation and management of the built heritage based on a participatory approach as part of the planning process, and raising community awareness and providing incentives for community mobilization for the sustainable conservation of cultural heritage.

Pillar 3: Enhance the Competitiveness of Strategic Urban Clusters

Sector-specific measures are required to enhance the competitiveness and to accelerate growth and job creation in the cultural tourism, handicraft production, and agroprocessing clusters. Although adequate infrastructure and services are necessary for local economic development, in most cases they are insufficient and need to be complemented by sector-specific initiatives and interventions to strengthen cluster competitiveness. Sector-specific interventions should be identified and prioritized through a coordinated effort between central agencies, local authorities, and the private sector. The study proposes a number of broad areas for intervention for each cluster, with the objective of exemplifying how a successful partnership between the public and private sectors can be developed to support local economic development.

- *Promote sustainable and responsible cultural tourism activities.* Cultural tourism has a strong potential to drive economic growth and job creation in urban areas, but its growth needs to be sustainably managed. Sustainable and responsible cultural tourism rests on the effective conservation and valorization of cities' cultural assets, the capacity of local governments to plan and provide adequate infrastructure and services, and reliable connective infrastructure. In addition to these fundamental building blocks for tourism development, a number of sector-specific interventions are required to support tourism initiatives and investments based on a partnership between private and public stakeholders. Strategic interventions would include improving and diversifying tourism products in the valley that respect local traditions, developing tourism strategies for heritage cities to enhance their market positioning, improving human resources capacity in the tourism sector, and strengthening the municipal capacity to partner with the private sector to promote sustainable tourism activities (such as the adaptive reuse of heritage buildings).

- *Support the modernization of the handicraft sector.* The growth of handicraft production and its contribution to the well-being of all social groups, including the most disadvantaged, will depend on the capacity of urban local governments to work with central agencies, local communities, and the private sector to develop a market-led strategy for the modernization of the sector, while creating a favorable and inclusive environment for artisans to carry out their activities and pass on their skills and their businesses to future generations. Strategic actions include promoting market research for handicraft product innovation and commercialization; developing an integrated program to support a few strategic handicraft product clusters on a pilot basis, based on a public-private partnership; and promoting initiatives in support of artisan communities to enhance their skills and facilitate access to the market, through training and microfinance programs.

- *Improve agroprocessing competitiveness.* Urban local governments have an important role to play in improving the competitiveness of the agroprocessing sector. In coordination with business associations and central agencies, municipalities can provide the market infrastructure together with the cluster support that is necessary to expand the agroprocessing sector from its current small-scale operation to industrial production and to support the growth of ancillary industries. Strategic interventions include developing and upgrading market infrastructure in strategic locations, strengthening agroprocessing cluster support through public-private partnership arrangements, and launching an action plan to improve production technology and commercialization in order to increase value addition.

Notes

1. The last local elections were held in May 1997. The elected local officials held office until July 2002.
2. Unless otherwise stated, Kathmandu refers to Kathmandu Metropolitan City; Biratnagar, Birgunj, Lalitpur, and Pokhara refer to the submetropolitan cities; and all other urban local governments are referred to as municipalities.
3. This section studies internal migration in Nepal based on data from the Labor Force Survey 2007/08 (CBS 2009).
4. *Lifetime migrants* are individuals whose place of residence on the survey date differs from their place of birth; *recent migrants* are individuals whose place of residence on the survey date differs from the place of enumeration at the census. Unless otherwise stated, the statistics presented in this chapter are for lifetime migration.
5. Data are from the Labor Force Surveys 1998–99 and 2008 (CBS 1999, 2009).
6. Artisans report that local retailers often keep 75 percent of the profit from the sale of their work.

References

ADB (Asian Development Bank). 2010. *Unleashing Economic Growth: Region-Based Urban Strategy for Nepal.* Manila: ADB.

Afram, Gabi G., and Angelica Salvi Del Pero. 2012. *Nepal's Investment Climate: Leveraging the Private Sector for Job Creation and Growth.* Washington, DC: World Bank.

Bhattarai, Keshav, and Dennis Conway. 2010. "Urban Vulnerabilities in the Kathmandu Valley, Nepal: Visualizations of Human/Hazard Interactions." *Journal of Geographic Information System* 2: 63–84.

CBS (Central Bureau of Statistics). 1996. *Nepal Living Standards Survey (1995/96).* Kathmandu: Government of Nepal.

————. 1999. *Report on the Nepal Labor Force Survey 1998/99*. Kathmandu: Government of Nepal.

————. 2007. *Nepal—Census of Manufacturing Establishments 2006–2007*. Kathmandu: Government of Nepal. http://www.cbs.gov.np/nada/index.php/catalog/3.

————. 2009. *Report on the Nepal Labor Force Survey 2008*. Kathmandu: Government of Nepal.

————. 2011. *Nepal Living Standards Survey (2010/11)*. Kathmandu: Government of Nepal.

————. 2012. *National Population and Housing Census 2011*. Kathmandu: Government of Nepal.

Dudwick, Nora, Katy Hull, Roy Katayama, Forhad Shilpi, and Kenneth Simler. 2011. *From Farm to Firm: Rural-Urban Transition in Developing Countries*. Washington, DC: World Bank.

ETG (Economic Transformations Group). 2012. "Kathmandu Valley Tourism Cluster Competitiveness Assessment and Action Plan." Background paper for this report, World Bank, Washington, DC.

Government of Nepal. 2010a. *Nepal Industrial Policy, 2010*. Kathmandu.

————, Ministry of Commerce and Supplies. 2010b. *Nepal Trade Integration Strategy 2010*. Kathmandu.

————, National Planning Commission. 2010c. "Three Year Plan Approach Paper 2010/11–2012/13." Kathmandu.

JICA (Japan International Cooperation Agency) and Ministry of Home Affairs. 2002. "The Study on Earthquake Disaster Mitigation in the Kathmandu Valley, Kingdom of Nepal." JICA, Tokyo.

World Bank. 2011a. "Large-Scale Migration and Remittance in Nepal: Issues, Challenges and Opportunities." Report No. 55390-NP, World Bank, Washington, DC.

————. 2011b. *World Development Indicators 2011*. Washington, DC: World Bank.

————. Forthcoming. *Bangladesh: The Path to Middle-Income Status from an Urban Perspective*. Directions in Development. Washington, DC: World Bank.

World Economic Forum. 2010. *The Global Competitiveness Report, 2010–2011*. Geneva: World Economic Forum.

CHAPTER 1

Urbanization and Growth

Nepal is the fastest-urbanizing country in South Asia. The country is undergoing a significant spatial transition, with an average urban population growth of approximately 6 percent per year since the 1970s. Despite the important contribution of urban areas to gross domestic product (GDP) and poverty alleviation, urbanization has historically been less correlated with economic growth in Nepal than in other South Asian countries. Nepal is caught in a cycle of political instability, poverty, and economic stagnation, with economic growth below 4 percent per year over the past decade. The pace of the economy's structural transformation has been relatively slow. Political instability, an unfavorable business climate for private sector development, and an internationally uncompetitive, remittance-dependent economy have suppressed economic growth. The lack of economic stimuli combined with the insecure political situation has resulted in a mass exodus of the Nepalese productive workforce from the country, and Nepal's growth is becoming increasingly reliant on highly volatile external remittance flows, rather than internal competitiveness. Nepal needs to leverage the comparative advantage of its cities to break the cycle of poverty and economic stagnation and to meet the government's target GDP growth of 5.5 percent per year. Only vibrant and competitive cities can attract high-return investments and generate the higher-productivity jobs required to accelerate growth to meet the government's target.

Nepal is undergoing a significant spatial transition. It is both the least urbanized country in South Asia, with about 17 percent of its population living in urban areas (based on 2011 census data, CBS 2012), and the fastest-urbanizing country, with an average urban population growth rate of about 6 percent per year since the 1970s.[1] The rapid spatial transformation has led to a population shift from rural to urban areas through rural-to-urban migration, reclassification (conversion of rural areas into urban areas), and the natural growth of urban areas. If Nepal's urban population growth rate continues at 3 percent per year as predicted, Nepal will become one-third urban by 2045 (UNDESA 2012; see figures 1.1 and 1.2).

The spatial demographic transition has been accompanied by an equally important spatial economic transformation, that is, a spatial shift of economic

Figure 1.1 Urbanization and Economic Development in South Asia, 1960–2010

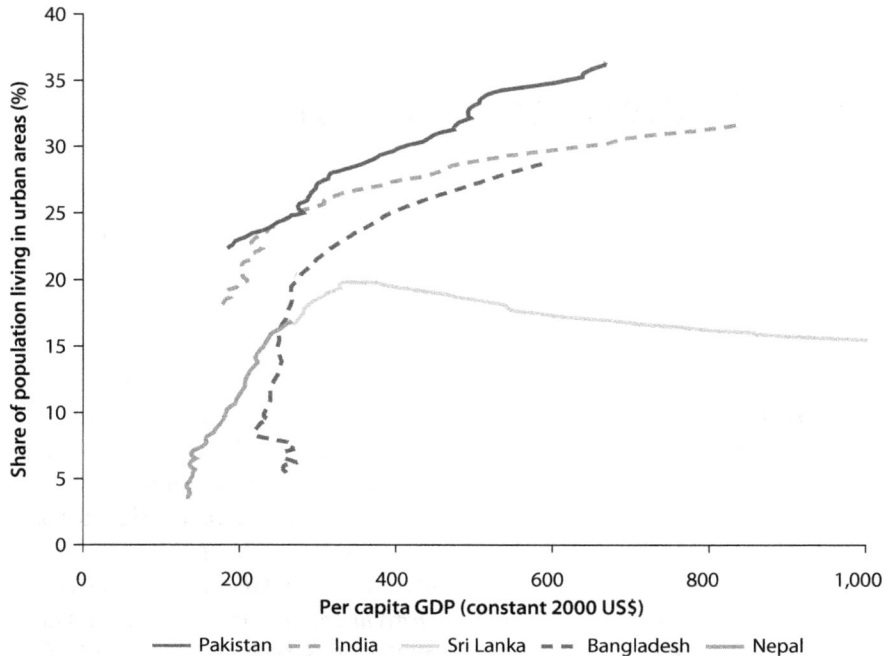

Sources: Based on data from UNDESA 2012 and World Bank 2011b.
Note: Urbanization is defined as the share of population living in settlements administratively designated as urban areas. Analysis excludes Afghanistan (because of lack of historic data) and Bhutan (because of lack of comparability given the country's small population). The decline in Sri Lanka's level of urbanization is associated with a change in that country's definition of urban areas, which led to the reclassification of urban centers in rural areas. GDP = gross domestic product.

production from rural to urban areas. Although Nepal's economy remains primarily agricultural and rural, urban areas are a major contributor to GDP growth and poverty alleviation. Accounting for 17 percent of the population, urban areas now contribute to about 62 percent of GDP according to the latest available estimates, compared with only 28 percent of GDP in 1975 (World Bank 2011b).[2] In 2008, urban areas had only 16 percent of the country's population, but as much as 36 percent of nonfarm employment, 28 percent of manufacturing employment, and 39 percent of service employment (see figure 1.3). The urban economy is growing significantly faster than the rural economy. The share of nonfarm income in total income increased from 22 percent to 37 percent, whereas farm income has declined from 61 percent to 28 percent from 1995/96 to 2010/11.[3] Urbanization is one of the main drivers of poverty reduction. About 15 percent of the urban population lives below the poverty line in urban areas, compared with 27 percent of the rural population. The incidence of poverty in urban areas declined from 22 percent to 15 percent from 1995/96 to 2010/11, compared with a decline from 43 percent to 27 percent in rural areas over the same period.[4]

Nepal's economy has undergone a structural shift over the last few decades, from agriculture to a mixed economy centered on services, as part of the

Figure 1.2 Urbanization and Annual Growth Rate of Urban Population in Nepal, 1950–2050

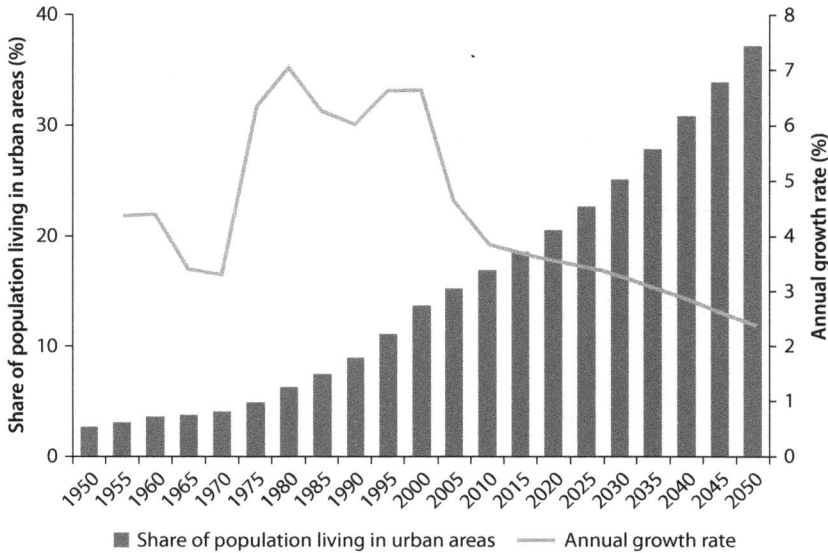

■ Share of population living in urban areas —— Annual growth rate

Source: UNDESA 2012.
Note: Urbanization is defined as the share of population living in settlements administratively designated as urban areas.
Growth rate of urban population includes reclassification (conversion of rural areas into urban areas).

Figure 1.3 Spatial Distribution of Population and Nonfarm Employment, 2008

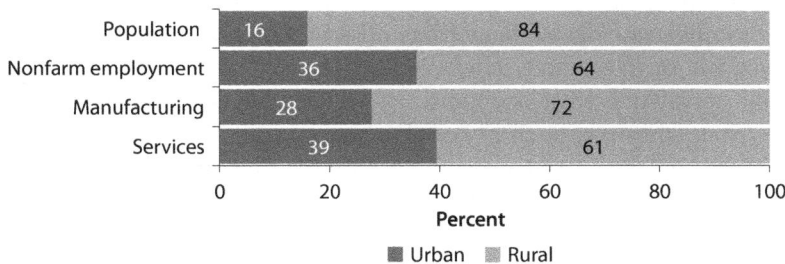

■ Urban ▨ Rural

Sources: CBS 2009; UNDESA 2012.
Note: Nonfarm employment includes service and manufacturing employment.

country's urban and spatial economic transformation. In the early 1970s, the country's agriculturally dominated economy started a rapid shift. By the mid-1990s, it had become a mixed economy, relying on agriculture, manufacturing, and services. Since then, further transformation has seen manufacturing lose out to services. Although Nepal's employment is still dominated by the agricultural sector, the employment pattern is shifting from agriculture to services, rather than to manufacturing. The broadly defined services sector is the only sector that has grown in both employment and GDP contribution over the last decade.

Figure 1.4 Sectoral Composition of GDP in Nepal, 1980–2011

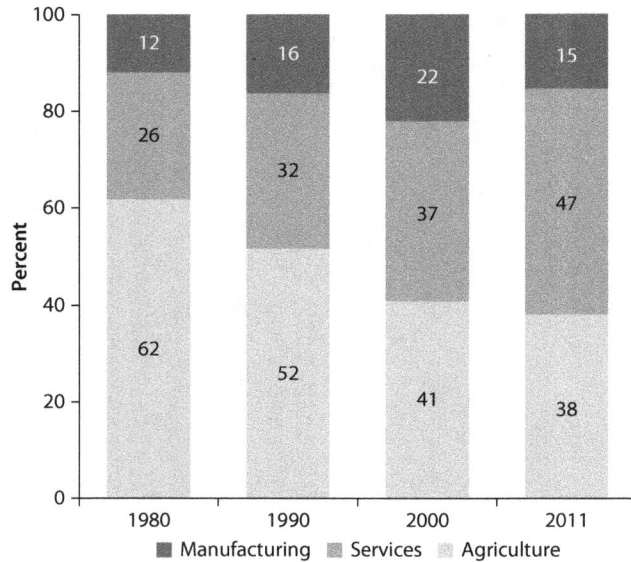

Source: World Bank 2011b.

The services sector now constitutes the largest share of GDP, at around 47 percent (see figure 1.4).

Urbanization, defined as the percentage of total population living in settlements administratively designated as urban areas, tends to be closely related to economic development. However, urbanization has been historically less strongly correlated with economic growth in Nepal compared with other South Asian countries, such as Bangladesh and India (see figure 1.1). On one hand, Nepal is the fastest-urbanizing country in South Asia. On the other hand, the country is caught in a cycle of political instability, poverty, and economic stagnation, in stark contrast with the booming South Asian economy. Economic growth has slowed in the last decade: real GDP growth averaged 3.8 percent over the past 10 years, compared with 7.5 percent in India, Nepal's main trading partner, and well below the government of Nepal's real GDP growth target of 5.5 percent per year (World Bank 2011b; Government of Nepal 2010). Nepal is among the poorest countries in the world, with per capita GDP of US$619 (2011 prices) and an estimated 25 percent of Nepalese falling below the international poverty line (US$1.25 per day). Overall, agriculture still contributes to more than one-third of Nepal's GDP (38 percent), compared with about 22 percent in Pakistan, 18 percent in Bangladesh, 17 percent in India, and 14 percent in Sri Lanka (World Bank 2011b).

Urbanization has taken place amid a conflict-ridden environment. Nepal has recently exited from a 10-year civil conflict that began in 1996 and escalated in 2001, ending only in 2006. The relatively weak correlation between economic growth and urbanization—and the slow pace of economic diversification—is in part the legacy of that conflict, which plunged the country into a prolonged period of political instability and retarded Nepal's economic development. In addition to the human toll from the conflict, the country experienced internal and external displacement of people, which affected the urban transition, and the destruction of economic infrastructure. The overall loss in economic growth associated with the conflict over the period from 1996 to 2006 is estimated at 3 percent of GDP per year (Pradhan 2009). Although a peace agreement was reached in 2006, the country remains in a state of political transition and is at a critical juncture in its history. Local elections have not been held in Nepal since 1997. The absence of elections of local government bodies has left urban local bodies without a platform for representation. A recent setback was the failure of the Constituent Assembly to ratify a new constitution by the deadline of May 27, 2012, and the subsequent dissolution of the assembly. The current transition is expected to culminate with the enactment of a new constitution, which will spell out the legal and institutional framework for establishing autonomous local entities within a federal state. The outcomes of these deliberations will have significant implications for defining the governance, financing, and management of urban local governments in Nepal.

Political instability, combined with weak infrastructure and labor market failures, has hindered private sector development and job creation. Political instability is still perceived as the main constraint across all industries, followed by infrastructure (in particular, infrastructure for connectivity and power supply). The power losses from civil unrest (44 days a year on average) and electricity shortages (of up to 27 percent of total sales) are prohibitively high for the private sector. Despite some positive signs of recovery in the years following the end of the conflict, private investments remain low. Nepalese enterprises also suffer from a multitude of failures in the labor markets, ranging from chronic work disruptions caused by political or union actions to poor labor relations, absenteeism, and poor skills. Not only do these failures hinder firm output and productivity, but they also stop firms from investing and from generating employment across all sectors (Afram and Salvi Del Pero 2012).

Nepal's growth is becoming increasingly reliant on highly volatile external remittance flows rather than internal competitiveness. The lack of economic stimuli, combined with political instability, has resulted in a mass exodus of the Nepalese productive workforce from the country. Labor is now Nepal's major export. One-third of the working male population is employed in overseas jobs and remits 25 percent of GDP. On average, remittances constitute one-fourth of the income of Nepalese households and almost two-thirds of the income of those receiving remittances (World Bank 2011a).

Remittances have led to improvements in living standards but stifled the international competitiveness of the Nepalese economy. On one hand, remittances from international migration have contributed significantly to the growth of the country's GDP and have now surpassed exports as the top contributor to

Creating jobs and economic opportunities in urban areas is a priority for sustainable
economic growth.

foreign exchange earnings. On the other hand, remittances have stifled the international competitiveness of the Nepalese economy and may constrain the country's long-term growth prospects. High remittances and lack of policy corrections
have exposed Nepal to the risks of Dutch Disease, as remittances have fueled
demand, causing overall prices to rise and leading to loss of international competitiveness (World Bank 2011a). Less than one-tenth of remittances are spent
on capital formation, including education,[5] while international migration has led
to a significant loss in the economically active workforce and to an increase in
wages because of a shortage of local manpower. In addition, remittances are
highly volatile. In 2011, growth in remittances suffered from the global crisis and
the recent turmoil in the Middle East (which accounts for about half of total
remittances) (IMF 2011; World Bank 2011a).

Nepal needs to leverage the comparative advantages of its cities to meet its
GDP growth target of 5.5 percent per year (Government of Nepal 2010).
Achieving that target would require broadening the base of economic activity
and job creation in urban areas—the main contributors to GDP growth. That
requirement in turn calls for tapping into the potential of Nepal's cities to turn
their comparative advantages into competitive advantages. Only vibrant and
competitive cities can attract high-return investments and generate the higher-
productivity jobs required to accelerate growth to meet the government's GDP
growth target.

Policy recognition of the importance of urban areas for growth and poverty alleviation is increasing. A critical urban policy initiative is the government's adoption of the National Urban Policy (NUP) in 2007 (Government of Nepal 2007). The objectives of the NUP are to promote a balanced urban structure, a sustainable urban environment, and effective urban management. The NUP views urban centers as catalysts for economic development and places urban local governments at the core of the urban development agenda, while recognizing that investments have not kept pace with urban growth.

Notes

1. Urban population data for South Asian countries are from the United Nations World Urbanization Prospects database (UNDESA 2012), based on the countries' official urban definition. Reclassification (conversion of rural areas into urban areas) is included in the figures and is also from the United Nations World Urbanization Prospects database (UNDESA 2012).
2. GDP contribution of nonfarm economic activities is used as a proxy for GDP contribution of urban areas.
3. The share of other income in total income increased from 16 to 35 percent from 1995/96 to 2010/11.
4. Data are from CBS (1996, 2011).
5. In the absence of productive investment opportunities, remittance recipients have nowhere to invest but in land and housing. The construction sector is booming, and land values continue to rise in small towns and cities.

References

Afram, Gabi G., and Angelica Salvi Del Pero. 2012. *Nepal's Investment Climate: Leveraging the Private Sector for Job Creation and Growth*. Washington, DC: World Bank.

CBS (Central Bureau of Statistics). 1996. *Nepal Living Standards Survey (1995/96)*. Kathmandu: Government of Nepal.

———. 2001. *National Population Census 2001*. Kathmandu: Government of Nepal.

———. 2009. *Report on the Nepal Labor Force Survey 2008*. Kathmandu: Government of Nepal.

———. 2011. *Nepal Living Standards Survey (2010/11)*. Kathmandu: Government of Nepal.

———. 2012. *National Population and Housing Census 2011*. Kathmandu: Government of Nepal.

Government of Nepal, Ministry of Physical Planning and Works. 2007. "National Urban Policy 2007." Department of Urban Development and Building Construction, Kathmandu.

———, National Planning Commission. 2010. "Three Year Plan Approach Paper 2010/11–2012/13." Kathmandu.

IMF (International Monetary Fund). 2011. "Nepal: Article IV Consultation." IMF Country Report 11/318, IMF, Washington, DC.

Pradhan, Gyan. 2009. "Nepal's Civil War and Its Economic Costs." *Journal of International and Global Studies*, 1 (1), 114–131.

UNDESA (United Nations, Department of Economic and Social Affairs). 2012. "World Urbanization Prospects. The 2011 Revision." New York: UNDESA.

World Bank. 2011a. "Large-Scale Migration and Remittance in Nepal: Issues, Challenges and Opportunities." Report No. 55390-NP, World Bank, Washington, DC.

———. 2011b. *World Development Indicators 2011*. Washington, DC: World Bank.

CHAPTER 2

The Spatial Transition

The spatial transformation is characterized by fast-growing population density in the Kathmandu Valley, along the main highways, and close to the border with India. The Kathmandu Valley, the largest urban agglomeration in Nepal, accounts for about one-third of the country's urban population and continues to sustain a fast pace of population growth, at about 4 percent per year. The boundaries of the Kathmandu Valley's urban agglomeration are also expanding rapidly as a result of sprawl at the periphery. Pokhara Submetropolitan City in the Central Hills is the largest and fastest-growing medium city, with growth exceeding 5 percent per year. A number of small and fast-growing urban centers are emerging along the main highways of the country and close to the border with India. And several emerging towns, which are classified as rural but have urban characteristics, are growing under the radar. Migration is a powerful force for urban change. The contribution of internal migration to urban growth is increasing over time. Although physical distance is a barrier to internal mobility, migrants in search of job opportunities are on the rise, are willing to travel longer distances, and tend to settle in urban areas. More and more migrants are pulled to the Kathmandu Valley by economic opportunities. Nonfarm economic production is concentrated in three main clusters in the Kathmandu Valley and in the Tarai zone close to the border with India—the Eastern Tarai cluster surrounding Biratnagar Submetropolitan City and the Central Tarai cluster surrounding Birgunj Submetropolitan City. These clusters make up a core urban center surrounded by a hinterland of small towns and rural areas, and they function as extended urban economic regions. This chapter presents an initial assessment of the demographic and economic trends of the spatial transformation. It highlights Nepal's urban growth patterns based on population census data, then makes an initial assessment of the country's internal migration trends and economic geography.

The Demographic Transition: Rapid and Concentrated Urban Growth

Nepal is a small, landlocked, mountainous country sandwiched between two Asian giants—India and China—and situated between the Himalayas and the plain of the Ganges River. Its mountainous terrain contains 8 of the world's 10 tallest mountains, including the highest point on earth, Mount Everest.

It has 75 administrative districts distributed across three ecological zones: the Mountains in the north, the Tarai in the south, and the Hills in between. Nepal has five development regions: the Far Western, Midwestern, Western, Central, and Eastern Regions. Three major river systems—the Koshi, the Narayani, and the Karnali—bisect the three ecological zones. With an estimated population of 26.4 million in 2011 (CBS 2012), Nepal extends over 800 kilometers from east to west and covers 147,181 square kilometers (see map 2.1).

Nepal's urban space includes one metropolitan city, four submetropolitan cities, and 53 municipalities (see box 2.1). Kathmandu Metropolitan City (hereafter, Kathmandu), the capital city and the largest urban settlement with a population of about one million in 2011, accounts for 22 percent of the country's urban population. Beyond Kathmandu, the urban hierarchy consists of four sub-metropolitan cities (Biratnagar, Birgunj, Lalitpur, and Pokhara) with populations ranging from 139,000 (Birgunj) to 265,000 (Pokhara), according to 2011 population census data. The 53 municipalities have populations ranging from 16,000 to 148,000.[1] Forty-one new municipalities have been proposed for conversion to urban local governments.[2] An additional 80 emerging towns are in the pipeline to become municipalities, and there are several hundred rural growth centers.[3] The 10 largest urban centers, with populations above 100,000 (including Kathmandu), account for 54 percent of the total urban population in 2011 (CBS 2012).

While overall population growth has slowed since 2001, urban population growth has kept its pace at 3.4 percent per year from 2001 to 2011, compared with 3.6 percent per year from 1991 to 2001 (reclassification—that is, the conversion of rural areas to urban areas—excluded).[4] The Central Region, where the Kathmandu Valley is located, has the highest proportion of urban population (50 percent of the total), followed by the Western (17 percent) and Eastern Regions (18 percent; see table 2.1). Kathmandu—the only city with a population above 1 million—is the fastest-growing city size category (4 percent per year), followed by small cities (50,000–100,000; 3.6 percent), and medium cities (100,000–300,000; 3.5 percent; see map 2.2 and figure 2.1). Significant variations in growth patterns occur within each city size category. The number of medium cities increased from four to nine between 2001 and 2011. Pokhara in the Central Hills is the largest and fastest-growing medium city, with a 2011 population of 265,000 and growth above 5 percent per year. Three medium cities have also sustained population growth in excess of 4 percent per year: Bharatpur (148,000) in the Central Tarai, Butwal (120,000) in the Western Tarai, and Dhangadhi (104,000) in the Far Western Tarai (CBS 2001, 2012; see figure 2.2 and appendix).

Rapid urbanization has transformed the Kathmandu Valley into a metro-politan region—an urban system anchored on a core city surrounded by suburban areas and satellite cities and towns whose economies are becoming highly integrated. The Kathmandu Valley is a bowl-shaped land mass, located at an average altitude of 1,350 meters above sea level, in the center of Nepal (see map 2.3). The Kathmandu Valley continues to sustain a fast-paced population growth, at about 4.3 percent per year. It is the most populated urban region

Map 2.1 Ecological Zones, Development Regions, and Districts

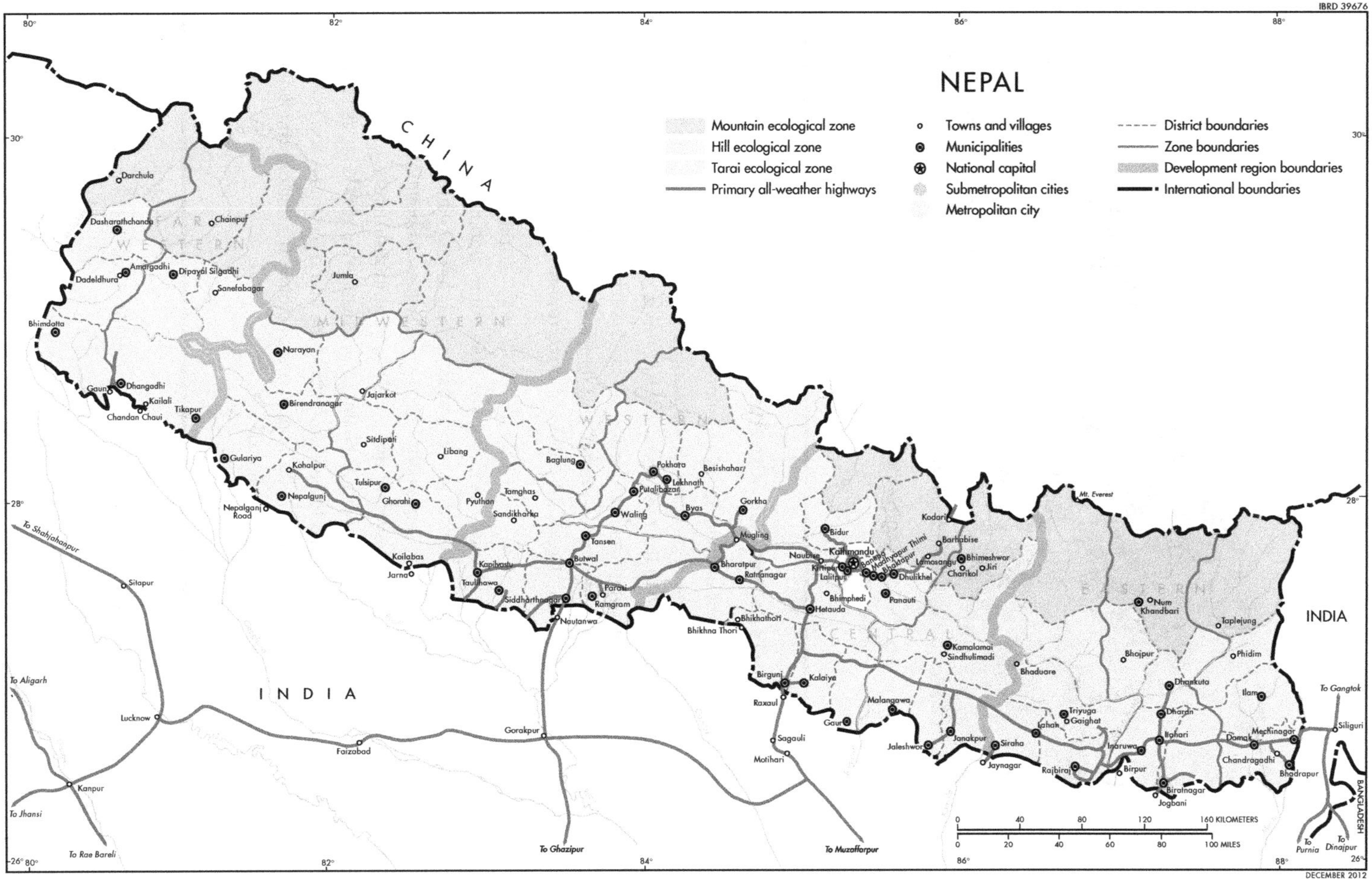

NEPAL

Mountain ecological zone
Hill ecological zone
Tarai ecological zone
Primary all-weather highways

o   Towns and villages
⊛   Municipalities
⊛   National capital
    Submetropolitan cities
    Metropolitan city

District boundaries
Zone boundaries
Development region boundaries
International boundaries

CHINA

INDIA

BANGLADESH

IBRD 39676

DECEMBER 2012

0 20 40 60 80 100 MILES
0 40 80 120 160 KILOMETERS

Pokhara is one of the fastest growing cities in Nepal.
© iStockphoto.com/Rajesh_KC.

Box 2.1 Nepal's Politico-Administrative Definition of Urban Areas

The Municipality Act of 1991, its 1997 amendment, and the Local Self-Governance Act of 1999 stipulated three criteria for designating urban local governments: (a) a minimum population of 10,000 in the Mountain and Hill zones and 20,000 in the Tarai, (b) the availability of basic urban infrastructure and services (such as a transportation link by road or air and access to telephone services), and (c) the size of internal revenues generated by the local government. Nepal's urban local governments are classified into the following three categories:

- *Metropolitan city:* a settlement with a minimum population of 300,000, at least Nr 400 million in annual revenue, and access to basic infrastructure.
- *Submetropolitan city:* a settlement with a minimum population of 100,000, at least Nr 100 million in annual revenue, and access to basic infrastructure.
- *Municipality:* a settlement with a minimum population of 20,000, at least Nr 5 million in annual revenue, and access to basic infrastructure. In the Mountain and Hill zones, a settlement with a population of 10,000, annual revenue of Nr 0.5 million, and limited infrastructure can also be declared a municipality.

Sources: Government of Nepal 1991, 1999.

---

of the country, with an urban population of about 1.5 million in 2011. The urban population of the valley has increased fivefold in just 60 years, from 197,000 people in 1952 to 996,000 in 2001 and to 1.5 million in 2011, accounting now for 32 percent of the country's urban population. The urban population in the Kathmandu Valley continues to grow at an annual rate

Table 2.1 Urbanization Patterns by Region and Ecological Zone, 1991–2011

	Urban centers (number)[a]	Distribution of urban population (%)		Population living in urban areas (%)		Annual urban population growth rate (%)		
		2001	2011	2001	2011	1991–2001 (reclassification excluded)	1991–2001 (reclassification included)	2001–11
Region								
Eastern	14	19	18	11	14	2.3	6.0	2.8
Central	20	50	50	25	24	4.0	5.5	3.5
Western	12	16	17	13	16	4.4	8.2	3.8
Midwestern	6	7	7	8	10	2.8	8.4	3.3
Far Western	6	8	7	13	13	3.6	7.2	3.1
Ecological zone								
Tarai	29	46	44	15	15	3.3	5.7	3.1
Hills	27	53	55	20	22	3.9	6.6	3.6
Mountains	2	1	1	3	3	n.a.	n.a.	1.3
Nepal	**58**	**100**	**100**	**14**	**17**	**3.6**	**6.4**	**3.4**

Sources: Based on 1991, 2001, and 2011 population census data (CBS 1991, 2001, 2012).

Note: n.a. = not applicable. Totals may not equal 100 percent due to rounding.

a. Urban centers correspond to urban local governments.

Map 2.2 Development Regions, Corridors, and Urban Centers, 2011 Population

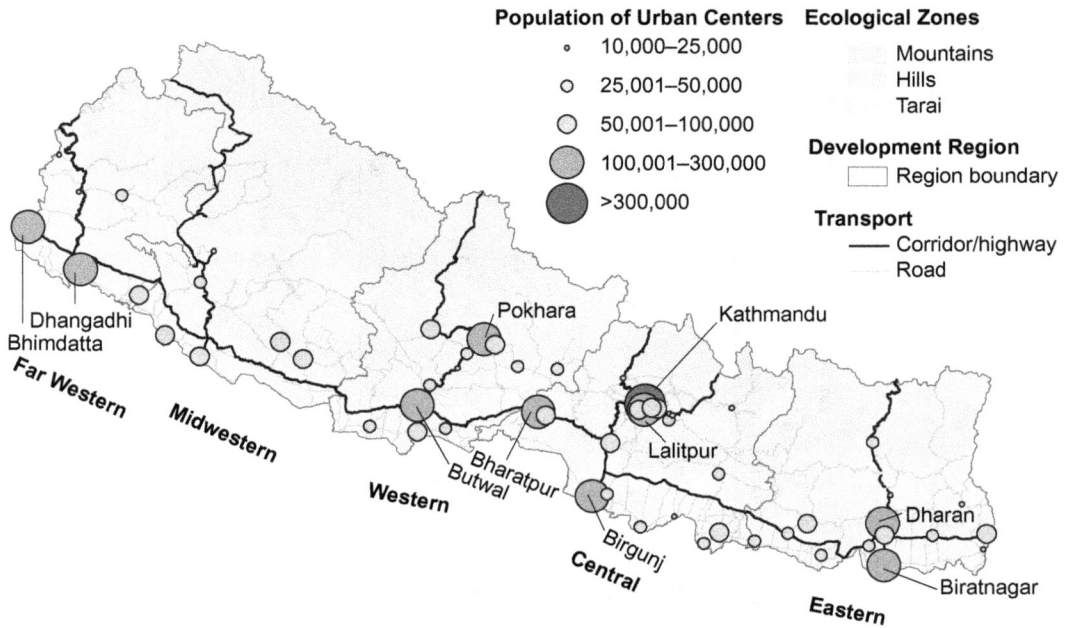

Population of Urban Centers
- ∘ 10,000–25,000
- ○ 25,001–50,000
- ◯ 50,001–100,000
- ⬤ 100,001–300,000
- ⬤ >300,000

Ecological Zones
- Mountains
- Hills
- Tarai

Development Region
- ☐ Region boundary

Transport
- —— Corridor/highway
- ⋯ Road

Source: Based on 2011 population census data (CBS 2012).
Note: Kathmandu refers to Kathmandu Metropolitan City; Biratnagar, Birgunj, Lalitpur, and Pokhara refer to the submetropolitan cities; and all other urban local governments are referred to as municipalities.

Figure 2.1 Population and Annual Population Growth of Urban Centers, 1991–2011

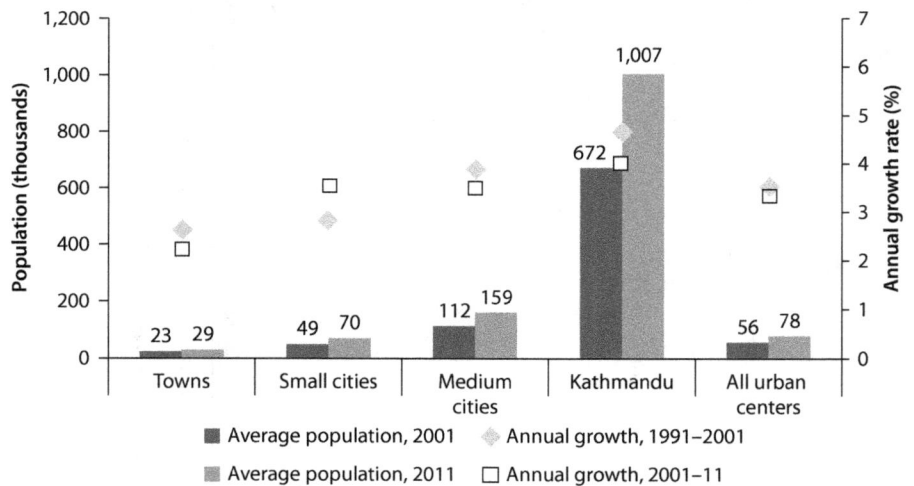

- ■ Average population, 2001   ◆ Annual growth, 1991–2001
- ■ Average population, 2011   ☐ Annual growth, 2001–11

Sources: Based on 2001 and 2011 population census data (CBS 2001, 2012).
Note: Kathmandu refers to Kathmandu Metropolitan City. Urban local governments are classified in four city size categories: 31 towns (with population below 50,000), 17 small cities (population of 50,000–100,000), 9 medium cities (population of 100,000–300,000), and Kathmandu. The classification of urban centers by population size is based on 2011 population census data. The population growth rate of urban centers from 1991 to 2001 excludes reclassification.

Figure 2.2 Population and Annual Population Growth Rate of the Largest Medium and Small Cities, 2001 and 2011

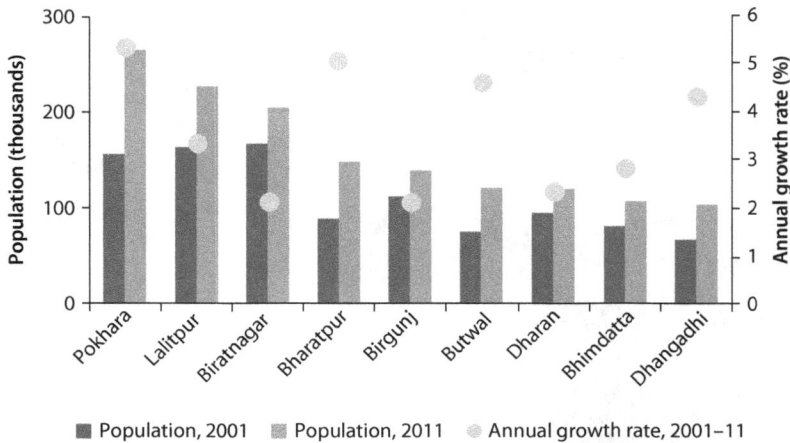

■ Population, 2001   ▦ Population, 2011   ● Annual growth rate, 2001–11

Sources: Based on 2001 and 2011 population census data (CBS 2001, 2012).
Note: Kathmandu excluded; Biratnagar, Birgunj, Lalitpur, and Pokhara refer to the submetropolitan cities; and all other urban local governments are referred to as municipalities.

Map 2.3 The Kathmandu Valley

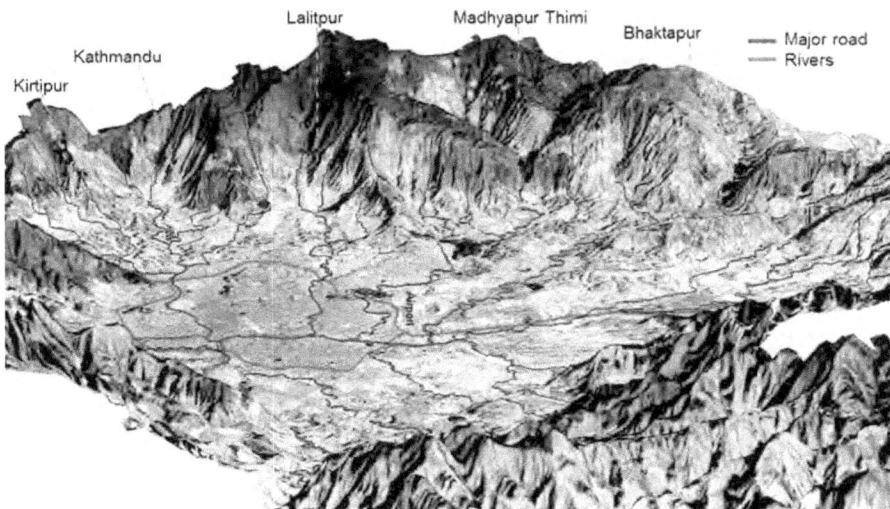

Source: Thapa and Murayama 2009.

of about 3.9 percent per year, according to 2011 population census data (see appendix). This growth rate makes the Kathmandu Valley one of the fastest-growing urban agglomerations in South Asia. By comparison, the Dhaka City Corporation, the urban core of the Dhaka metropolitan area, has an annual growth rate of about 3.0–3.5 percent per year, according to 2010 unpublished population survey data (World Bank, forthcoming).

Modernity blends with traditions in the streets of Kathmandu Metropolitan City.
© ECS Nepal. Used with permission. Permission required for further re-use.

The Kathmandu Valley is characterized by sustained population growth in the urban core and rapid urban sprawl. The Kathmandu Valley comprises five urban settlements (Bhaktapur, Kathmandu, Kirtipur, Lalitpur, and Madhyapur Thimi) and peri-urban areas (administratively classified as rural local governments). The largest urban settlement in the valley—Kathmandu—contains 40 percent of the valley's population and has recorded a rapid population growth rate of over 4 percent since the late 1970s. Such a fast rate of growth is expected to continue until 2020, when Kathmandu alone will reach more than 1.5 million people. The boundaries of the Kathmandu Valley's urban agglomeration are also expanding fast as a result of sprawl at the periphery. Annual population growth is very high in the peripheral municipalities of Kirtipur (5.0 percent) and Madhyapur Thimi (5.7 percent) and in the peri-urban areas officially classified as rural space, where population grew at 4.8 percent per year from 2001 to 2011 (see figure 2.3 and table 2.2).

Although larger urban centers, such as Kathmandu and Pokhara,[5] continue to grow steadily, significant growth is also happening in "gateway" settlements, such as market towns and border towns strategically located on major highway junctures between the east-west highway and the five main north-south corridors. Throughout the Tarai zone, which accounts for about 44 percent of total urban population (see table 2.1), a number of urban growth centers have developed at railheads on the border with India. Each north-south corridor consists of a main arterial linking a number of towns. The main urban centers in each corridor are Biratnagar (east), Birgunj (center), Butwal (west),

Figure 2.3 Population and Annual Population Growth Rate of Kathmandu Metropolitan City, 1950–2025

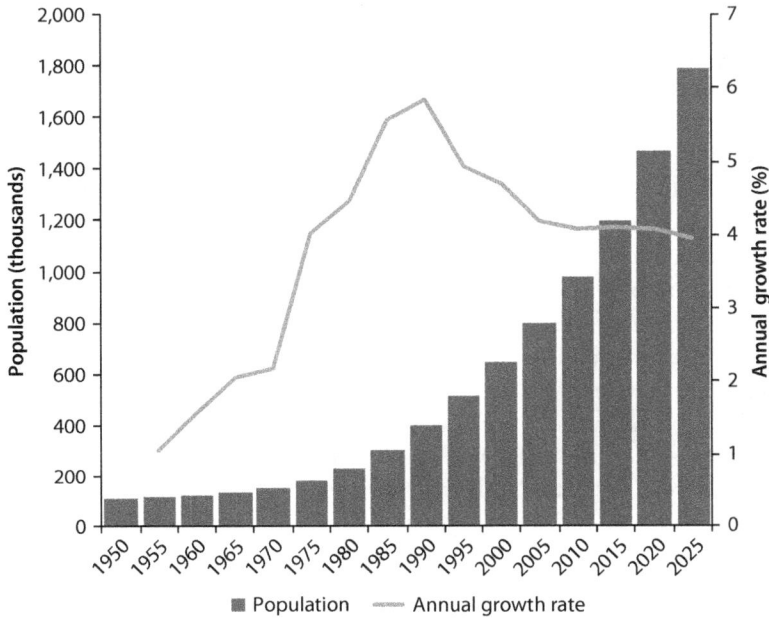

Source: Based on UNDESA 2012.

Table 2.2 Population of the Kathmandu Valley, 1991–2011

	Average annual growth rate (%)		Population (thousands)		Distribution of population (%)	
	1991–2001	2001–11	2001	2011	2001	2011
Kathmandu	4.7	4.0	672	1,007	41	40
Lalitpur	3.4	3.3	163	223	10	9
Bhaktapur	1.6	1.4	72	84	4	3
Kirtipur	2.4	5.0	40	67	2	3
Madhyapur Thimi[a]	4.1	5.7	48	84	3	3
Kathmandu Valley (urban)	4.1	3.9	996	1,465	61	58
Kathmandu Valley (peri-urban)[b]	3.8	4.8	649	1,047	39	42
Kathmandu Valley (total)	**4.0**	**4.3**	**1,645**	**2,517**	**100**	**100**

Sources: Based on 1991, 2001, and 2011 population census data (CBS 1991, 2001, and 2012).
Note: Kathmandu refers to Kathmandu Metropolitan City; Lalitpur refers to the submetropolitan city; and Kirtipur and Madhyapur Thimi refer to the municipalities.
a. Declared municipalities after 1991.
b. Peri-urban areas are administratively classified as rural areas.

Nepalgunj (midwest), and Dhangadhi (far west). Most growth centers are constituted as *urban economic regions*—larger zones where a city exercises an economic influence over the surrounding rural hinterland and where rural inhabitants can reach the urban center within a day by nonmotorized transportation (ADB 2010). On the map, urban economic regions comprise agglomerations of cities or larger towns surrounded by a string of smaller settlements, all of which function as a single economic unit. Along the main highways, the fastest-growing small urban settlements with populations below 100,000 and growth in excess of 4 percent include Damak and Itahari (Eastern Tarai); Banepa (Central Hills); Byas and Tansen (Western Hills); Gorahi and Tulsipur (Midwestern Tarai); and Birendranagar (Midwestern Hills) (see appendix).

Reclassification of rural into urban areas is an important driver of urban growth in Nepal. The urban population growth rate increases from 3.6 percent to 6.5 percent over the period from 1991 to 2001 if reclassification is included. Twenty-five new municipalities were declared between 1991 and 2001, and reclassification accounted for 50 percent of total urban growth. With the proposed creation of 41 new municipalities, reclassification will continue to be an important driver of urban growth in the future. The establishment of the proposed new municipalities, when effective, will result in an increase in the proportion of population residing in urban area by 4 percentage points, from 17 to 21 percent.[6] About 54 percent of the population in the proposed new municipalities is in the Tarai zone, and 34 percent is in the Central Region (see table 2.1). From 2001 to 2011, the proposed new municipalities had a population growth rate of 2.1 percent per year—above the growth rate for rural areas (1.2 percent) but significantly below the rate for existing urban areas (3.4 percent) (CBS 1991, 2001, 2012).

On the ground, the spatial transformation is not fully captured by the politico-administrative definition of urban areas. In Nepal, a municipality with rural characteristics may be located in the vicinity of rural-classified urbanlike emerging towns. The disconnect between urban geography on the ground and

Lekhnath, a municipality of nearly 60,000 inhabitants close to Pokhara Submetropolitan City still presents rural characteristics.

the politico-administrative definition of urban areas is the result of Nepal's legal definition of urban settlements, as spelled out in the Municipality Act and the Local Self-Governance Act, which overemphasizes the role of population size while assigning little weight to other urban criteria, such as population density and economic structure of urban areas (Government of Nepal 1991, 1999) (see box 2.1).

On one hand, a number of Nepal's existing municipalities present large shares of land area with rural characteristics. Many of Nepal's municipalities have attained urban status through the amalgamation of a number of village development committees (VDCs), which taken together had a sufficiently large population to meet the act's criteria. As a result, a number of municipalities have not yet experienced the demographic and economic transformations that characterize urban areas, and they continue to exhibit rural characteristics. In 2011, the population density (defined as people per square kilometer and shown in parentheses) in a number of municipalities, such as Amargadhi (160), Kamalamai (198), and Triyuga (223), was comparable or only slightly above the density of rural areas (153 people per square kilometer) and the OECD's (Organisation for Economic Co-operation and Development) population density threshold for urban areas of 150 people per square kilometer (OECD 1994).[7]

On the other hand, several rural-classified emerging towns, with urban characteristics, are growing under the radar. In Nepal, towns classified as rural not uncommonly have populations and industrial production densities comparable with or higher than those of municipalities. About 300 VDCs exhibit population and employment densities that are almost as high as those of municipalities. Further, three VDCs—Baliya, Jorpati, and Krishnapur—have manufacturing employment densities that are higher than those of any municipality.[8] The Department of Urban Development and Building Construction (DUDBC) and the Department of Water Supply and Sewerage (DWSS) have identified a number of emerging towns with urban characteristics, yet many of those towns remain administratively classified as rural.[9] The large number of rural-classified emerging towns suggests that Nepal's urbanization level may be understated. According to the *World Development Report 2009* agglomeration index of urbanization, which classifies urban areas by population density and distance to centers of human settlement of 50,000 or more, Nepal's urbanization level (the percentage of the population living in urban areas) was as high as 26 percent in 2000 (World Bank 2009). This rate is higher than the 13 percent recognized by the government and the Central Bureau of Statistics for that year, and even higher than the current estimated urbanization rate of 17 percent.

The proposed creation of 41 new municipalities is a reflection of Nepal's sustained process of urbanization, but the reclassification would not contribute to making Nepal's urban structure more consistent, because the criteria for municipal selection remain unchanged. Developing a new urban classification, taking into account such features as population density, economic links, road access, and infrastructure, may help obtain a better understanding of the spatial transition that is under way in Nepal.

Internal Migration: A Powerful Force for Urban Change

Internal migration is an important livelihood strategy, although it is not as prevalent as international migration.[10] This section studies internal migration patterns and drivers of migration in Nepal based on data from the Labor Force Survey 2008 (CBS 2009). Both recent migration (during the period from 2002 to 2007) and lifetime migration (up to 2007) are considered.[11]

Migration: A Driver of the Urban Transformation

Migration is an important driver of Nepal's urban transformation and is increasing over time. A net inflow of migrants to urban areas is balanced by a net outflow from rural areas. The inflow of migrants to urban areas represents 45 percent of Nepal's urban population compared with an outflow of 16 percent of the urban population (see box 2.2). These high levels of inbound urban migrants are an important source of urban growth. During the 1990s, migration contributed 30 percent to total urban growth, on average, and as much as 40 percent to urban growth in Kathmandu, which has the largest net inflow of migrants among urban areas (ADB 2010). The contribution of internal migration to urbanization is growing over time, because urban areas are becoming more common migration destinations: 34 percent of recent migrants have moved to urban areas, compared with 23 percent of lifetime migrants.

Box 2.2 Internal Mobility and Migration Flows

Turnover or gross migration—calculated as the total number of people moving in and out of a given area—is a measure of total population mobility in Nepal. Gross lifetime migration amounts to 11.5 million people in rural areas, compared with only 2.1 million people in urban areas. Thus, the magnitude of migratory flows suggests that rural-to-rural migration is the prevailing form of internal mobility in Nepal.

When migration is measured as a percentage of local population rather than in absolute terms, mobility is slightly higher in urban areas than in rural areas. Turnover accounts for 61 percent of urban population compared with 56 percent of rural population when lifetime migration is considered. (This turnover means that the total number of people who moved into and out of urban areas is equivalent to 61 percent of the current urban population.) A similar picture emerges for recent migration: turnover is estimated at 17 percent of urban population and 9 percent of rural population.

---

box continues next page

Box 2.2 Internal Mobility and Migration Flows *(continued)*

Figure B2.2.1 Internal Urban and Rural Migration Flows, Lifetime Migration, 2008

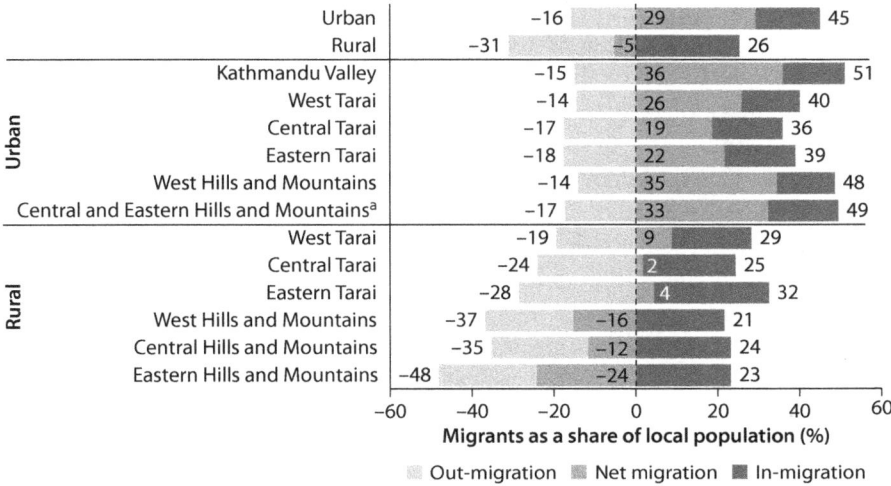

Source: Based on Labor Force Survey 2008 (CBS 2009).
Note: West includes Western, Midwestern, and Far Western Regions.
a. Central Hills excludes Kathmandu Valley.

Moreover, a net inflow of migrants to urban areas is balanced by a net outflow from rural areas. Urban areas in all ecological zones and development regions registered a net inflow of migrants. Only rural areas in the Tarai zone have experienced a net inflow of lifetime migrants (542,000 people). The Hills and the more remote rural Mountains have a net outflow of migrants (1.6 million people) (see figure B2.2.1).

The Kathmandu Valley has the largest net inflow of migrants among urban areas. Lifetime net migration to the Kathmandu Valley, estimated at 419,000 people, is more than twice the net level of migration to any other urban region. The urban areas in the Mountain and Hill zones of West Nepal, which have the second-largest net inflow of migrants, have a net migration of only 176,000 people. Similar patterns hold when population shares are considered. The net inflow of migrants in the Kathmandu Valley accounts for 36 percent of the valley's urban population. In the West Nepal Hills and Mountains, there is a net inflow of migrants to urban areas equivalent to 35 percent of the urban population, and a net outflow of migrants to rural areas, equivalent to 16 percent of the rural population (see figure B2.2.1).

Source: Based on Labor Force Survey 2008 (CBS 2009).
Note: West Nepal includes the Western, Midwestern, and Far Western Regions.

Migration and Barriers to Mobility

Physical barriers to mobility constrain migrants to move locally. Because economic opportunities tend to decrease with distance from major urban centers, migrants in search of job opportunities would benefit the most from traveling long distances—from remote areas all the way to the most prosperous cities—but migration costs constrain many migrants to move locally. In Nepal, physical distance constitutes an important barrier to internal mobility. Within any development region, 68 percent of migrants travel locally, that is, within the same region and ecological zone (see figure 2.4).[12] A significantly lower percentage of migrants (equivalent to about 13 percent of lifetime migrants) travel to a different region from the one in which they were born (see figure 2.5). This migration pattern can be partially explained by the country's rugged topography and limited connectivity, which make travel across regions difficult. About half of Nepal's road network is concentrated in the Tarai—including the only highway in the east-west direction (ADB 2010). Moreover, those living in the Mountain zone, where only two urban centers are located, find reaching distant urban centers located in the Hills and the Tarai particularly difficult.

Migrants to the Kathmandu Valley travel longer distances. The influence of physical distance on migrants' choice of destination varies by region. The Central Region, where the Kathmandu Valley is located, is the largest gravity center for long-distance migration. That fact suggests that those who can afford long-distance migration move to the one location in Nepal where economic opportunities are greatest. The Central Region accounts for about 36 percent of total lifetime migrants in Nepal. About 20 percent of lifetime migrants in the Central Region are from a different region, compared with only 6 percent and 8 percent of lifetime migrants in the Eastern and Western Regions, respectively (see figure 2.5).

Migrants may prefer to remain in areas with a shared linguistic, ethnic, religious, and cultural background. However, the analysis finds that *social distance*—the difference between a migrant's ethnic group and the share of that ethnic group in the population of a given area—is not a significant barrier

Figure 2.4 Percentage of Migrants Who Travel Locally, by Region, Lifetime Migration, 2008

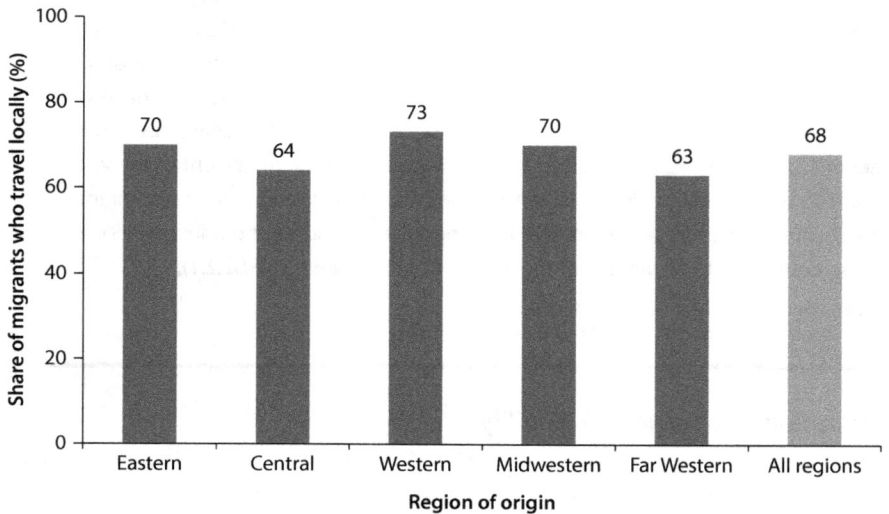

Source: Based on Labor Force Survey 2008 (CBS 2009).
Note: Local migration is defined as intraregional and intraecological-zone migration; that is, local migrants are those traveling within the same region and the same ecological zone. Trends among recent migrants are similar to those for lifetime migrants.

Figure 2.5 Regional Migration Patterns, by Origin and Destination, Lifetime Migration, 2008

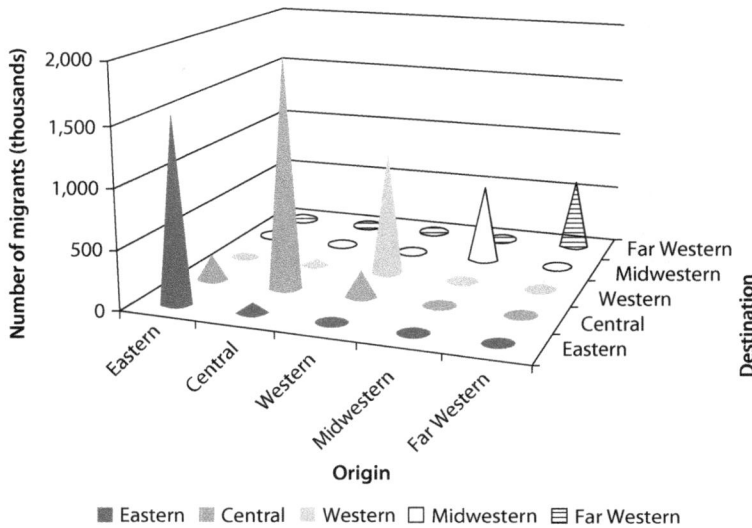

Source: Based on Labor Force Survey 2008 (CBS 2009).

to mobility.[13] In Nepal, only 20 percent of migrants chose destinations where social distance is low. The remaining 80 percent of migrants is equally split between those choosing a destination where social distance is medium or where it is high (see figure 2.6). Internal migrants may move to socially distant locations because of Nepal's diverse social structure: the population is composed of many different ethnic groups inhabiting distinctive pockets of territory across the country. An important consequence of migrating long social distances is that large socioeconomic differences may exist between migrants and locals, which may limit the ability of migrants to integrate the local population well. However, empirical evidence suggests that in spite of social distance, migrants have the means to tap into local economic opportunities—on average migrants are more educated and have better access to services than the locals. (see box 2.3).

Push and Pull Factors of Internal Migration

Migrants are made up of those in search of better living standards—the "pull" migrants—and those who have been forced out of their birthplace by a lack of job opportunities, poor public services, and natural disasters—the "push" migrants (Fafchamps and Shilpi 2009). Push factors are the predominant force driving internal migration in Nepal, accounting for as much as 88 percent of lifetime migration. However, important gender differences exist in the migration patterns and the forces driving migration. Migration is twice as common among females as males: the 2001 rate of lifetime migration for males and females is 21 and 44 percent, respectively. Females reportedly migrate for social reasons 97 percent of the time, compared with 64 percent of the time

Figure 2.6 Percentage of Migrants with Medium or Large Social Distance, by Region, Lifetime Migration, 2008

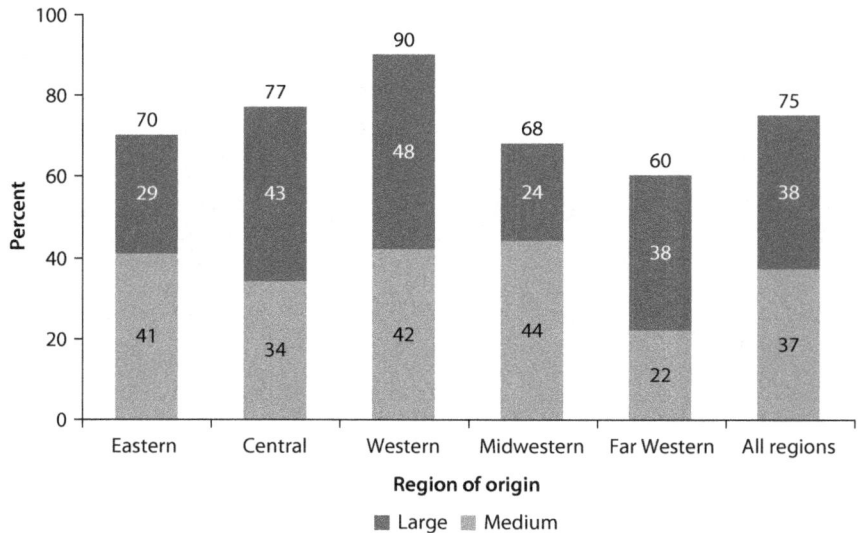

Source: Based on Labor Force Survey 2008 (CBS 2009).
Note: Social distance is defined as the difference between a migrant's ethnic group and the share of that ethnic group in the population of a given area. It captures differences in linguistics, ethnicity, religion, and cultural background.

for males. Another push factor driving recent migration is the decadelong civil conflict. Although exact figures are not available, the civil conflict forced an estimated 1 million or more people to flee their homes, resulting in an escalation of migration (ADB 2010; Sengupta and Sharma 2006; Williams and Pradhan 2008).

The number of migrants who move for economic reasons is increasing. Economic migration has gained importance as a livelihood strategy in recent years: pull factors—that is, the search for better employment and education opportunities—account for 43 percent of recent urban migration, compared with 32 percent of lifetime urban migration. Economic migration presents two distinct geographic patterns. First, those who move for economic reasons tend to settle in urban areas. Pull factors account for 32 percent of lifetime migration to urban areas but only 8 percent of lifetime migration to rural areas. Second, migrants who move for economic reasons are willing to travel longer distances than migrants pushed by social reasons. As many as 44 percent of nonlocal migrants to urban areas moved in search of jobs or for study and training purposes, compared with only 28 percent of local migrants to urban areas (see figure 2.7).

More and more migrants are pulled to the Kathmandu Valley by economic opportunities. Large differences in economic opportunities across locations motivate people to migrate and to reap the benefits of living in a more prosperous place. Compared with other urban areas, the Kathmandu Valley exhibits a larger

Box 2.3 Migrants' Socioeconomic Profile

Empirical evidence suggests that migrants tend to be more educated than locals across all regions and across both urban and rural areas. Recent migrants have the highest levels of education, followed by lifetime migrants, whereas locals lag behind. On average, 71 percent of lifetime migrants have completed primary education, compared to 48 percent of nonmigrants. In the Kathmandu Valley, however, the educational differences between migrants and nonmigrants are fewer than in other areas of the country.

Migrants seek better access to public services. Access to public services is an important consideration in migrants' choice of destination (Fafchamps and Shilpi 2009). Nepal's internal migrants have better access to public services than locals, on average. Nevertheless, important variations across regions remain. Differences in access to public services between migrants and nonmigrants are greater in urban areas than in rural areas. In the Kathmandu Valley, however, migrants have similar access to services as locals. Interestingly, recent migrants have greater access to public services than lifetime migrants, which may reflect the fact that recent migrants are better educated and more skilled (see figure B2.3.1).

Figure B2.3.1 Percentage of Migrant and Nonmigrant Population with Access to Services, 2008

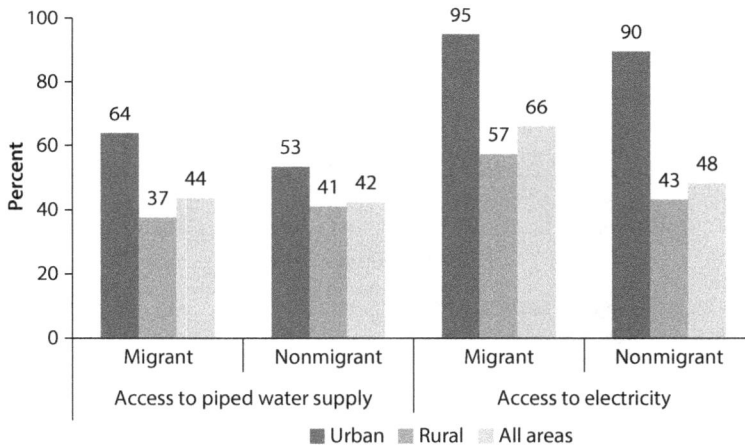

Source: Based on Labor Force Survey 2008 (CBS 2009).

share of migrants who are pulled by economic reasons. More than 25 percent of lifetime migration to the Kathmandu Valley is for job-related reasons, against an average of 19 percent for urban areas. The percentage is significantly higher, at 50 percent, for recent migrants. In addition, education-related migration to the Kathmandu Valley is on the rise, increasing from 17 percent of lifetime migration to as much as 27 percent of recent migration.

A strong correlation exists between long-distance urban migration and returns to mobility. In urban areas, economic opportunities are greatest and nonfarm

Figure 2.7 Economic Drivers of Migration, by Distance, Lifetime and Recent Migration, 2008

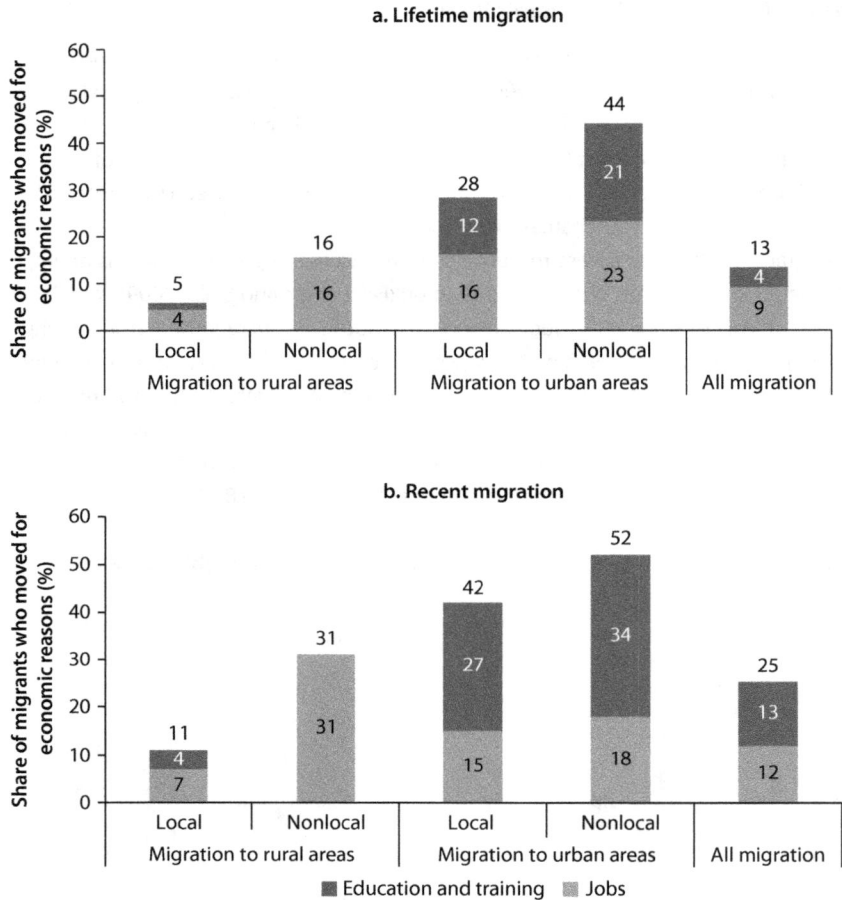

a. Lifetime migration

b. Recent migration

Education and training ■ Jobs

Source: Based on Labor Force Survey 2008 (CBS 2009).
Note: *Local migration* is defined as intraregional and intraecological-zone migration; that is, local migrants are those
traveling within the same region and the same ecological zone. *Nonlocal migration* includes short-distance migration
(to a neighboring ecological zone or region), medium-distance migration (to the second-closest neighboring area),
and long-distance migration (to the third-closest neighboring area).

employment is more common, allowing migrants to escape survival agriculture
and to join the ranks of the service or industrial workforce. The large majority
(85 percent) of local rural-to-rural migrants work in their own or family businesses, which provide insurance against unemployment, and only 15 percent
work in paid employment, whereas a higher share (39 percent) of local rural-to-
urban migrants succeed in finding paid employment. Long-distance migrants are
also more likely to work in paid employment than local migrants. Only about
30 percent of long-distance migrants moving from rural to urban areas work in
their own or family businesses, compared to as many as 60 percent of local
migrants moving from rural to urban areas.

Main Patterns and Emerging Trends of Nepal's Spatial Economy

Nonfarm economic activity decreases with distance from towns and with geographic isolation, an association that carries particular significance in Nepal because of its difficult topography dominated by mountains and rivers. Rural areas account for 83 percent of the country's population based on 2011 census of population data and 64 percent of nonfarm employment (CBS 2012; see figure 2.8). However, on average, the share of nonfarm activities relative to overall employment is only 16 percent in rural areas, compared with 59 percent in urban areas, and 82 percent in the Kathmandu Valley (see figure 2.9). Within rural areas, nonfarm economic activities are more prevalent in proximity to urban centers. This prevalence indicates a distinct spatial division of labor in Nepal: nonfarm employment predominates in and around cities and markets, whereas farm employment is concentrated in more distant rural areas (Fafchamps and Shilpi 2002).

Nonfarm economic production is concentrated in three main clusters in the Kathmandu Valley, the Central Tarai, and the Eastern Tarai. These clusters form a core urban center surrounded by a hinterland of small towns and rural areas and function as extended urban economic regions. Within such extended regions, firms are able to reap the benefits from demand-and-supply links between rural and urban areas (World Bank 2010), as well as to exploit agglomeration economies. The main cluster, located in the Kathmandu Valley within the Central Hills, accounts for 25 percent of nonfarm employment, equivalent to as many as 631,000 employees. The second cluster, located in the Eastern Tarai surrounding Biratnagar, accounts for another 18 percent of nonfarm

Figure 2.8 Rural Share of Nonfarm Employment, by Region and Ecological Zone, 2008

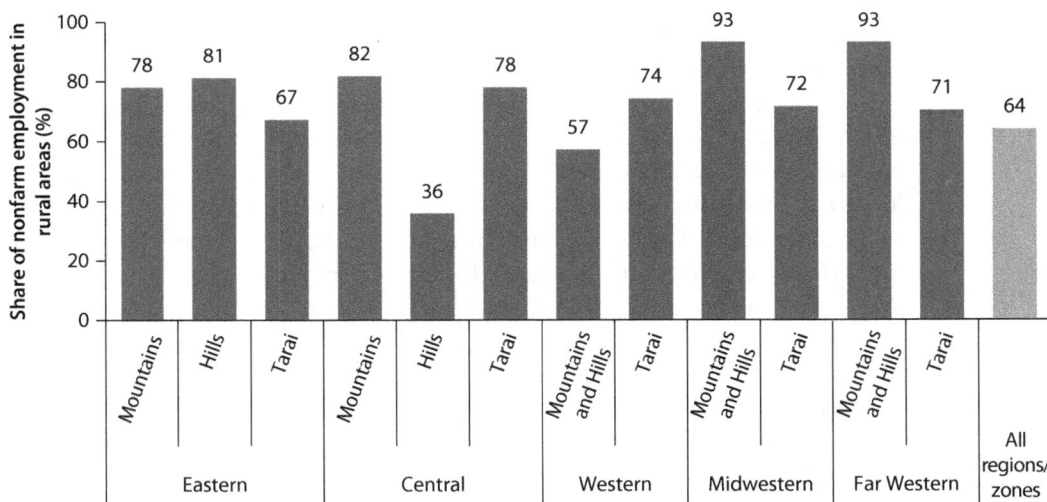

Source: Based on Labor Force Survey 2008 (CBS 2009).

Figure 2.9 Nonfarm Employment as a Share of Total Employment, by Region, 2008

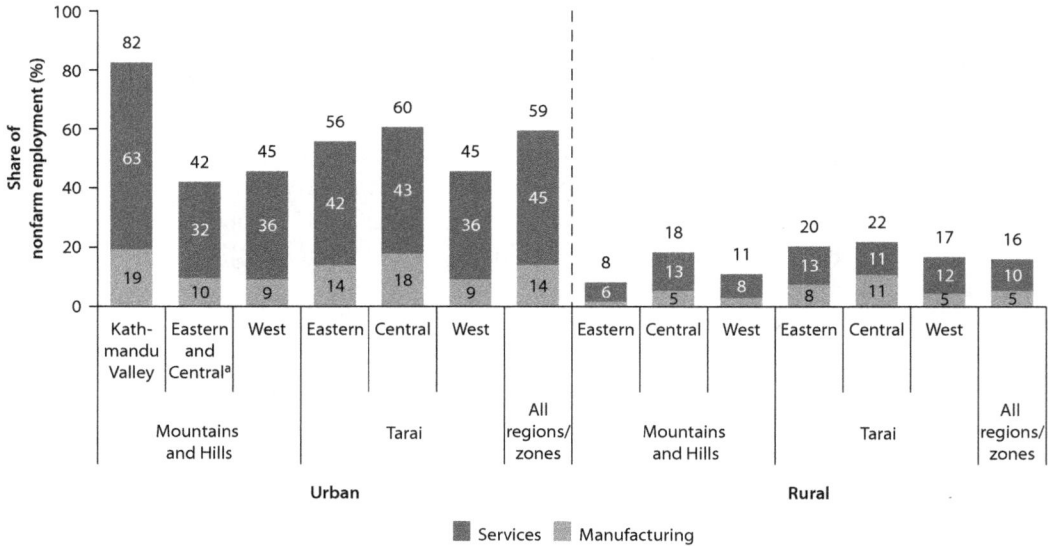

Source: Based on Labor Force Survey 2008 (CBS 2009).
Note: Nonfarm employment includes services and manufacturing. West includes the Western, Midwestern, and Far Western Regions.
a. Central Hills excludes Kathmandu Valley.

employment, equivalent to 446,000 employees. The third cluster, located in the Central Tarai surrounding Birgunj, accounts for 19 percent of nonfarm employment, equivalent to another 478,000 employees (see figures 2.10 and 2.11).

The Spatial Geography of the Services Sector

The services sector is the largest contributor to gross domestic product (GDP), accounting for 47 percent of GDP and as much as 72 percent of nonfarm employment. The services sector is also the main driver of economic growth: services' contribution to GDP doubled from 26 to 47 percent over the last 30 years (World Bank 2011b). However, the services sector still accounts for only 15 percent of overall employment, and it remains concentrated in low-value-added trading activities (with the exception of tourism-related services). The sector's performance has been constrained by the low growth rate of the overall economy (below 4 percent on average, since 2001). Moreover, in recent years, tourism has declined in relative importance as a foreign exchange earner because of growth in other sources of foreign exchange, such as remittances (UNCTAD 2011).

Services and manufacturing activities tend to locate in the vicinity of each other to benefit from agglomeration economies. For example, artisans may benefit from locating in areas where tourism and financial services are available. In Nepal, the overall distribution of service employment is similar to that of nonfarm employment: service employment is geographically concentrated in the three main clusters of the Kathmandu Valley, the Central Tarai, and the

Figure 2.10 Nonfarm Employment, by Region and Ecological Zone, 2008

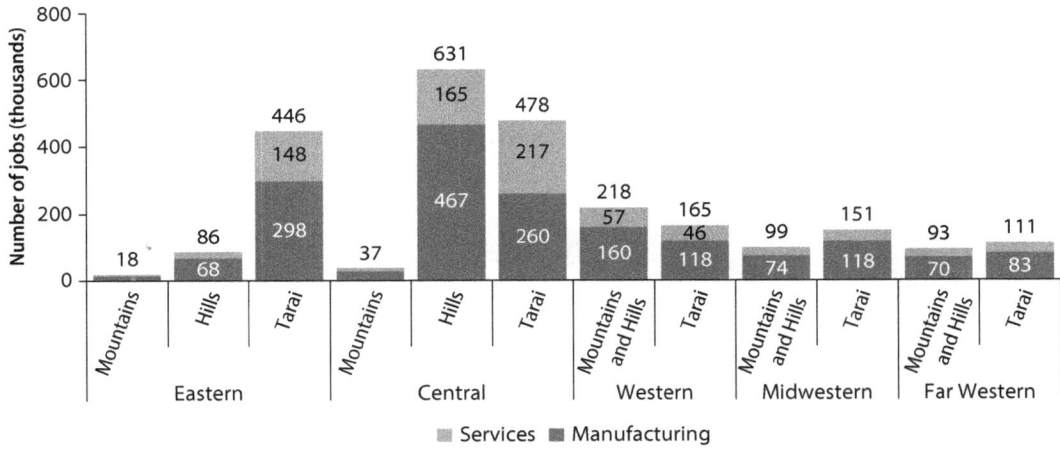

Source: Based on Labor Force Survey 2008 (CBS 2009).

Figure 2.11 Regional Share of Urban Nonfarm Employment, 2008

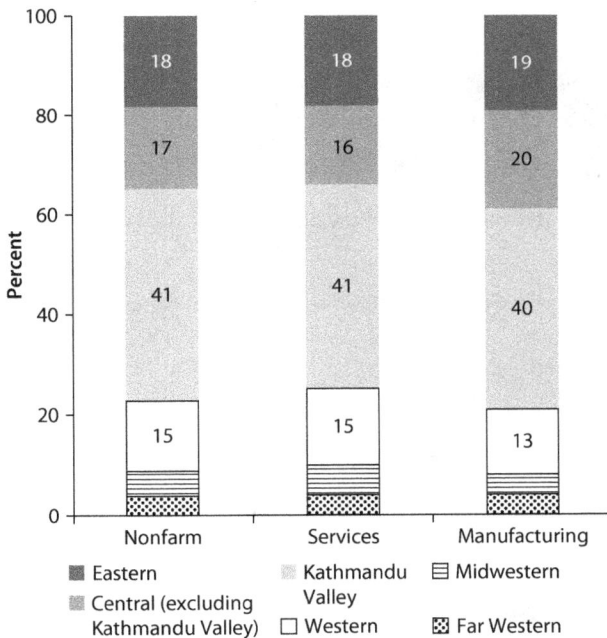

Source: Based on Labor Force Survey 2008 (CBS 2009).

Eastern Tarai. The concentration of service activities is particularly pronounced within the Kathmandu Valley (41 percent of total, see figure 2.11). The Central Hills—where the valley is located—has almost twice as many service employees as any other region (see figure 2.12). The sectoral composition of Nepal's economic clusters shows that, at the heart of each economic cluster, is an urban core, which plays the role of a service center for an extended economic region with manufacturing concentrated in the rural hinterland. Relative to manufacturing employment, service employment is predominantly urban. On average, the urban share of service employment (39 percent) is larger than the urban share of manufacturing employment (28 percent) and this holds across most regions of Nepal (see figures 2.12 and 2.16).

The economic base of the services sector in urban areas is dominated by small wholesale and retail services. Small retail activities, which have mushroomed in many Nepalese towns, constitute the bulk of trading services, which account for over one-third of overall service employment and represent an important livelihood

Tansen, a municipality in the Western Province, is the main service center for the district population.

Figure 2.12 Employment in the Service Sector, by Region and Ecological Zone, 2008

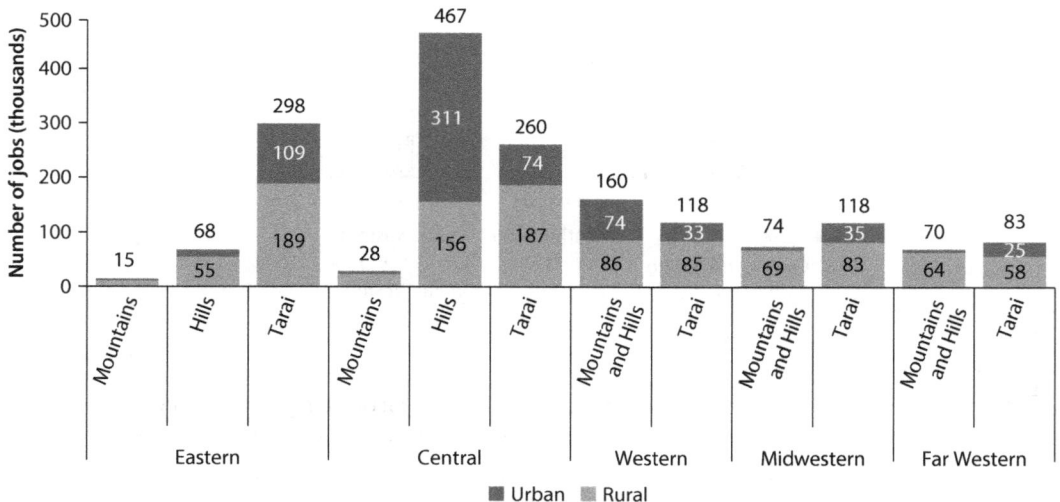

Source: Based on Labor Force Survey 2008 (CBS 2009).

strategy for much of Nepal's population. The second main component of service employment is public administration and social services, which account for as much as 27 percent of service employment. Although financial services and the tourism industry account for only 9 percent and 11 percent of service employment, respectively, both sectors have important potential for development. The tourism industry has been held back by the decadelong conflict, but Nepal has a strong comparative advantage in tourism, given its stunning physical beauty and distinctive cultural and spiritual diversity (see chapter 3). The financial sector also has potential for development because of strong remittance flows. In spite of its potential, however, the economic base of the services sector in urban areas remains weak, and the urban composition of service employment is very similar to the rural composition. Little variation occurs across regions (see figure 2.13).

The Spatial Geography of the Manufacturing Sector

Manufacturing is characterized by small-scale industries whose performance has been declining over time. The performance of the manufacturing sector has been sluggish since 2001, and its contribution to GDP has declined to about 15 percent—down from 22 percent in 2000. Over the period from 2002 to 2007, employment in 10+[14] manufacturing fell by 2 percent annually and declined for most subsectors (with the exception of wood, chemicals, and machinery), and value added fell by 1 percent per year (see figure 2.14). This decline encompasses both urban and rural areas, with the exception of the rural Central Tarai. Small firms account for most of manufacturing employment. Even when only 10+ enterprises are considered, small firms, with fewer than

Figure 2.13 Sectoral Composition of Employment in the Service Sector, 2008

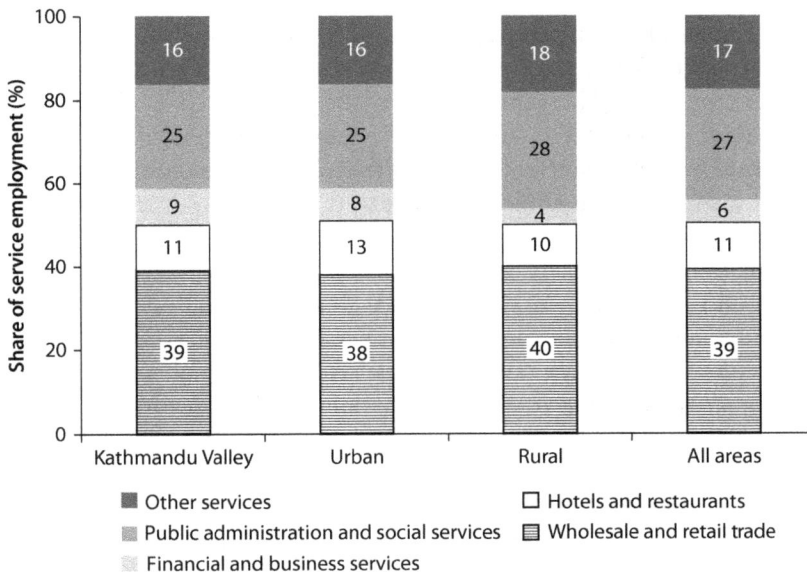

Source: Based on Labor Force Survey 2008 (CBS 2009).

Figure 2.14 Manufacturing Employment and Growth, by Sector, 2002–07

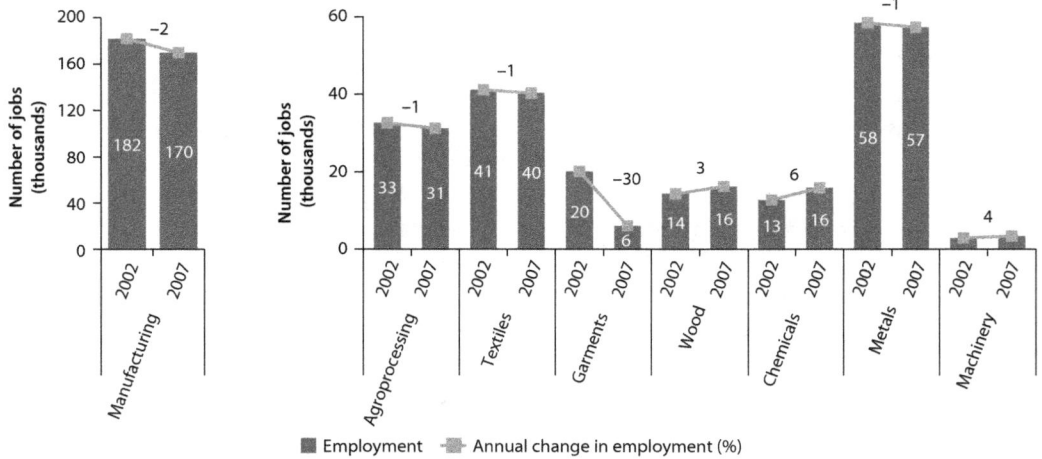

Sources: Based on Census of Manufacturing 2002 and 2007 (CBS 2003, 2007).
Note: Analysis includes firms with more than 10 employees.

20 employees, make up the bulk of the manufacturing base, and the proportion of small firms has increased slightly from 2002 to 2007 (see figure 2.15).

Manufacturing firms are clustered in the Kathmandu Valley and in proximity to the Indian border (see figure 2.16). The geographic distribution of manufacturing employment and output is similar to that of nonfarm employment, which indicates complementarities that exist between manufacturing and services. Maps 2.4 and 2.5 show an important concentration of 10+ manufacturing employment close to the Kathmandu Valley in the Central Region, and also in the vicinity of Birgunj and Biratnagar in the Eastern and Central Tarai. Smaller clusters can also be seen throughout the Tarai. The main cluster, located within the Kathmandu Valley, accounts for as much as 40 percent of overall manufacturing employment. The remaining two clusters, located in the Eastern and Central Tarai, account for another 17 percent and 15 percent of overall manufacturing employment, respectively. Each of these three main clusters has more than 100,000 manufacturing employees, close to three times as many manufacturing employees as any other region in Nepal (see map 2.4).

Manufacturing is spatially concentrated in rural areas. Given the concentration of the country's road network, including the east-west highway, in the Tarai and near the Indian border, the clustering of manufacturing activity within the Tarai zone is not surprising. Across all regions of Nepal, over half the manufacturing employment is located in rural areas. The only notable exception is the Central Hills—which includes the Kathmandu Valley—where the urban share of total manufacturing is nearly 60 percent. The small urban share of manufacturing employment may be explained in part by the classification of urban areas. As noted earlier, many areas designated as rural exhibit population and industrial production densities that are comparable to or higher than those of urban areas (see chapter 1 and map 2.5).

Figure 2.15 Firm Size Distribution of Manufacturing Firms, by Sector, 2002 and 2007

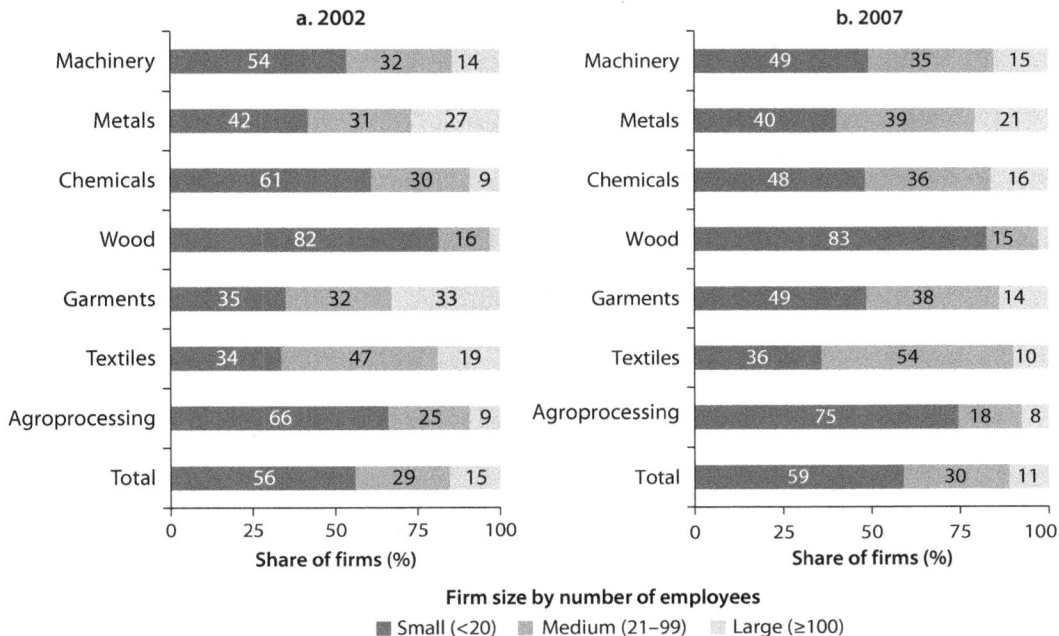

a. 2002

Sector	Small	Medium	Large
Machinery	54	32	14
Metals	42	31	27
Chemicals	61	30	9
Wood	82		16
Garments	35	32	33
Textiles	34	47	19
Agroprocessing	66	25	9
Total	56	29	15

Share of firms (%)

b. 2007

Sector	Small	Medium	Large
Machinery	49	35	15
Metals	40	39	21
Chemicals	48	36	16
Wood	83		15
Garments	49	38	14
Textiles	36	54	10
Agroprocessing	75	18	8
Total	59	30	11

Share of firms (%)

Firm size by number of employees

■ Small (<20)   ■ Medium (21–99)   Large (≥100)

Sources: Based on Census of Manufacturing 2002 and 2007 (CBS 2003, 2007).
Note: Analysis includes firms with more than 10 employees.

Figure 2.16 Manufacturing Employment, by Region and Ecological Zone, 2008

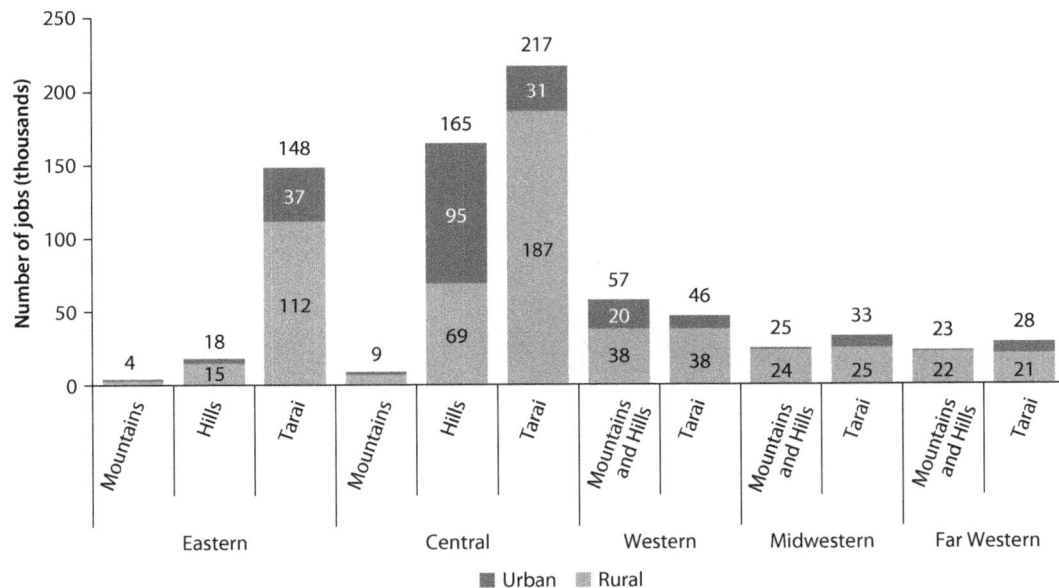

Region	Zone	Urban	Rural	Total
Eastern	Mountains			4
Eastern	Hills		15	18
Eastern	Tarai	37	112	148
Central	Mountains			9
Central	Hills	95	69	165
Central	Tarai	31	187	217
Western	Mountains and Hills	20	38	57
Western	Tarai		38	46
Midwestern	Mountains and Hills		24	25
Midwestern	Tarai		25	33
Far Western	Mountains and Hills		22	23
Far Western	Tarai		21	28

■ Urban   ■ Rural

Source: Based on Labor Force Survey 2008 (CBS 2009).

Urban Growth and Spatial Transition in Nepal • http://dx.doi.org/10.1596/978-0-8213-9659-9

Map 2.4 Manufacturing Employment Density, 2007

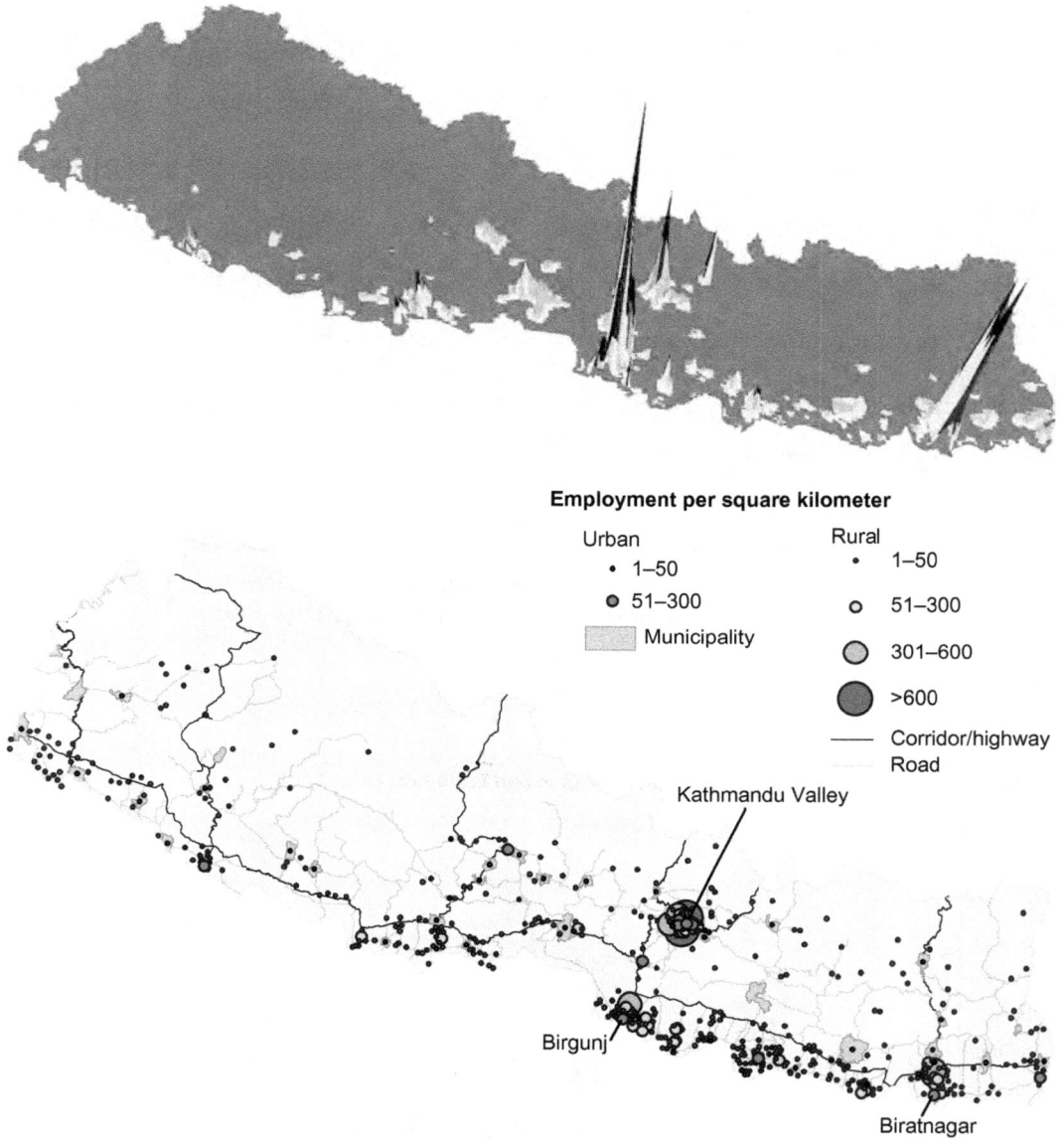

Source: Based on Census of Manufacturing 2007 (CBS 2007).
Note: Analysis includes firms with more than 10 employees. Biratnagar and Birgunj refer to the submetropolitan cities.

A new government industrial policy went into effect in 2010 with the objective of increasing employment opportunities in the manufacturing sector while promoting industrial growth. The 2010 industrial policy provides fiscal incentives and facilitation measures for industrial development and serves as an important stepping stone toward implementation of special economic zones (SEZs). Among the fiscal incentives for industrial growth, the 2010 industrial policy

Map 2.5 Manufacturing Output Density, 2007

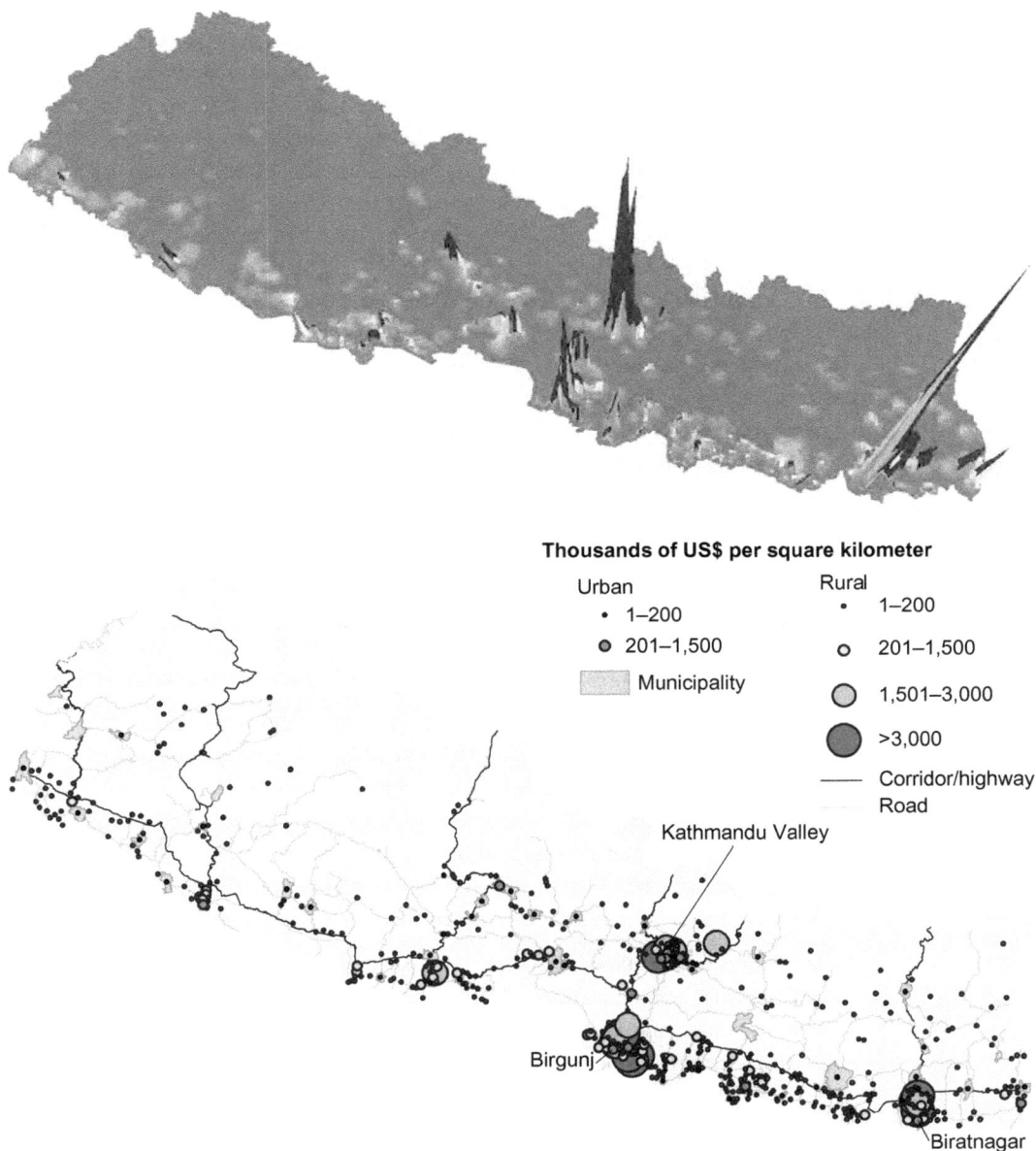

Thousands of US$ per square kilometer

Urban
- 1–200
- 201–1,500
- Municipality

Rural
- 1–200
- 201–1,500
- 1,501–3,000
- >3,000

— Corridor/highway
Road

Kathmandu Valley

Birgunj

Biratnagar

Source: Based on Census of Manufacturing 2007 (CBS 2007).
Note: Analysis includes firms with more than 10 employees. Biratnagar and Birgunj refer to the submetropolitan cities.

provides for tax incentives and government subsidies for infrastructure development in factory sites to firms that locate in lagging districts. Given that firms benefit from agglomeration economies and proximity to markets, fiscal incentives encouraging them to locate in districts with low population densities and

Urban Growth and Spatial Transition in Nepal • http://dx.doi.org/10.1596/978-0-8213-9659-9

far from major urban centers seldom yield the intended results. Policies aimed at deconcentrating manufacturing employment—from manufacturing clusters with strong comparative advantages to remote locations—may also harm Nepal's industrialization process in the long term. Policy interventions to address the main constraints to industrial expansion, such as infrastructure, in strategic growth centers with the potential to drive economic growth in an extended region are likely to be more effective. Although the establishment of SEZs in strategic locations could be instrumental in improving the investment climate, SEZs have not yet taken off, given delays in the Parliament's approval of the 2006 SEZ bill (see box 2.4).

Manufacturing activities are dominated by handicrafts and agroprocessing. Labor-intensive manufacturing (handicrafts) accounts for about 60 percent of total industrial production (see chapter 4). Agroprocessing accounts for as much as 19 percent of urban manufacturing employment, lower than the rural share of 28 percent. Garment manufacturing, at 19 percent of overall employment, is an important component of the urban manufacturing base (see table 2.3). However, this subsector has experienced a significant loss in export competitiveness in recent years (see box 2.5). Textiles, particularly jute, account for another 18 percent of overall employment. About 7 percent

---

Box 2.4 Key Features of Nepal's 2010 Industrial Policy and Its Implementation

The main objective of the 2010 industrial policy is to enhance the contribution of the industrial sector in national and regional employment by (a) boosting the export of competitive industrial products; (b) increasing the use of local resources, raw materials, and skills; (c) sustaining industrialization through the application of new technologies and environmentally friendly production processes; and (d) creating the enabling environment for Nepal to become an attractive destination in South Asia for investment. The 2010 industrial policy provides a number of facilitation and incentive measures to achieve these objectives.

- *Incentives and facilities.* Promotional incentive packages are available for export industries, particularly small and medium enterprises. Income tax concessions of 25 percent are given to small, medium, and large industries that directly employ 100, 300, and 600 people, respectively. Income tax deductions are provided for research and development expenditure and marketing. Different tariff rates are set for imports of raw materials and finished products to favor local manufacturing over direct imports. Income tax incentives are available for industries promoted by women.
- *Special economic zones.* The industrial policy grants firms located in SEZs and agro-export promotion zones exemptions from customs duty, excise duty, and value added taxes. Special incentive packages are available to develop new industrial villages.
- *Incentives for firms located in lagging districts.* Tax holidays are provided for 10, 7, and 5 years to firms that locate in 23 "highly underdeveloped" districts, 15 "undeveloped" districts, and 24 "less developed" districts, respectively.

Box 2.4 Key Features of Nepal's 2010 Industrial Policy and Its Implementation *(continued)*

Although the policy is an important stepping stone toward implementation of SEZs in Nepal, the SEZs remain a concept on paper. The government has proposed SEZs in eight districts in the country. Among the proposed SEZ locations are Bhairahawa (Rupandehi District), Birgunj (Parsa District), Ratmate-Tiling-Devighat (Nuwakot District), and Panchkhal (Kavre District). Work on developing SEZ infrastructure, such as roads, water supply, and electricity lines, is nearly complete in Bhairahawa, and prefeasibility studies of other SEZs are in progress. However, the future of these zones is uncertain. An SEZ bill was drafted in 2006 to provide for the establishment and development of the zones, but it is still awaiting approval by the Parliament.

Source: Government of Nepal 2010.

Table 2.3 Sectoral Composition of Manufacturing Employment in Urban and Rural Areas, 2008
Percentage of total manufacturing employment

Manufacturing sector	Urban	Rural
Machinery, equipment, vehicles, and furniture	14	9
Paper, minerals, plastics, chemicals, and wood	30	30
Garments	19	17
Textiles	18	16
Agroprocessing	19	28
Total manufacturing employment	100	100

Source: CBS 2009.

Box 2.5 The Decline of Nepal's Ready-Made Garment Industry

The large-scale garment industry in Nepal has lost competitiveness. Ready-made garments were one of the country's top exports, but the industry began to decline after 2001. As a share of total merchandise exported, the industry's exports fell from 23.0 percent in 2003 to 6.7 percent in 2007. The industry has been hit especially hard by the expiry of the World Trade Organization Agreement on Textiles and Clothing in 2004. Export earnings declined by 14.2 percent a year from 2000 to 2007, in large measure from falling exports in the U.S. market. Employment in the industry declined from a peak of 50,000 in 1999 to 4,450 in 2006. Between 2003 and 2007, annual output and employment in the garment industry fell by about 30 percent. Increased competition from other countries in the region has hurt the industry, given its dependency on imports of raw materials from India and China. Equally important, however, are the common domestic impediments that plague much of the economy: low productivity, inflexible labor markets, poor transport services, inadequate and unreliable electricity, red tape, and frequent strikes.

Source: Belbase and Kharel 2009.

Figure 2.17 Sectoral Composition of Urban Manufacturing Employment, 2002 and 2007

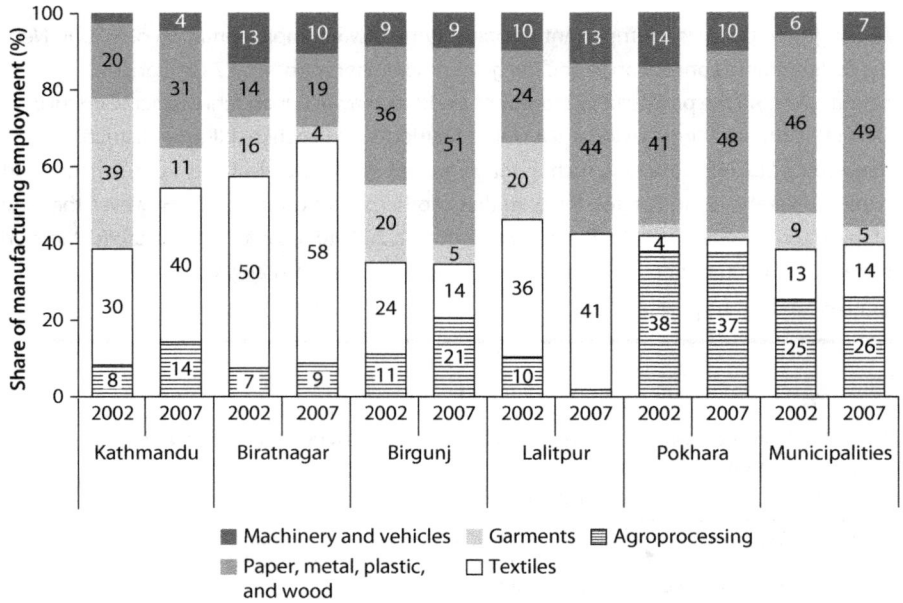

Sources: Based on Census of Manufacturing 2002 and 2007 (CBS 2003, 2007).
Note: Analysis includes firms with more than 10 employees. Kathmandu refers to Kathmandu Metropolitan City; Biratnagar, Birgunj, Lalitpur, and Pokhara refer to submetropolitan cities.

of the urban manufacturing workforce is engaged in wood carving and the manufacturing of wood products (see chapter 4). Taken together, the manufacture of paper products, minerals, chemical products, and wood accounts for as much as 30 percent of urban manufacturing employment (see table 2.3). In Kathmandu, Biratnagar, and Lalitpur, textiles account for the largest share of manufacturing employment. Pokhara stands out for its large share of agroprocessing employment (37 percent) (see figure 2.17).

Notes

1. Unless otherwise stated, Kathmandu refers to Kathmandu Metropolitan City; Biratnagar, Birgunj, Lalitpur, and Pokhara refer to the submetropolitan cities; and all other urban local governments are referred to as municipalities.

2. In the 2011 Budget Speech delivered to the Parliament, the government declared the formation of 41 new municipalities, effective as of July 17, 2011, per the recommendation of the Technical Committee established in 1994 (Government of Nepal 2011). A new Technical Committee was formed immediately after the Budget Speech to define the boundaries of the newly declared municipalities. The Technical Committee has completed the study and submitted its recommendations for approval to the government of Nepal. The newly declared municipalities have not yet been formally established and therefore are not included in the 2011 population census data.

3. The rural settlements of the country are organized into 3,783 village development committees.

4. Population growth has slowed from 2.25 percent over 1991–2001 to 1.35 percent per year over 2001–2011 (CBS 2001, 2012).

5. Pokhara experienced a growth rate of 4.9 percent per year between 1991 and 2001, and a growth rate of 5.3 percent per year between 2001 and 2011.

6. The 2011 population census results do not include the 41 newly declared municipalities.

7. Analysis is based on 2001 census of population data; see CBS (2001).

8. Analysis is based on 2007 census of manufacturing data; see CBS (2007).

9. Of the emerging towns identified by the DUDBC and the DWSS, about 70 percent are classified as rural.

10. Almost half of Nepalese households have at least one migrant abroad or a returnee (World Bank 2011a).

11. Unless otherwise stated, the statistics presented in this chapter are for lifetime migration. *Lifetime migrants* are individuals whose place of residence on the survey date differs from their place of birth; *recent migrants* are individuals whose place of residence on the survey date differs from the place of enumeration at the census.

12. *Local migration* is defined as intraregional and intraecological-zone migration, that is, local migrants are those traveling within the same region and the same ecological zone. *Nonlocal migration* includes short-distance migration (to a neighboring ecological zone or region), medium-distance migration (to the second-closest neighboring area), and long-distance migration (to the third-closest neighboring area).

13. Social distance is calculated as the average exclusion measure weighted by the share of ethnic group in the area population. The exclusion measure is based on Bennett and Parajuli (2011). The 25th and 75th percentiles of the absolute difference between the average exclusion measure (MEM) and the exclusion measure for each migrant are estimated. Social distance is low if the difference between the migrant ethnic group and the MEM is smaller or equal to the 25th percentile. Social distance is medium if the difference between the migrant ethnic group and the MEM is between the 25th percentile and the 75th percentile. Social distance is high if the difference between the migrant ethnic group and the MEM is larger than the 75th percentile. Trends among recent migrants are similar to those for lifetime migrants.

14. The Census of Manufacturing carried out by the Nepal Central Bureau of Statistics (CBS 2007) covers all manufacturing establishments located within the geographic boundary of Nepal engaging 10 or more persons; thus, this chapter uses the designation "10+" to describe them.

References

ADB (Asian Development Bank). 2010. *Unleashing Economic Growth: Region-Based Urban Strategy for Nepal.* Manila: ADB.

Belbase, Anil, and Paras Kharel. 2009. "Competitiveness of Nepalese Ready-Made Garments after Expiry of the Agreements on Textiles and Clothing." ARTNeT Working Paper 70, Asia-Pacific Research and Training Network on Trade, Bangkok.

Bennett, Lynn, and Dilip Parajuli. 2011. "Nepal Multidimensional Exclusion Measure: Methodology, First Round Findings, and Implications for Action." World Bank, Washington, DC.

CBS (Central Bureau of Statistics). 1991. *National Population Census 1991*. Kathmandu: Government of Nepal.

———. 2001. *National Population Census 2001*. Kathmandu: Government of Nepal.

———. 2003. *Nepal—Census of Manufacturing Establishments 2001–2002*. Kathmandu: Government of Nepal.

———. 2006. "Small Area Estimation of Poverty, Caloric Intake and Malnutrition in Nepal." Central Bureau of Statistics, Nepal; United Nations Food Programme, Nepal; and World Bank.

———. 2007. *Nepal—Census of Manufacturing Establishments 2006–2007*. Kathmandu: Government of Nepal.

———. 2009. *Report on the Nepal Labor Force Survey 2008*. Kathmandu: Government of Nepal.

———. 2012. *National Population and Housing Census 2011*. Kathmandu: Government of Nepal.

Fafchamps, Marcel, and Shilpi, Forhad. 2002. "The Spatial Division of Labor in Nepal." Policy Research Working Paper 2845, World Bank, Washington, DC.

———. 2009. "Determinants of the Choice of Migration Destination." CEPR Discussion Paper 7407, Centre for Economic Policy Research, London.

Government of Nepal, Ministry of Law, Justice and Parliamentary Affairs. 1991. Municipality Act, 2048 (1991). Nepal: Law Books Management Board.

———, Ministry of Law, Justice and Parliamentary Affairs. 1999. Local Self-Governance Act, 2055 (1999). Nepal: Law Books Management Board.

———. 2010. *Nepal Industrial Policy, 2010*. Kathmandu.

———, Ministry of Finance. 2011. *Budget Speech of Fiscal Year 2011–12*. Kathmandu.

OECD (Organisation for Economic Co-operation and Development). 1994. *Creating Rural Indicators for Shaping Territorial Policy*. Paris: OECD.

Sengupta, Urmi, and Sujeet Sharma. 2006. "The Challenge of Squatter Settlements in Kathmandu: Addressing a Policy Vacuum." *International Development Planning Review* 28 (1): 105–26.

Thapa, Rajesh Bahadur, and Yuji Murayama. 2009. "Examining Spatiotemporal Urbanization Patterns in Kathmandu Valley, Nepal: Remote Sensing and Spatial Metrics Approaches." *Remote Sensing* 1: 534–56.

UNCTAD (United Nations Conference on Trade and Development). 2011. *National Services Policy Review: Nepal*. Geneva: UNCTAD. http://www.unctad.org/en/docs/ditctncd20103_en.pdf.

UNDESA (United Nations, Department of Economic and Social Affairs). 2012. "World Urbanization Prospects. The 2011 Revision." New York: UNDESA.

Williams, Nathalie, and Meeta Sainju Pradhan. 2008. "Political Conflict and Migration: How Has Violence and Political Stability Affected Migration Patterns in Nepal?" Presented at the Third Annual Himalayan Research Policy Conference, Madison, WI, October 16.

World Bank. 2009. *World Development Report 2009: Reshaping Economic Geography*. Washington, DC: World Bank.

————. 2010. "Managing Rural-Urban Transformation in South Asia." World Bank, Washington, DC.

————. 2011a. "Large Scale Migration and Remittances in Nepal: Issues, Challenges, and Opportunities." World Bank, Washington, DC.

————. 2011b. *World Development Indicators 2011*. Washington, DC: World Bank.

————. Forthcoming. *Bangladesh: The Path to Middle-Income Status from an Urban Perspective*. Directions in Development. Washington, DC: World Bank.

CHAPTER 3

Urban Growth, Planning, and Infrastructure

Lack of effective planning and inadequate infrastructure are major constraints for sustainable urban growth and city competitiveness. The challenges of urban planning are particularly complex in the Kathmandu Valley, where rapid urbanization is overtaking the capacities of existing institutions to manage spatial growth at the metropolitan level. Nepal has the lowest road density in South Asia. Limited connectivity is a constraint for the expansion of nonfarm activities, such as agroprocessing, whereas intermittent electricity supply is a major impediment to the expansion of Nepal's industrial base. Municipal infrastructure—for example, water, sanitation, and solid waste management—is as important for city competitiveness as it is for city livability. Rapid urbanization is intensifying the municipal infrastructure deficit. Access to piped water supply is declining in urban areas, and the Kathmandu Valley faces an imminent water crisis. Inadequate sanitation in urban areas is an obstacle to city livability and sustainable tourism development. Solid waste management is a major environmental problem that undermines efforts to develop sustainable tourism activities in urban areas. For example, the sacred Bagmati river in the Kathmandu Valley has been turned into an open sewer and garbage dump for nearby urban centers. Public capital expenditure for municipal infrastructure, averaging US$11 per capita, is inadequate to meet the growing needs of urban areas. It has declined slightly in real terms over time (from US$14 per capita in fiscal 2008)[1] and is biased against Kathmandu Metropolitan City and the submetropolitan cities, where infrastructure needs are the greatest. This chapter presents a brief overview of urban development planning, infrastructure access and quality, and public capital expenditure for municipal infrastructure from a spatial perspective.

Urban Growth and Planning: The Challenges of Managing a Fast-Growing Metropolitan Region

Land patterns in urban areas are rapidly changing, and urban development planning usually lags behind actual growth. Agricultural land and forest cover a significant share of the territory of a large number of urban local bodies. However, urban growth has led to a rapid loss of agricultural land. The growth of the built-up areas in most urban settlements is haphazard and uncontrolled. Five-year development plans are required of all urban local governments in Nepal, but because of inadequate funding, the plans are seldom implemented. Statutory land-use plans are woefully out-of-date and are often not coordinated spatially. With lack of land-use zoning and plans, managing rapid changes in land patterns is a major challenge for most urban local governments. Squatter settlements are rising in fast-growing cities such as Kathmandu Metropolitan City (hereafter, Kathmandu) and Pokhara Submetropolitan City (hereafter, Pokhara), as well as in small settlements such as Mechinagar.[2] The informal and unplanned development is compromising the natural beauty of historic settlements, such as Lekhnath, Pokhara, and Tansen.

The challenges of spatial planning are particularly complex in the Kathmandu Valley. Rapid population growth is overtaking the capacities of existing institutions to manage urbanization in the valley. The "Kathmandu Valley Long Term Development Plan," prepared by the Kathmandu Valley Town Development Committee in 2002, projected a population of 2.6 million in 2021. However, urbanization has been much more rapid than predicted, given that the population of the Kathmandu Valley had already reached 2.5 million in 2011.

The Kathmandu Valley metropolitan region crosses local administrative boundaries, like most metropolitan regions around the world, making effective governance and metropolitan management far more complex than in self-contained cities. Lacking effective mechanisms for coordination at the metropolitan level, the Kathmandu Valley suffers from fragmentation and an overlap of institutional responsibilities between central and local authorities in the planning and delivery of infrastructure and services. The 2002 plan never received statutory authority, and municipal land-use plans are out-of-date and are not prepared within the context of an overall statutory plan for the valley. This lack of coordination jeopardizes the efficient provision of transportation and infrastructure services across jurisdictions and the enforcement of development control tools at the metropolitan level. Institutional fragmentation and lack of cooperation on a territorial basis also create dysfunctional labor and housing markets and socioeconomic imbalances within the metropolitan region. Such imbalances are manifested in low rates of innovation and job creation, social segregation, and deterioration of the urban fabric.

The urban development pattern in the Kathmandu Valley is environmentally unsustainable. Unplanned urban development has led to rapid and uncontrolled urban sprawl and has contributed to dramatic changes in the urban footprint of the valley. The historic spatial patterns of land change show that the rate of conversion from nonbuilt to built areas has been rapid, with scattered patches of urban development in peri-urban and rural areas characterizing the urban sprawl in the valley (see map 3.1) (Chreod Ltd. 2012; Thapa and Murayama 2012). If urban development continues through both infill in existing urban areas and outward expansion, the valley will face unprecedented stress on land resources, losing river and forest ecosystems and other environmentally sensitive areas by the next decade.

Map 3.1 Population Density in the Kathmandu Valley, 2001 and 2011

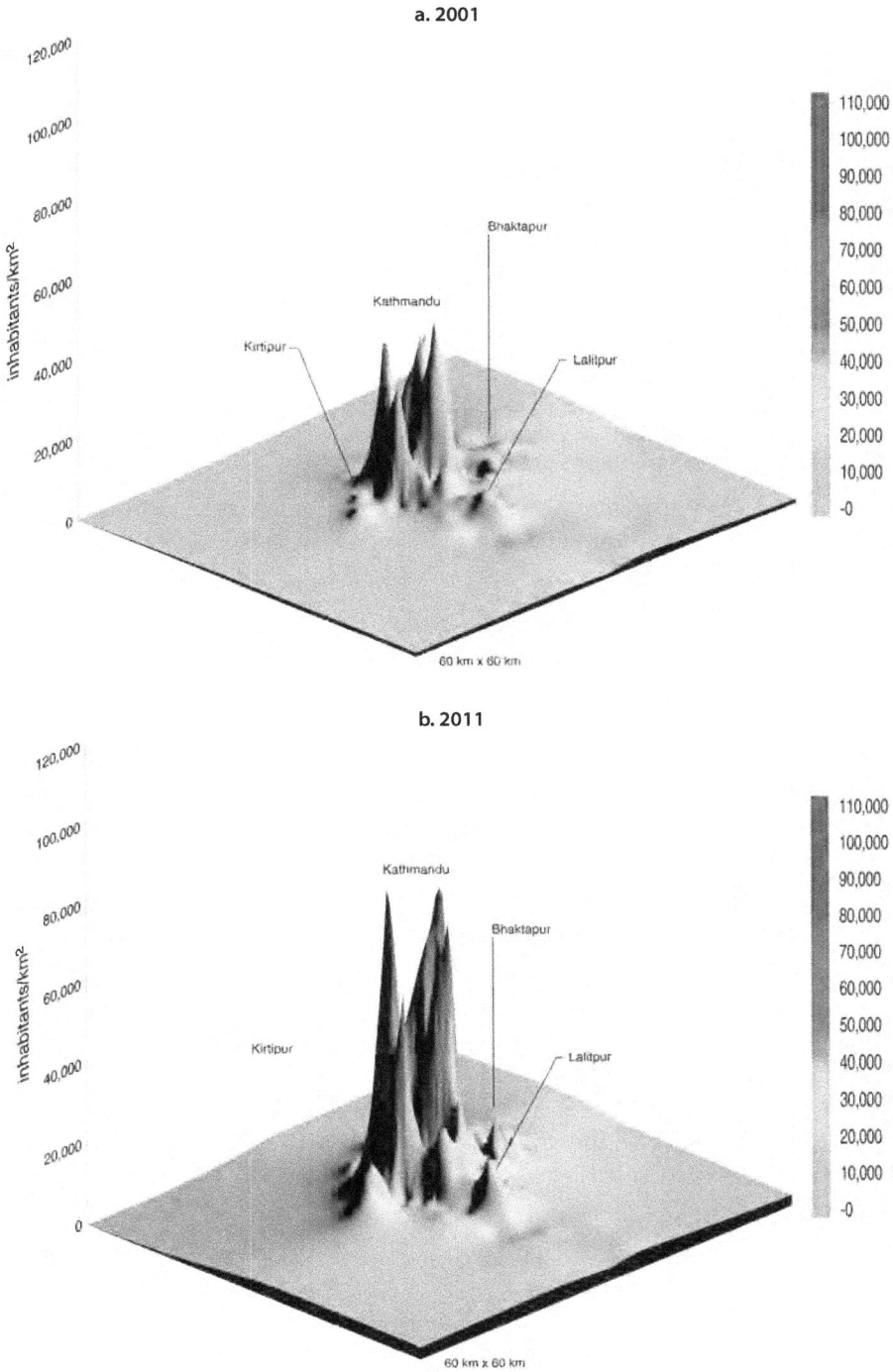

a. 2001

b. 2011

Source: Chreod Ltd. 2012.

Urban Growth and Spatial Transition in Nepal • http://dx.doi.org/10.1596/978-0-8213-9659-9

Unplanned growth and poor enforcement of regulation have led to irregular, substandard, and inaccessible housing patterns, and loss of open space (see box 3.1). They have also significantly increased vulnerability to disasters. Seismic hazard is very high in the Kathmandu Valley. Geologically, the Kathmandu Valley is as vulnerable as Haiti, which experienced a devastating 7.0 earthquake on January 13, 2010, that resulted in the loss of over 200,000 lives and left 500,000 people homeless (Bhattarai and Conway 2010). Haphazard urban development has exposed an increasing percentage of the population to seismic hazards and has decreased the capacity of emergency services to cope with the challenges associated with disasters. In most parts of the Kathmandu Valley, buildings stand side by side on narrow alleys. Fire brigades and ambulances are unable to provide services. Moreover, in the aftermath of a big earthquake,

---

Box 3.1 Urban Vulnerabilities of the Kathmandu Valley

The main factors affecting urban vulnerabilities in the valley include (a) uncontrolled densifica-tion and land subdivisions, (b) substandard housing, (c) loss of open space, and (d) lack of accessibility.

Uncontrolled Densification and Land Subdivisions

The valley's residential density has exceeded 1,000 people per hectare as new three- and four-story buildings are constructed on farmland and small open spaces to accommodate the increasing population in densely built structures. Ongoing development patterns in the valley have also resulted in land subdivisions. Although the recommended official plot size for the Kathmandu Valley is 100 square meters, many houses in the valley are built on plots as small as 15 to 45 square meters.

Substandard Housing

Most of the informal housing in the Kathmandu Valley is built with local materials at substan-dard levels, sometimes without the basic necessities, and it does not meet requirements of health, safety, seismic scales, and external environment. On average, three to four people share a room of 12–15 square meters. Most housing is unaffordable to the Nepalese, leaving them with no alternative but to squat on open land. Spontaneous slum settlements are mush-rooming along the ecologically sensitive and marginal areas, such as riverbeds and lowlands, and along dangerous or untenable flood areas (see figure B3.1.1). Furthermore, squatters often occupy heritage sites, such as temples and monasteries, or live near dumps, making them extremely vulnerable to life-threatening events and conditions.

Loss of Open Space

New houses are built on any available space, and infill housing has resulted in a significant decrease in open space. The loss of open space and vegetation owing to the construction of substandard buildings has hindered vehicular accessibility to houses. Moreover, that loss has made the bowl-like valley with its generally low-velocity wind a sink for pollutants

---

box continues next page

Box 3.1 Urban Vulnerabilities of the Kathmandu Valley *(continued)*

during the winter. Open spaces are not sufficient to protect people from seismic risk. Given the valley's seismic vulnerability, planners in the valley recommend adopting a 40:60 ratio for built-up and non-built-up land by 2021, compared to the 32:68 ratio that planners envisioned in 2001.

Lack of Accessibility

Narrow streets limit vehicular accessibility to individual houses. In the inner areas of the valley's city centers, the narrow streets (less than or equal to 2.5 meters in width) and sturdy fences erected for security reasons are posing problems of accessibility. The subdivision of inner-city land to maximize profits has further narrowed the width of roads. Three-dimensional (3-D) visualization techniques are very useful for examining adjacency, proximity, accessibility, and environmental conditions within the uncontrolled and unevenly patterned agglomeration of the Kathmandu Valley (see map B3.1.2).

Source: Bhattarai and Conway 2010.

Map B3.1.1 Squatter Settlements in Kathmandu Metropolitan City, 2007

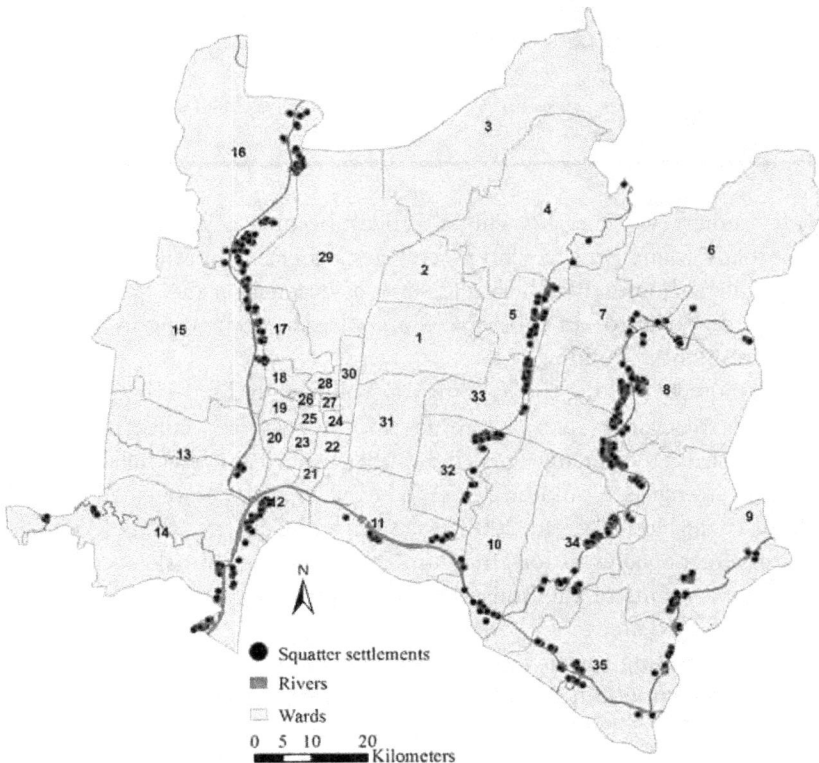

Source: Bhattarai and Conway 2010.

box continues next page

Box 3.1 Urban Vulnerabilities of the Kathmandu Valley *(continued)*

Map B3.1.2 3-D Simulation of Accessibility in the Kathmandu Valley

Source: Bhattarai and Conway 2010.
Note: Visualization of housing typology without proper access by emergency vehicles (New Baneshwor area of Kathmandu Metropolitan City, digitized and converted into 3-D).

providing emergency services will be difficult because of accumulated debris on narrow roads. Many private schools, colleges, other educational institutions, and private nursing homes, which should serve as evacuation shelters and treatment centers in the event of an earthquake, are currently operating in ordinary, substandard residential buildings.

An earthquake striking the Kathmandu Valley would have devastating effects. Many large structures (such as temples and monasteries) constructed of heavy rock, bricks, mud mortar, masonry, and timber, as well as individual houses having low tensile strengths, would be destroyed even in a moderate earthquake (JICA and Ministry of Home Affairs 2002; Bhattarai and Conway 2010). Map 3.2 identifies areas in the valley at low, medium, and high seismic risk, according to the spatial arrangements of the houses. The high-risk areas coincide with the most densely populated areas.

The deteriorating urban environment resulting from ineffective coordination at the metropolitan level provided the impetus for the establishment of the Kathmandu Valley Development Authority (KVDA). The KVDA was legally established on April 13, 2012 based on the Kathmandu Valley Development Authority Act of 1988, replacing the Kathmandu Valley Town Development Committee (Government of Nepal 1988a).[3] The establishment

Map 3.2 Seismic Hazard in the Kathmandu Valley

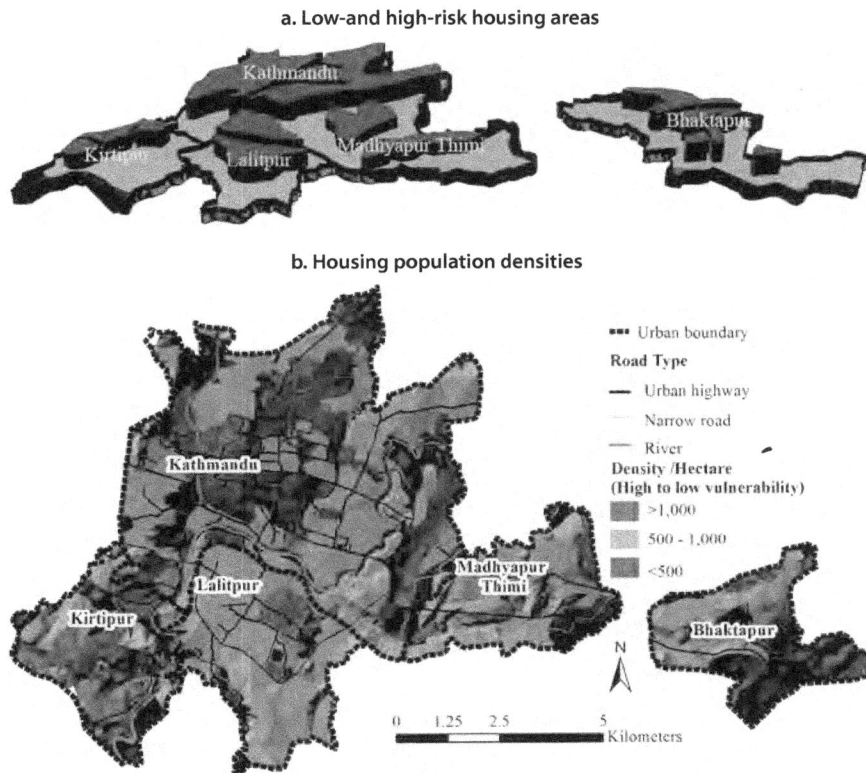

a. Low-and high-risk housing areas

b. Housing population densities

Source: Bhattarai and Conway 2010.
Note: Density is people per hectare.

of the new Authority responds to the need to create institutional stability in the valley, and also coincides with the creation of a new Ministry of Urban Development in May 2012. There is now the pressing need to articulate and codify the responsibilities of the newly created Ministry of Urban Development, the KVDA, sector agencies, and local governments in the management of the Kathmandu Valley metropolitan region (Chreod Ltd. 2012).

Infrastructure Access and Quality in Urban Areas

Connective infrastructure and power supply are two major constraints to economic growth and city competitiveness. Nepal's national and regional infrastructure is in dismal condition. In 2010–11, the *Global Competitiveness Report* ranked Nepal as the country with the least competitive stock of infrastructure (with a score of 1.7 out of 7.0) among the 139 countries covered by the Global Competitiveness Index (World Economic Forum 2010). The low ranking is mainly driven by the poor quality of Nepal's road network, rail, and air transport infrastructure and the limited reliability of Nepal's electricity supply. The quality of the electricity supply received the lowest score (1.2 of 7.0). The index ranking is particularly worrisome given the strategic importance of tourism for the economic development of the country and urban areas. Insufficient infrastructure not only limits the capacity to absorb tourists but also suppresses the average receipt per tourist.

Rapid urbanization is intensifying the municipal infrastructure deficit, in particular in the Kathmandu Valley. Nepal's urban areas face an imminent infrastructure crisis. The scale and quality of municipal infrastructure are inadequate to meet the needs of the existing urban population and to sustain current urban population growth rates. The quality of the water supply is inadequate in most urban areas, and many municipalities have barely enough water for subsistence. The Kathmandu Valley is facing a severe water crisis. Less than half the municipal waste is collected, and only half the urban population has access to improved sanitation. Although the Kathmandu Valley has some sewerage facilities, sewage treatment is still very poor and most wastewater flows untreated into the Bagmati River. The rest of this section discusses the status of connective and municipal infrastructure from a spatial perspective.

Connective Infrastructure

Nepal has the lowest road density in South Asia (0.6 kilometer per 1,000 people). Nepal's rugged terrain makes road access particularly problematic. On average, a person must walk more than three hours to reach a paved road. About 50 percent of Nepal's roads are concentrated in the less rugged Tarai zone, which has 23 percent of the country's land area (ADB 2010a). Additionally, much of the existing road network is not trafficable; 45 percent of the road network is unpaved; and more than half the population lacks year-round ready access to a road (Afram and Salvi Del Pero 2012). Road quality is better and accessibility is higher in more wealthy and more urbanized areas. In Nepal's urban areas, the average travel time to a paved road is about 11 minutes, and to a commercial bank it is 21 minutes. For the country as a whole, the corresponding figures are significantly higher, 4.9 hours and 3.5 hours, respectively (Dudwick and others 2011).

Nepal's limited connectivity is an obstacle for urban competitiveness, trade, and market integration. Nepal's poor accessibility is particularly troubling because connective infrastructure is critical for supporting the agglomeration forces that fuel urbanization. Research suggests that proximity to major highways tends to affect municipalities' level of development (Portnov, Adhikari, and Schwartz 2007). Lack of road links between urban and rural areas, particularly in the Hill and Mountain zones, is the most crucial problem. Lack of connectivity hurts both rural and urban development by increasing transport costs and limiting commercial agriculture, agroprocessing, and trade (Reja and Kutzbach 2007). In the manufacturing sector, 1.4 percent of shipments to domestic markets are lost as a result of breakage and spoilage (Afram and Salvi Del Pero 2012).

Nepal's accessibility by air is limited. The constraints at Tribhuvan International Airport (TIA) in Kathmandu constitute a major impediment to economic development, in particular tourism. Despite airport upgrades in previous decades, the current number and the expected growth of tourist arrivals necessitate reducing the constraints on increasing passenger traffic. Because of the difficult geographic limitations of TIA, a second international airport has been proposed in Nijgadh in Bara District as a long-term solution to the constraints at TIA. According to the feasibility study presented in 2011, this second international airport will cover 3,000 hectares of land[4] and will have the capacity to handle 15 million passengers until 2022 (ETG 2012; Global Travel Industry News 2011).[5] In addition, domestic air transportation is limited and unable to effectively connect the Kathmandu Valley with the country's other cities and tourism destinations, whose airport facilities also require major improvements. Finally, TIA needs significant quality improvements. Currently, it ranks 8th in the top 10 most disliked airports of the world (with London's Heathrow, New York's JFK, and Australia's Perth), according to a recent CNNGo rating (Rane 2011). The quality of airport services is in part a reflection of the challenges in coordinating the more than 200 different government and private organizations involved in performing functions at the international airport (ETG 2012).

Electricity

Intermittent electricity supply is a major impediment to the expansion of Nepal's industrial base. Urban access to electricity is high (see figure 3.1). As of 2010, 96 percent of urban households have access to electricity, and the coverage is comparable to that of other countries in the region, such as Bangladesh, India, and Pakistan (WHO and UNICEF 2012). However, the electricity sector faces a number of problems, the most important of which is intermittent service. Ninety-nine percent of businesses suffer from frequent power outages, at an average of 16 hours per day from winter until spring, which cost them an estimated 22 percent of their annual sales. The losses are significantly higher for the tourism sector, at 31 percent of annual sales, than those for manufacturing and services (Afram and Salvi Del Pero 2012). Nepal has significant hydropower potential, and commercially exploitable hydropower generation is estimated to be roughly 43,000 megawatts. Despite this generation potential, only about 600 megawatts have been developed so far (ESMAP 2008).

Water

Urban access to improved water supply is high. Ninety-three percent of Nepal's urban population had access to an improved source for drinking water as of 2010, in line with other countries in the region, such as Bangladesh (85 percent), India (97 percent), and Pakistan (96 percent), and Nepal is on

Figure 3.1 Household Access to Electricity, 2003–10

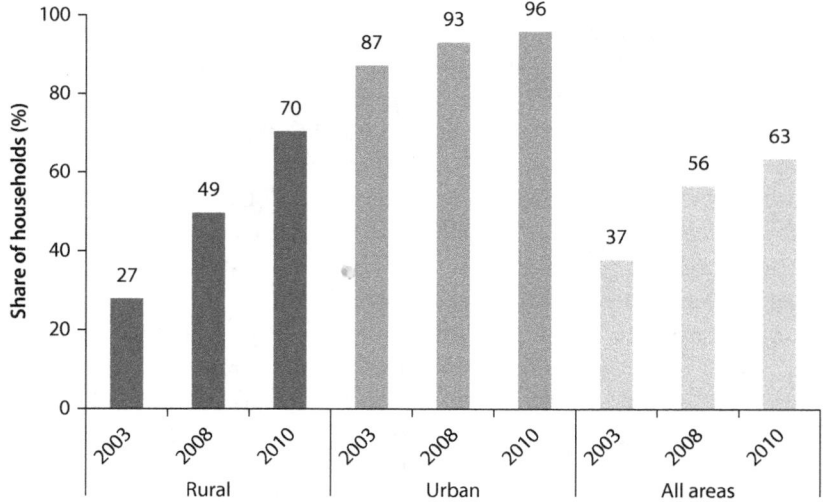

Sources: CBS 2004, 2009, 2011.

track to reach the Millennium Development Goal of near universal access to drinking water by 2015 (WHO and UNICEF 2012).[6] However, the quality of service remains inadequate, and access to drinking water does not necessarily imply access to "safe" or "sufficient" drinking water. Access to piped water supply in urban areas decreased from 68 to 58 percent from 2003 to 2010 (see figure 3.2). Much of the decrease is driven by the high growth in urban population, combined with a lack of expansion of the piped network. Nepal's piped drinking water is unsafe in most locations and throughout most of the year, and several cities are facing a chronic shortage of water owing to unplanned urban growth. Many urban households receive barely enough water for subsistence at less than 50 liters per capita per day. As urban populations continue to increase, improving urban infrastructure and service delivery in the water sector will become essential for Nepal.

The Kathmandu Valley, the largest urban agglomeration in Nepal, has the worst water supply system. Although urbanization has contributed to intensifying infrastructure bottlenecks in the valley, one of the most prominent problems is the shortage of domestic water supply. The daily demand for water in the valley is around 220 million liters, but the supply is less than half that—approximately 100 million liters a day (Federation of Canadian Municipalities 2002; Bhushal 2011). The rapid increase in the valley's population during the last decade and a lack of investment in water supply provision and system maintenance have resulted in less than 20 percent of the population receiving a reliable supply of piped drinking water (ADB 2010b). Most traditional supplies (for example, communal water tanks) have ceased to function, and households and businesses have responded to the shortfall by investing in individual local supplies and in-house

Figure 3.2 Household Access to Piped Water Supply, 2003–10

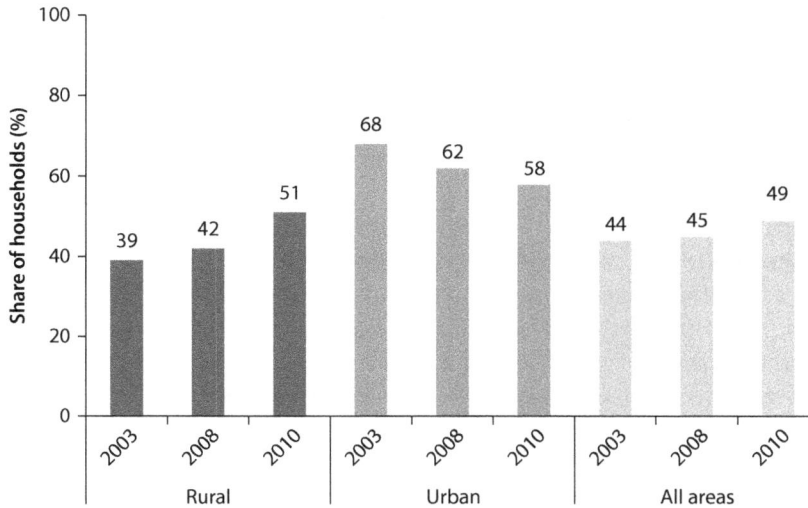

Sources: CBS 2004, 2009, 2011.

storage, exploiting local groundwater resources, and relying on water being delivered by tankers at considerable socioeconomic costs. To address extreme water shortage, communities have revived the use of *hitis*—traditional communal water sources—as an alternative water source throughout the valley, although many *hitis* have fallen into disrepair (see box 3.2). Moreover, water supply is lost through leakage from old, rusty, and broken pipes; water quality is poor, with intermittent supply; and groundwater is polluted. The existing distribution networks are reported to be inadequate for current needs, and unaccounted-for water and losses are over 50 percent. Although the designated authorities (the Kathmandu Valley Water Supply Management Board and the service provider, KUKL— Kathmandu Upatyaka Khanepani Limited) have put plans in place to address these deficits, considerable additional investments and policy interventions will be needed for their successful implementation.

Environmental Infrastructure and Services

Nepal's municipal solid waste management—including waste collection, treatment, and disposal—is inadequate. Most urban residents consider solid waste management the most important environmental problem in the urban areas of Nepal (Government of Nepal 2008; WaterAid 2008). According to a recent survey carried out in eight municipalities across Nepal, households with regular garbage collection range from 25 percent to 45 percent. In Mechinagar, only 25 percent of households report having regular garbage collection (Government of Nepal 2012). Households ranked solid waste, together with drainage, as the lowest-performing infrastructure sector in their municipalities and expressed concerns about the deterioration of services resulting from haphazard development. Only two municipalities in Nepal (Pokhara and Ghorahi) dispose of waste

Box 3.2 Traditional Stone Spouts and Community Mobilization Increase Well-Being for Low-Income Households

An example of the power of community mobilization to provide basic services is the revitalization of the traditional water sources known as *hitis*. The extreme shortage of water in the Kathmandu Valley has revived the use of *hitis*, especially on the part of the poor who have limited access to piped water.

Traditional *hitis* are sunken courtyards, usually surrounded by a wall with one or more decorative stone spouts through which water flows continuously. The *hiti* is an ancient and highly sophisticated water management system, usually sourced by aquifers. Water arrives at *hitis* via natural subsurface flow or constructed channels. In earlier times, aquifers acting as the water source were continuously recharged by the construction of ponds nearby, and those ponds were often fed by water from faraway sources through canals.

Unfortunately, when piped water became available in the valley and was abundant, maintenance of the traditional system was ignored and the intricacies of its design forgotten. In 2005, the NGO Forum for Urban Water and Sanitation carried out a survey and mapping of traditional stone spouts in the five urban areas of the valley. The study found 389 *hitis*, but only about half were in good working order. In total, the stone spouts are supplying about 3 million to 8 million liters of water per day in the dry and wet seasons, respectively. That amount is enough to supply

Revitalization of the traditional *hiti* is helping solve problems of water scarcity in the Kathmandu Valley.

box continues next page

Box 3.2 Traditional Stone Spouts and Community Mobilization Increase Well-Being for Low-Income Households *(continued)*

about 300,000 people living in the core city areas. The water is free from chemical contamination, but it must be treated with disinfectant before drinking because of bacterial contamination.

More recently, communities have revived traditional *hitis* to provide water to the valley. Interest in conserving *hitis* was triggered by the Ikhachhen community in Lalitpur, which made arrangements to collect water from the Alko *hiti* late at night when it had few users. As a result, about 250 households receive one hour of water per day through pipes for Nr 100 a month. Their success led to the formation of the Historic Stone Spout and Source Conservation Association, which has generated similar initiatives in other urban areas in the valley and has led to the development of a 12-point declaration on the importance and means of conserving this traditional water resource. The stone spout water sources of the Kathmandu Valley are unique because they not only demonstrate human ingenuity in harnessing subsurface flows but also provide an example of outstanding social accomplishment in the form of community collaboration. Besides providing water to the people of the valley, their conservation and restoration are important for their historic and cultural significance.

Sources: NGFUWS 2007; UNESCO 2006.

---

at a sanitary landfill.[7] In most cases, the main waste disposal sites are riverbanks, depressed land and dumps, open pits, or temporary open piles. More than two-thirds of municipalities are resource-constrained in equipment, technical manpower, capacity building, and specialized human resources. Similarly, almost half the municipalities have insufficient budgets allocated for solid waste management and drainage (Government of Nepal 2008). Inadequate solid waste management and drainage are also major constraints for tourist destinations.

In the Kathmandu Valley, solid waste management deserves urgent attention. The lack of adequate waste management infrastructure and a poor regulatory environment have allowed the sacred Bagmati River to become a garbage dump for nearby urban centers (see box 3.3). In the valley, domestic solid waste is collected by both small-scale private sector contractors and by the respective municipal and town authorities. An estimated 484 tons per day is generated, of which about 414 tons per day is collected (Government of Nepal 2008). The waste is then either dumped informally along the riverbanks or taken to the overloaded municipal transfer station at the confluence of the Bagmati and Bishnumati Rivers. There, a portion is recycled and the remainder is transported (by both public and private operators) to the municipal landfill at Sisdol. The Sisdol landfill, managed by Kathmandu, is currently at capacity and in need of formal and environmentally responsive closure. An additional appropriate site with long-term capacity has been identified nearby. A feasibility study for a new landfill was prepared in 2011; that site, together with improvements to the access road, should be developed urgently in conjunction with improvements to the municipal solid waste recycling, collection, and transportation systems.

Urban Growth and Spatial Transition in Nepal • http://dx.doi.org/10.1596/978-0-8213-9659-9

Municipal solid waste management is inadequate in Nepal.

Sanitation

Inadequate sanitation in urban areas is an obstacle not only for city livability but also for sustainable local economic development. Although Nepal's access to improved sanitation has been increasing over time, further improvements are needed. Access to toilets in urban Nepal increased from 81 percent to 85 percent from 2003 to 2010, yet many toilets remain unsanitary (see figure 3.3). When toilet quality is considered, the share of urban households with access to *improved sanitation* is 48 percent (as of 2010), lower than in other countries in the region, such as India (58 percent), Bangladesh (57 percent), Pakistan (72 percent), and Sri Lanka (88 percent) (WHO and UNICEF 2012). Furthermore, only the Kathmandu Valley has some sewerage facilities. All other urban areas have on-site sanitation. Inadequate sanitation is a constraint for the expansion of the tourism sector, in particular cultural tourism in urban areas. As a result of inadequate water and sanitation facilities, waterborne epidemics occur regularly in Nepal, affecting the poor and marginalized the most. Also, the urban environment is becoming highly degraded, owing to the discharge of untreated wastewater into water bodies and unmanaged solid waste.

With increased urbanization, the socioeconomic costs of inadequate wastewater collection and treatment are rising in the Kathmandu Valley. Over the years, wastewater systems have been constructed in much of the urban area of the Kathmandu Valley. Limited information is available on the extent and condition of the existing wastewater system; much of the system is understood to be in poor

Figure 3.3 Household Access to Sanitation, 2003–10

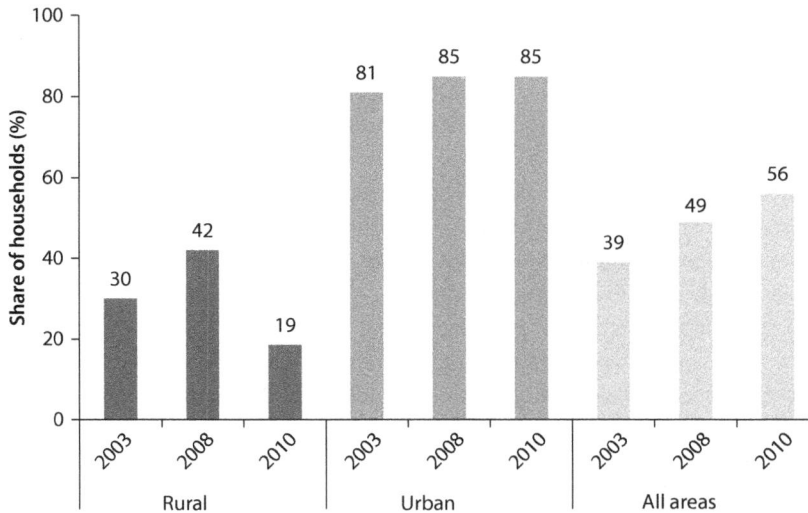

Sources: CBS 2004, 2009, 2011.
Note: Sanitation includes flush toilets (connected to public drainage or septic tanks), pit latrines, and communal toilets.

condition and has exceeded its normal working life, needing to be replaced. Groundwater infiltration is considerable; hence collected wastewater volumes are larger than would be expected from reticulated networks. Where pipe networks are not functional or available (estimated for more than 30 percent of households) (CBS 2012), wastewater disposal is on site, through leach pits and septic tanks. The conveyor and treatment investments of the wastewater systems have also not been developed in parallel. The few treatment plants constructed have not been maintained and are mostly inoperative. Most wastewater flows in the urban areas are untreated, resulting in the highly polluted streams and watercourses flowing through the valley and causing significant public risk and nuisance (ADB 2010b). The sacred rivers in the Kathmandu Valley have been turned into open sewers because of the discharge of untreated wastewater. The ecosystems and biosystems in these formerly pristine watercourses are therefore currently totally nonviable. Many scientists have declared the rivers "dead" because hardly any fish can survive in them. For example, recent studies show that the fish population has been completely wiped out in the 10- to 15-kilometer stretch of the Bagmati River flowing through the Kathmandu Valley. This contaminated waterway is one of the holiest sites in Nepal, which flows past one of the most sacred Hindu shrines, the Pashupatinath Temple (Bhushal 2011; see box 3.3).

Urban Transport

Core and suburban transport infrastructure have not kept pace with rapid urbanization. The Kathmandu Valley faces severe congestion that constrains accessibility to residences and enterprises and undermines economic efficiencies across the

Box 3.3 The Bagmati River: An Ecological Crisis Undermining Sustainable Urbanization

Together with its tributaries, the Bagmati River plays an important role in the ecological, socioeconomic, cultural, and religious life of the Kathmandu Valley. The sacred river originates in the Shivapuri Hills of the valley and forms a natural boundary between two of Nepal's most important urban centers, Kathmandu and Lalitpur. In addition to being a water source for drinking and for agricultural purposes, it is the site of religious burial rituals. Many of Nepal's most important temples, shrines, and *ghats* are located on the riverbanks. However, the river's extreme state of pollution, a critical depletion of the groundwater supply, and unbridled urbanization trends along the riverbed are causing irreparable damage to its already fragile ecosystem and jeopardizing the sustainability of life in the valley.

Lack of adequate waste management infrastructure and a poor regulatory environment have allowed the Bagmati River to become an open sewer and garbage dump for nearby urban centers. The discharge of toxic industrial waste from small industries and solid waste from private households in the nearby urban areas in the valley is severely affecting the river's water quality and destroying its ecosystem. The resulting pollution of the river is the cause of many waterborne diseases and is becoming a serious health concern. The lack of adequate infrastructure also contributes to the severe water crisis in the valley. Adding to the ecological crisis, the deteriorating condition of monuments and temples along the riverbanks seriously

The Bagmati River faces an ecological crisis.

box continues next page

Box 3.3 The Bagmati River: An Ecological Crisis Undermining Sustainable Urbanization
(continued)

undermines efforts to develop sustainable tourism activities along the river, and their restoration is vital to the Bagmati River's renewal.

Restoring the Bagmati River is critical to ensure that urbanization in the valley is sustainable. The High Powered Committee for the Integrated Development of the Bagmati Civilization (HPCIDBC)[a] was created in 1995 to develop a plan for improving the quality of water in the river system through priority investments in sewer lines and treatment plants. Together with the National Trust for Natural Conservation, the HPCIDBC has laid out a five-year action plan to restore the Bagmati River's fragile ecosystem and to address the septage, solid waste, and wastewater needs of the valley in response to rapid urbanization demands. The HPCIDBC and the National Trust also support restoration efforts of heritage buildings that lie on the Bagmati's banks with the aim of developing sustainable cultural tourism in this area. The plan calls for tapping into carbon financing under the Clean Development Mechanism of the Kyoto Protocol to address solid waste disposal and public-private partnerships to fund investments in wastewater treatment. Many of the activities outlined in the Bagmati action plan are, however, still unfunded.

Source: Bhushal 2011.
a. The HPCIDBC was previously known as the High Powered Committee for Implementation and Monitoring of the Bagmati Area Sewerage Construction/Rehabilitation Project.

valley. Traffic and road conditions in the valley have deteriorated as a result of rapid increase in both urban growth and motorized transport. In-city journey times have reportedly increased significantly, as have traffic and pedestrian accidents. The poor condition of the city streets and sidewalks highlights both lack of maintenance and rapid traffic growth beyond the capacity of the current infrastructure. These conditions are clearly causing a reduction in urban efficiency, increasing the costs of all aspects of logistics within the valley. Negligible traffic management data are available for the Kathmandu Valley. Transport planning needs to be fully integrated with land-use planning across the valley if accessibility to residences and businesses is to be improved. The valley's landlocked location increases logistics costs for imports and exports: logistics efficiencies are essential if enterprises are to be competitive in regional and global markets. In the late 1970s, a ring road was built in the core peripheral areas of Kathmandu and at first reduced core area traffic. Currently, almost all the areas of the old ring road are filled with new structures. The planned development of a new ring road in the hinterland of the Kathmandu Valley may help alleviate the valley's core congestion problems in the short term, but the current situation may very well repeat itself unless regulatory measures are implemented and enforced (see map 3.3).

Public Capital Expenditure for Municipal Infrastructure

This section documents and analyzes the spatial distribution of public capital expenditure for municipal infrastructure across urban areas based on expenditure data (hereafter referred to as public infrastructure expenditure survey

Map 3.3 Existing and Proposed Ring Roads in the Kathmandu Valley

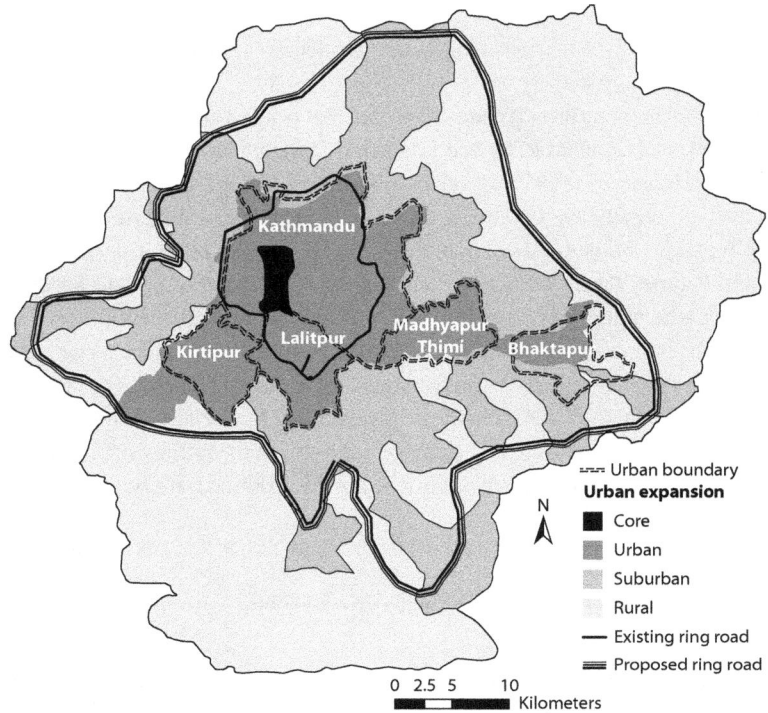

Source: Bhattarai and Conway 2010.

data) collected from central agencies and urban local authorities for three consecutive fiscal years—from fiscal 2008 to fiscal 2010. For the purpose of the analysis, municipal infrastructure is categorized in the broad and complementary categories of physical infrastructure and social infrastructure. Physical infrastructure includes water, sewerage, drainage, local roads, and solid waste. Social infrastructure comprises health and education (i.e., schools and hospitals). Municipal infrastructure that does not fall into these two categories is classified as residual (for example, parks and market infrastructure). The first part of the analysis studies the spatial distribution of public capital expenditure for municipal infrastructure[8] within urban areas, whereas the second part examines the spatial distribution of countrywide public infrastructure expenditure falling under national investment programs between urban and rural areas.

Spatial Allocation of Capital Expenditure for Municipal Infrastructure within Urban Areas

Nepal has three main modalities for funding public investments in municipal infrastructure. First, municipal investments can be funded as project-based progams financed by central agencies. The programs can in turn be classified into two main categories, according to the prevailing financing and implementation arrangements: centrally sponsored investment programs can either be channeled through the

The social costs of haphazard urbanization are rising in the Kathmandu Valley.

urban local bodies or be implemented directly by central agencies. Second, municipal investments can be financed through the intergovernmental fiscal transfer system as capital block grants. Third, urban local governments can use own-source revenues to fund municipal infrastructure investments. Project-based programs account for about 49 percent of the total capital expenditure for municipal infrastructure; block grant revenues account for an additional 46 percent in fiscal 2010. The percentage of capital expenditure for municipal infrastructure funded by own-source revenues is small, and declining over time—from 8 percent of total expenditure in fiscal 2008 to 5 percent in fiscal 2010. Information on own-source revenues has been collected only for Kathmandu and the submetropolitan cities because own-source revenues represent a small share of the municipalities' total revenues and they are largely used to fund recurrent expenditures.

Project-based programs are the main form of infrastructure-financing modalities in municipalities, whereas blocks grants prevail in Kathmandu and the submetropolitan cities. From fiscal 2008 to fiscal 2010, project-based programs accounted for a large share of municipal infrastructure expenditure in the 53 municipalities, ranging from 68 percent in fiscal 2008 to 58 percent in fiscal 2010. In contrast, in both Biratnagar and Lalitpur, the share of project-based programs was consistently below 20 percent of total capital expenditure for municipal infrastructure during the same period. In Kathmandu, the share of project-based programs was 17 percent in fiscal 2008 and then it increased to 33 percent in fiscal 2010 (see figure 3.4). Lower project-based expenditure in Kathmandu and the submetropolitan cities may be partly explained by lower levels of involvement from development partners.

Significant variations also occur in the implementation arrangements for project-based programs across urban areas. Although most project-based programs are implemented and managed directly by central agencies in Kathmandu, the bulk of project-based funds are channeled through the local governments in the municipalities. For example, in fiscal 2010, funds channeled through municipalities accounted for 67 percent of overall project-based capital expenditure, whereas only 33 percent of overall project-based capital infrastructure expenditure in those same municipalities was directly implemented by central agencies. Map 3.4 shows the location of urban infrastructure programs funded by development partners and channeled through the local governments.

Public expenditure in municipal infrastructure is inadequate to meet the high and growing demand for urban services. Public capital expenditure for municipal infrastructure averages only US$11 per capita across the 58 urban local governments (2010 prices). Capital expenditure has slightly declined in real terms from US$14 per capita in fiscal 2008 (see figure 3.5). The current level of capital

Figure 3.4 Public Expenditure for Municipal Infrastructure, by Funding Modality, Fiscal 2008 and 2010

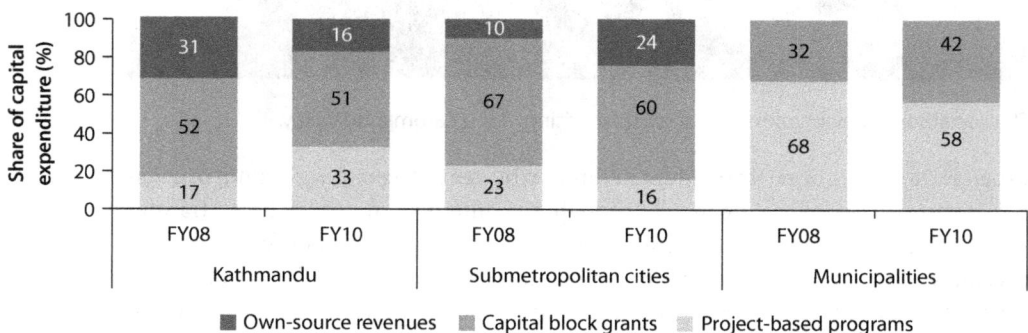

Source: Public infrastructure expenditure survey data.
Note: FY = fiscal year. A fiscal year is from July 1 through June 30 (for example, July 1, 2007, through June 30, 2008, constitutes fiscal 2008). Kathmandu refers to Kathmandu Metropolitan City; submetropolitan cities include Biratnagar, Birgunj, Lalitpur, and Pokhara.

Map 3.4 Location of Urban Infrastructure Programs Funded by Development Partners and Channeled through Local Governments, Fiscal 2010

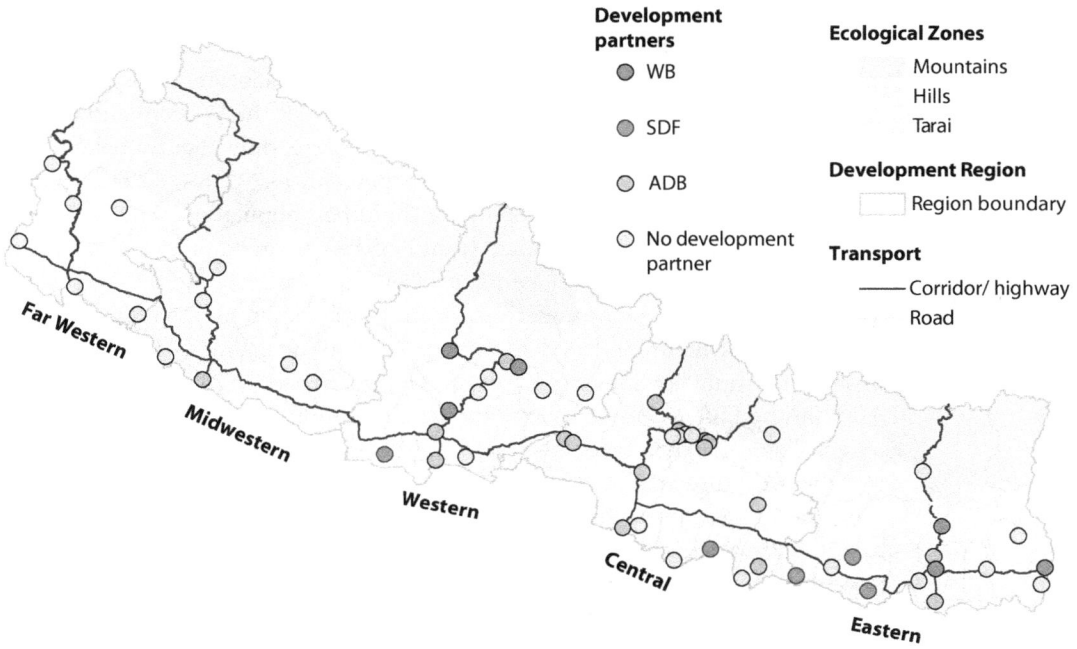

Development partners
- ◉ WB
- ◉ SDF
- ◎ ADB
- ○ No development partner

Ecological Zones
- Mountains
- Hills
- Tarai

Development Region
- Region boundary

Transport
- —— Corridor/ highway
- Road

Source: Public infrastructure expenditure survey data.
Note: WB = World Bank; SDF = Saudi Development Fund; ADB = Asian Development Bank.

Figure 3.5 Per Capita Public Expenditure for Municipal Infrastructure, by Urban Area and Funding Modality, Fiscal 2008 and 2010

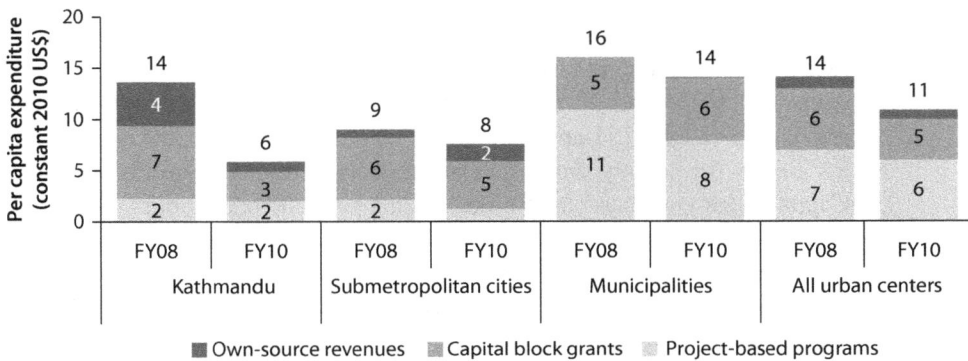

■ Own-source revenues   ▨ Capital block grants   ▥ Project-based programs

Source: Public infrastructure expenditure survey data.
Note: FY = fiscal year. A fiscal year is from July 1 through June 30 (for example, July 1, 2008, through June 30, 2008, constitutes fiscal 2008). Kathmandu refers to Kathmandu Metropolitan City; submetropolitan cities include Biratnagar, Birgunj, Lalitpur, and Pokhara.

expenditure is inadequate to even close the high backlog in service delivery that characterizes Nepal's cities. The recent decline in expenditure from an already-low base is particularly worrisome, given the pressure on urban infrastructure posed by migration and urban growth.

The regional distribution of overall capital expenditure for municipal infrastructure is broadly in line with the regional share of urban population. Capital expenditure for municipal infrastructure varies from US$10.1 per capita in the Far Western Region to US$14.7 per capita in the Central Region (see figure 3.6). The limited regional variation indicates that investments are allocated broadly according to population distribution. The expenditure share of the Western and Eastern Regions, at 16 percent and 17 percent, respectively, is only slightly below their urban population share (17 percent and 18 percent, respectively). The Central Region's share (51 percent) is in line with the urban population's share (51 percent) (see table 3.1). Spending ranges from US$11 per capita in the Tarai zone to US$16 in the Mountain zone (see figure 3.6). The relatively higher level of per capita expenditure in the Mountain zone can be explained by the higher costs of providing infrastructure in less densely populated municipalities—the population threshold for municipalities located in the Mountains is only 10,000, compared to 20,000 in the Hill and Tarai zones. The distribution of capital expenditure across ecological zones slightly favors the Hill zone, which accounts for 61 percent of the capital expenditure and 54 percent of the total urban population (see table 3.1).

Significant variations occur in the regional allocation of capital expenditure for physical and social infrastructure. On one hand, the bulk of centrally sponsored project-based programs for physical infrastructure investment goes to the Central Region. The share of physical infrastructure spending directed to the Central Region increased from 40 percent in fiscal 2008 to 62 percent in fiscal 2010 and is well above the Central Region's share of urban population (51 percent). The bias in favor of the Central Region can be justified by its strategic importance for Nepal's economic development, because two of Nepal's three main clusters of economic production are located in the Central Region—the Kathmandu Valley and the Central Tarai cluster surrounding Birgunj. On the other hand, centrally funded project-based programs for social infrastructure are biased against the Central Region—the Central and Midwestern Regions receive a similar share of spending, equivalent to 24 and 22 percent, respectively, of the total, despite the different population weights (51 and 7 percent, respectively). The spatial allocation can be justified by the equity dimension of social investments in health and education. Capital block grants also have an equalizing effect across regions (see table 3.1).

The spatial distribution of capital expenditure for municipal infrastructure is biased against Kathmandu—the city with the greatest infrastructure needs. On a per capita basis, municipalities benefit from a higher level of capital expenditure for municipal infrastructure than Kathmandu and the submetropolitan cities. In fiscal 2010, infrastructure (physical and social) capital expenditure averaged US$11 per capita in the 53 municipalities, compared with US$6.3 per capita in Biratnagar, US$7.9 in Birgunj, US$9.2 in Lalitpur and US$6.8 in Pokhara. Spending in Kathmandu declined from US$14 per capita in fiscal 2008 to US$6 per capita in fiscal 2010. Higher per capita expenditures in the 53 municipalities are driven partly by a more substantial presence of project-based investments funded by development partners in these localities. The level of per capita expenditure for physical infrastructure projects is worrisomely low in submetropolitan

Figure 3.6 Per Capita Public Expenditure for Municipal Infrastructure, by Region or Ecological Zone, Fiscal 2008 and 2010

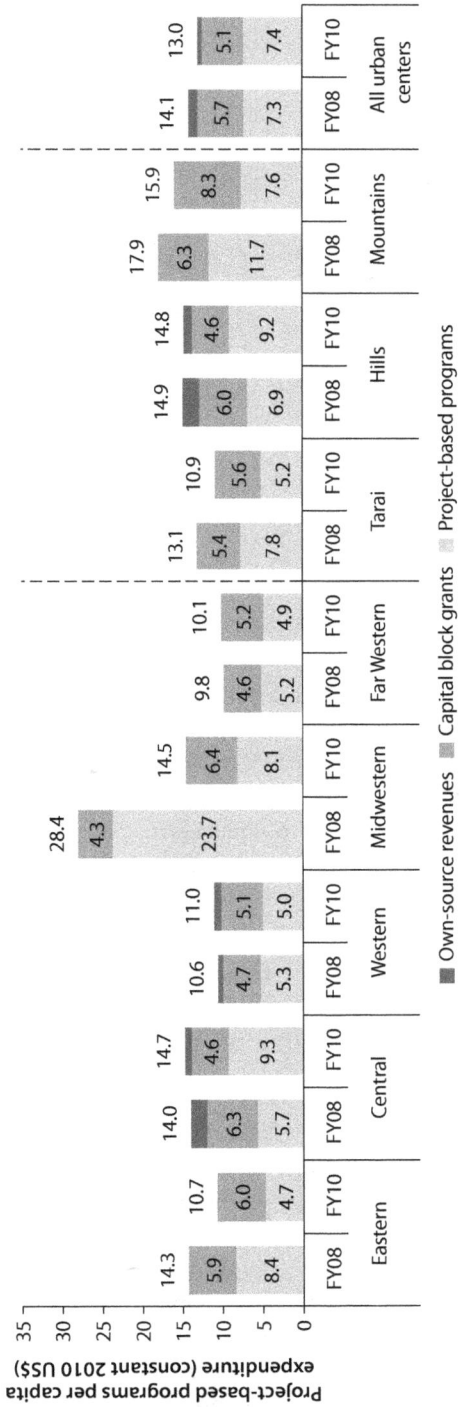

Project-based programs per capita expenditure (constant 2010 US$)

	Eastern		Central		Western		Midwestern		Far Western		Tarai		Hills		Mountains		All urban centers	
	FY08	FY10	FY08	FY10	FY08	FY10	FY08	FY10	FY08	FY10	FY08	FY10	FY08	FY10	FY08	FY10	FY08	FY10
Total	14.3	10.7	14.0	14.7	10.6	11.0	28.4	14.5	9.8	10.1	13.1	10.9	14.9	14.8	17.9	15.9	14.1	13.0
Own-source revenues	5.9	6.0	6.3	4.6	4.7	5.1	4.3	6.4	4.6	5.2	5.4	5.6	6.0	4.6	6.3	8.3	5.7	5.1
Capital block grants	8.4	4.7	5.7	9.3	5.3	5.0	23.7	8.1	5.2	4.9	7.8	5.2	6.9	9.2	11.7	7.6	7.3	7.4

■ Own-source revenues ■ Capital block grants ■ Project-based programs

Source: Public infrastructure expenditure survey data.
Note: FY = fiscal year. A fiscal year is from July 1 through June 30 (for example, July 1, 2007, through June 30, 2008, constitutes fiscal 2008).

83

Table 3.1 Spatial Allocation of Capital Expenditure for Municipal Infrastructure by Region and Ecological Zone, Fiscal 2010
Percent of total

Region or ecological zone	Project-based programs		Capital block grants	All funding modalities	Urban population share
	Physical infrastructure	*Social infrastructure*	*Capital block grants*	*All funding modalities*	*Urban population share*
Region					
Eastern	13	23	21	17	18
Central	62	24	46	51	50
Western	13	21	17	16	17
Midwestern	6	22	9	9	7
Far Western	6	9	8	7	7
Ecological zone					
Tarai	40	45	50	44	45
Hills	58	54	49	55	54
Mountains	2	1	2	1	1

Source: Public infrastructure expenditure survey data and CBS 2012.
Note: Totals may not equal 100 percent due to rounding.

cities, where spending ranged from US$0.5 to US$1.0 per capita in fiscal 2010, considering the critical role submetropolitan cities play in driving economic growth in Nepal's main extended urban economic regions (see figure 3.5).

The sectoral composition of capital expenditure varies significantly across urban areas. The bulk of municipal infrastructure expenditure funded through project-based programs is allocated to municipal roads in Kathmandu and the submetropolitan cities. Solid waste management expenditure is mostly concentrated in Kathmandu; in fiscal 2008, solid waste accounted for 65 percent of total capital expenditure for municipal infrastructure in Kathmandu, whereas it accounted for 2 percent in the municipalities. In the municipalities, the bulk of municipal infrastructure expenditure is allocated to municipal roads, water, and sanitation. Capital expenditure for municipal water supply in the municipalities has been declining over time, despite the growing needs (see figure 3.7).

Spatial Allocation of Capital Infrastructure Expenditure between Urban and Rural Areas

This section focuses on the spatial distribution of national capital expenditure programs for local infrastructure (covering both urban and rural areas).[9] For purposes of analysis, national-level capital expenditure programs are categorized by funding modality into two categories: (a) project-based investment programs and (b) capital block grants. The main project-based national-level investment programs for local infrastructure include the programs managed by the Department of Urban Development and Building Construction, the Ministry of Federal Affairs and Local Development, the Roads Board Nepal, the Ministry of Health and Population, the Department of Water Supply and Sewerage, and the Town Development Fund. National capital block grants are administered by the Ministry

Figure 3.7 Sectoral Allocation of Public Expenditure for Physical Infrastructure, by Urban Area, Fiscal 2008 and 2010

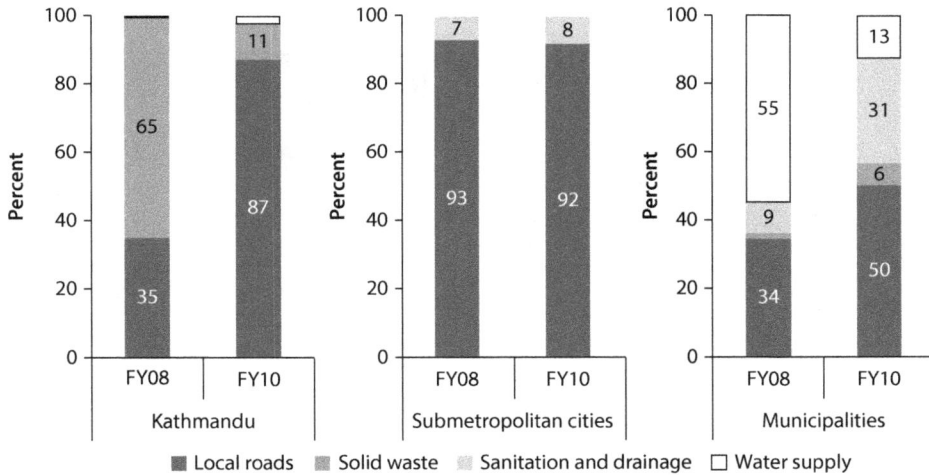

Source: Public infrastructure expenditure survey data.
Note: Totals may not equal 100 percent due to rounding. The sectoral analysis is based on project-based programs only, because the sectoral composition of infrastructure funded through own-source revenues and capital block grants is unknown.
FY = fiscal year. A fiscal year is from July 1 through June 30 (for example, July 1, 2007, through June 30, 2008, constitutes fiscal 2008).
Kathmandu refers to Kathmandu Metropolitan City; submetropolitan cities include Biratnagar, Birgunj, Lalitpur, and Pokhara.

of Federal Affairs and Local Development.[10] In fiscal 2008, the allocation of national-level expenditure for local infrastructure to urban areas was 18 percent, slightly above the proportion of the population living in urban areas (16 percent). However, in fiscal 2010, the urban share of national-level capital expenditures shrank to only 12 percent at the same time that the share of the urban population increased to 17 percent (see figure 3.8). In fiscal 2010, capital expenditure for local infrastructure funded by national programs amounted to US$7 per capita (2010 prices) in rural areas, compared with US$5 in urban areas (see figure 3.9).

Urban areas are the main recipients of project-based capital expenditures under national-level programs; rural areas are the main recipients of block grant allocations. On a per capita basis, project-based capital expenditure funded by national-level programs is higher in urban areas than in rural ones. In fiscal 2008, project-based capital expenditure in urban areas amounted to US$2.7 per capita under national programs, compared with US$1.1 per capita in rural areas. In fiscal 2010, differences in capital expenditures between urban and rural areas continued to be pronounced: urban per capita project-based expenditure was roughly twice the equivalent figure for rural areas (US$2.7 per capita in urban areas, compared with only US$1.6 in rural areas). Although project-based capital expenditures tend to favor urban areas, the difference in project-based expenditures is more than compensated for by higher capital block grant allocations in rural areas in fiscal 2010 (see figure 3.9).

The main fiscal transfer program is the capital block grant to local bodies from the Ministry of Federal Affairs and Local Development. The block grant

Figure 3.8 Urban and Rural Allocation of National Expenditure for Local Infrastructure Compared with Population, Fiscal 2008 and 2010

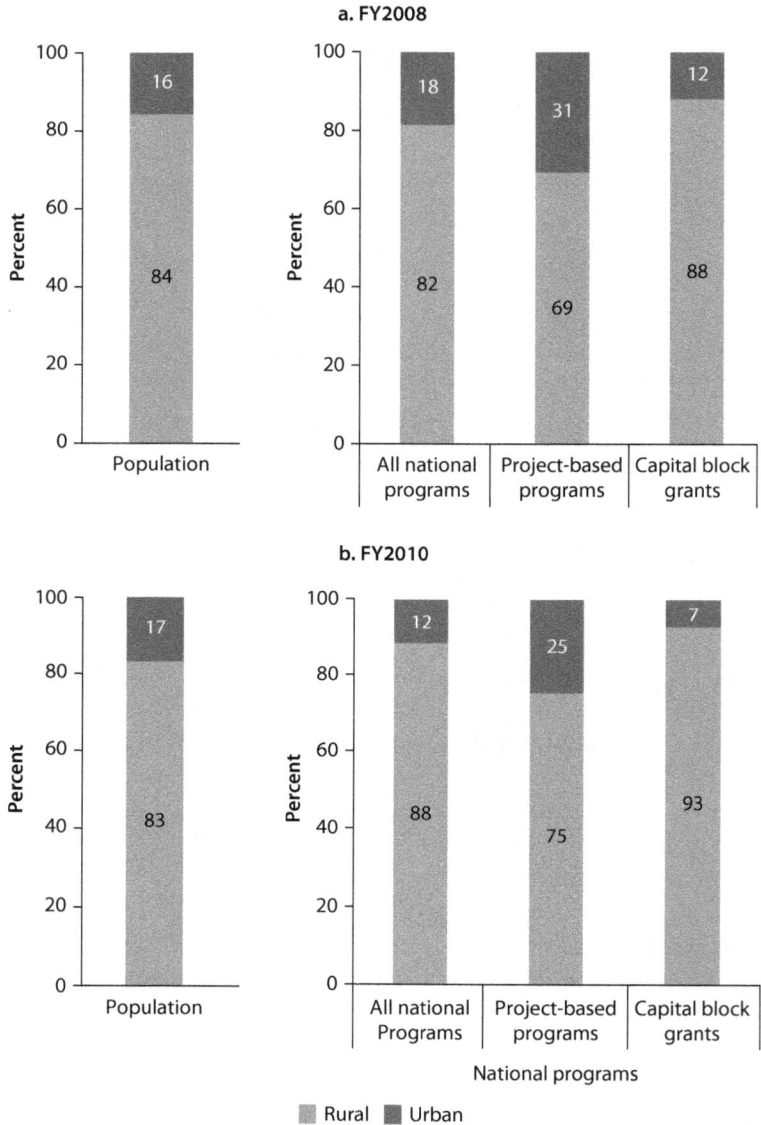

a. FY2008

b. FY2010

Rural Urban

Source: Public infrastructure expenditure survey data; UNDESA 2012.
Note: National programs include project-based programs and capital block grants. FY = fiscal year. A fiscal year is from July 1 through June 30 (for example, July 1, 2007, through June 30, 2008, constitutes fiscal 2008).

allocation between urban and rural areas is based on historical data as well as discretionary evaluations.[11] Urban and rural local governments are authorized to use capital block grants on a discretionary basis for infrastructure projects based on local priorities. From fiscal 2008 to fiscal 2010, the per capita block grant for rural areas increased relative to the per capita block

Figure 3.9 Per Capita Public Expenditure for Local Infrastructure, National Programs, Fiscal 2008 and 2010

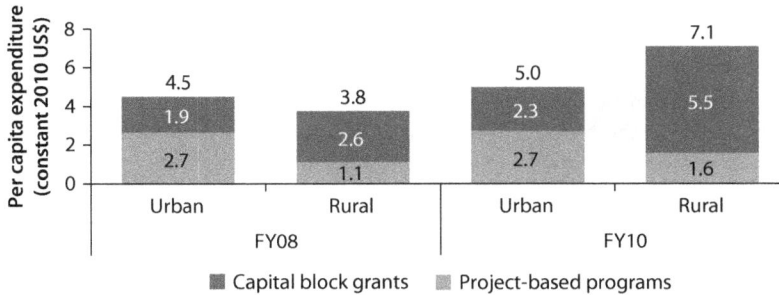

Source: Public infrastructure expenditure survey data.
Note: FY = fiscal year. A fiscal year is from July 1 through June 30 (for example, July 1, 2007, through June 30, 2008, constitutes fiscal 2008).

grant for urban areas, and in fiscal 2010, it was biased against urban areas, being significantly below the share of urban population. In fiscal 2008, 88 percent of capital block grants went to rural areas, accounting for 84 percent of the population. In fiscal 2010, the rural share of capital block grants increased to 93 percent (see figure 3.8).

Notes

1. A fiscal year is from July 1 through June 30 (for example, July 1, 2007, through June 30, 2008, constitutes fiscal 2008).

2. Unless otherwise stated, Kathmandu refers to Kathmandu Metropolitan City; Biratnagar, Birgunj, Lalitpur, and Pokhara refer to the submetropolitan cities; and all other urban local governments are referred to as municipalities.

3. The Nepal Supreme Court in 2012 annulled the Kathmandu Town Develpment Committee established under the Town Development Act of 1988 (Government of Nepal 1988b). The Committee continued to operate following the Supreme Court decision, but in a legal limbo.

4. The project includes 2,000 hectares for building the airport (runways and terminals) and the remaining land for building an "airport city."

5. The proposed airport apron will have 15 stands for international carriers, four stands for domestic carriers, and two stands for cargo flights.

6. Data are from the World Health Organization (WHO)/UNICEF Joint Monitoring Programme (JMP) for Water Supply and Sanitation (WHO and UNICEF 2012).

7. Although the Sisdol landfill in Kathmandu is considered sanitary, its operation does not meet the standards required by a sanitary landfill. Data provided by the Solid Waste Management Technical Center.

8. The analysis of the spatial allocation of public expenditure for municipal infrastructure across urban areas includes expenditure under both municipal and national programs.

9. This section analyzes national programs covering urban and rural areas, while the previous section focused on urban areas only.

10. The Ministry of Federal Affairs and Local Development block grant is augmented by a smaller block grant from the Local Governance and Community Development Program.

11. The distribution of capital block grants among urban and rural areas is based on a formula set by the Ministry of Federal Affairs and Local Development that includes population, area, internal revenue, and administrative expenditure.

References

ADB (Asian Development Bank). 2010a. *Unleashing Economic Growth: Region-Based Urban Strategy for Nepal*. Manila: ADB.

———. 2010b. Project Preparatory Technical Assistance. Consultants' Report for Kathmandu Valley Water Supply and Wastewater System Improvement Study. TA 4893-Nep, Manila.

Afram, Gabi G., and Angelica Salvi Del Pero. 2012. *Nepal's Investment Climate: Leveraging the Private Sector for Job Creation and Growth*. Washington, DC: World Bank.

Bhattarai, Keshav, and Dennis Conway. 2010. "Urban Vulnerabilities in the Kathmandu Valley, Nepal: Visualizations of Human/Hazard Interactions." *Journal of Geographic Information System* 2: 63–84.

Bhushal, Ramesh Prasad. 2011. "The Dead Rivers of Kathmandu." chinadialogue, London. http://www.chinadialogue.net/article/show/single/en/4321-The-dead-rivers-of-Kathmandu.

CBS (Central Bureau of Statistics). 2004. *Nepal Living Standards Survey 2003/04*. Kathmandu: Government of Nepal.

———. 2009. *Report on the Nepal Labor Force Survey 2008*. Kathmandu: Government of Nepal.

———. 2011. *Nepal Living Standards Survey 2010/11*. Kathmandu: Government of Nepal.

———. 2012. *National Population and Housing Census 2011*. Kathmandu: Government of Nepal.

Chreod Ltd. 2012. "Metropolitan Trends and Issues in the Kathmandu Valley." Background paper for this report, World Bank, Washington, DC.

Dudwick, Nora, Katy Hull, Roy Katayama, Forhad Shilpi, and Kenneth Simler. 2011. *From Farm to Firm: Rural-Urban Transition in Developing Countries*. Washington, DC: World Bank.

ESMAP (Energy Sector Management Assistance Program). 2008. "Nepal: Assessing the Social Impacts of Rural Energy Services." World Bank, Washington, DC.

ETG (Economic Transformations Group). 2012. "Kathmandu Valley Tourism Cluster Competitiveness Assessment and Action Plan." Background paper for this report, World Bank, Washington, DC.

Federation of Canadian Municipalities. 2002. "Nepal: Country Profile—Urban Sector and Municipal Governance." Federation of Canadian Municipalities, Ottawa.

Global Travel Industry News. 2011. "Second International Airport in Nepal to Be Operational by 2015." eTurboNews, April 11. http://www.eturbonews.com/22258/second-international-airport-nepal-be-operational-2015.

Government of Nepal, Ministry of Law, Justice and Parliamentary Affairs. 1988a. Kathmandu Valley Development Authority Act 2045 (1988). Kathmandu.

————, Ministry of Law, Justice and Parliamentary Affairs. 1988b. Town Development Act 2045 (1988). Kathmandu.

————, Ministry of Local Development, Solid Waste Management and Resource Mobilization Center. 2008. "Baseline Study on Solid Waste Management in Municipalities of Nepal." Kathmandu.

————, Ministry of Urban Development. 2012. "Emerging Towns Project: Baseline Survey." Kathmandu.

JICA (Japan International Cooperation Agency) and Ministry of Home Affairs. 2002. "The Study on Earthquake Disaster Mitigation in the Kathmandu Valley, Kingdom of Nepal." JICA, Tokyo.

NGFUWS (NGO Forum for Urban Water and Sanitation). 2007. Informational brochure. NGFUWS, Kathmandu.

Portnov, Boris A., Madhav Adhikari, and Moshe Schwartz. 2007. "Urban Growth in Nepal: Does Location Matter?" *Urban Studies* 44 (5–6): 915–37.

Rane, Jordan. 2011. "10 of the World's Most Hated Airports." CNN Travel, November 9. http://travel.cnn.com/explorations/life/10-most-hated-airports-324645.

Reja, Ben, and Mark Kutzbach. 2007. "Transport Accessibility and Economic Development in Nepal: A Survey of the Current Situation." University of California, Irvine.

Thapa, Rajesh Bahadur, and Yuji Murayama. 2012. "Scenario Based Urban Growth Allocation in Kathmandu Valley, Nepal." *Landscape and Urban Planning* 105 (1–2): 140–48.

UNDESA (United Nations, Department of Economic and Social Affairs). 2012. "World Urbanization Prospects. The 2011 Revision." New York: UNDESA.

UNESCO (United Nations Educational, Scientific, and Cultural Organization). 2006. *Cultural Portrait Handbook*. Vols. 1–7. Kathmandu: UNESCO.

WaterAid. 2008. "Solid Waste Management in Nepal." WaterAid, Kathmandu. http://www.wateraid.org/documents/plugin_documents/solid_waste_management_in_nepal.pdf.

WHO (World Health Organization) and UNICEF (United Nations Children's Fund). 2012. "Progress on Drinking Water and Sanitation—2012 Update." WHO and UNICEF.

World Economic Forum. 2010. *The Global Competitiveness Report, 2010–2011*. Geneva: World Economic Forum.

CHAPTER 4

The Comparative Advantages of Urban Areas

Urban areas have a comparative advantage in cultural tourism services, handicrafts, and agroprocessing. The challenge is turning these comparative advantages into competitive advantages. Rich in cultural heritage and located amid unparalleled natural scenery, cities in Nepal maintain a considerable appeal and potential for expansion of cultural tourism, and tourist arrivals are steadily increasing as Nepal's political situation stabilizes. However, the evolution of tourism in the Kathmandu Valley—the country's most important heritage destination—is characterized by an increasing number of tourists but a decreasing quality of the tourism experience. Similar to the Kathmandu Valley at large, the World Heritage site and buffer zones are suffering from deteriorating infrastructure, lack of basic urban services, traffic congestion, and intense population and commercial development pressure. Nepal has a comparative advantage in the handicraft sector and the related craft industry, which accounts for 6 percent of gross domestic product (GDP). Urban centers are not only the places where most artisans create and produce but also the natural location of wholesalers and retailers. Nepal's domestic handicraft market is led by sales to tourists, but handicraft exports are losing competitiveness because of the sector's inability to modernize in response to international competition. Agroprocessing is an important source of job creation in urban areas, and rural agroprocessing firms benefit from proximity to urban areas. However, agroprocessing remains a small-scale operation in Nepal and suffers from inadequate connective and market infrastructure, low productivity, and limited cluster support. This chapter provides an initial assessment of the growth drivers of urban areas, with a focus on opportunities and challenges faced by cultural tourism, handicrafts, and agroprocessing.

An Initial Assessment of Growth Drivers of Urban Areas

Urban areas have a comparative advantage in cultural tourism services, handicrafts, and agroprocessing—three sectors that hold significant potential for the growth of Nepal's cities. These sectors have a comparative advantage from both an international perspective (export competitiveness) and a regional perspective (contribution to regional job creation and local economic development). Export competitiveness was assessed using evidence from existing studies and the findings of the *Nepal Trade Integration Strategy 2010* (Government of Nepal 2010a). A location quotient analysis was carried out to estimate the contribution of a given sector to regional job creation.

Export Competitiveness

In the broadest sense, Nepal's comparative advantages from an international perspective can be identified by considering what makes Nepal "unique." Some of Nepal's main attributes include its ecological diversity and its rich cultural heritage, which give Nepal a comparative advantage in the tourism sector (ADB 2010). A complementary way of identifying Nepal's comparative advantages is to compare the export competitiveness of its products and services. The *Nepal Trade Integration Strategy 2010* identifies tourism, handicrafts, and agroproducts as strategic export markets. It identifies 19 products with the highest potential for export growth based on an assessment of domestic and international demand-and-supply trends. Among those products, tourism and labor services (remittances) are identified as the sectors with the highest export potential and socioeconomic impact on the national economy, followed by agroproducts and handicrafts. Among the other export products with the highest potential for expansion, seven are agrofood products (cardamom, ginger, honey, lentils, tea, noodles, and medicinal herbs), and five are handicraft industries (handmade paper, silver jewelry, pashmina and wool products). The other sectors with export potential are iron and steel, information technology and business process outsourcing services, health and education, hydroelectric power, and engineering.

Manufacturing in Nepal has a comparative advantage in resource-intensive and labor-intensive products. As much as 95 percent of Nepal's manufactured exports are concentrated in resource-intensive and labor-intensive product areas (World Bank 2003). Using the nominal protection coefficient—defined as the ratio of a product's domestic price to the export parity price at the border—Karmacharya (2000) finds that Nepal has a comparative advantage in stone carving, leather and leather products, essential oils, paper, and knotted carpets, as well as specialty teas and cardamom. Most of these products—from carpets to stone carvings—are manufactured using traditional labor- and resource-intensive skills passed on from generation to generation. The results are consistent with the findings of a recent regional competitiveness study carried out by the Asian Development Bank (ADB 2010). The study finds that urban regions have a competitive advantage in herbs and spices, carpets and pashmina, and fruits, in addition to tourism.[1]

Growth Drivers of Urban Regions

Urban areas have a comparative advantage in the products and services that hold the largest potential for export. A location quotient analysis was carried out to identify the growth drivers of the main urban areas. The location quotient measures the degree of employment concentration of an economic activity in a region relative to the entire country. A location quotient above one indicates higher concentration in the region relative to the rest of the country. A regional economic growth driver is a sector that has higher employment concentration and is growing faster in the region compared to the national average. The results of the location quotient analysis are presented in figures 4.1 to 4.6. The size of the bubble in the figures indicates the employment size of the sector (total number of employees). The analysis confirms that urban areas are service-oriented economies, with wholesale and retail trades being by far the main contributors to urban employment. The analysis also highlights the important contribution of tourism, agroprocessing, and handicrafts—three of the sectors with the largest potential for export growth—to local economic development in Nepal's cities. Jobs in hotels and restaurants are on the rise, and the sector is an important source of job creation for urban areas in the Kathmandu Valley, the Hills and Mountains of the Central and Eastern Regions, and the Tarai of the Eastern Region and West Nepal.[2] The agroprocessing sector is a growth driver in the urban areas of the Central Tarai, and an emerging sector in the urban areas of West Nepal. Handicrafts are an important growth driver for urban areas in the Kathmandu Valley, the Eastern and Central Tarai, and the Central and Eastern Hill and Mountain zones. Information and communication technology is a relatively small sector, but important with regard to value addition, and saw important growth in employment from 2003 to 2007 in urban areas, particularly in the Kathmandu Valley.

The comparative advantage of cities in Nepal ultimately rests on the effective conservation of their cultural heritage. A common characteristic of Nepal's growth drivers is their linkages with the country's tangible and intangible cultural heritage. The effective management of Nepal's cultural heritage—which encompasses both monuments and sites of outstanding universal value (tangible heritage) and skills, knowledge, and instruments transmitted from generation to generation (intangible heritage)—is vital for the competitiveness of cultural tourism, traditional handicraft production, and some agroproducts. The conservation of Nepal's cultural heritage can be a catalyst for urban revitalization by enhancing city livability; increasing competitiveness; creating a wide range of income-earning opportunities, such as improved cultural tourism services; and generating wealth to the poor. The poverty reduction effect of cultural heritage can also be far-reaching, from the promotion of job creation and income diversification to the preservation of the social identity of poor local communities.

The rest of this section discusses the potential for expansion and the constraints for three sectors important to local economic development in Nepal's cities: cultural tourism, handicrafts, and agroprocessing.

Figure 4.1   Economic Base of the Kathmandu Valley, 1998–2008

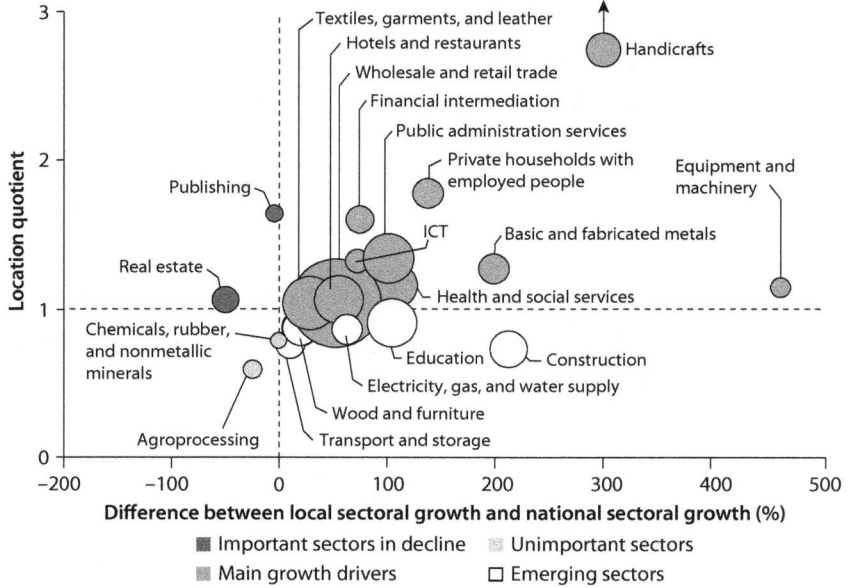

Sources: Based on CBS 1999, 2009.
Note: The analysis includes sectors with more than 1,000 employees in the Kathmandu Valley. ICT = information and communication technology.

Figure 4.2   Economic Base of Urban Areas in the Hill and Mountain Zones of the Central and Eastern Regions, 1998–2008

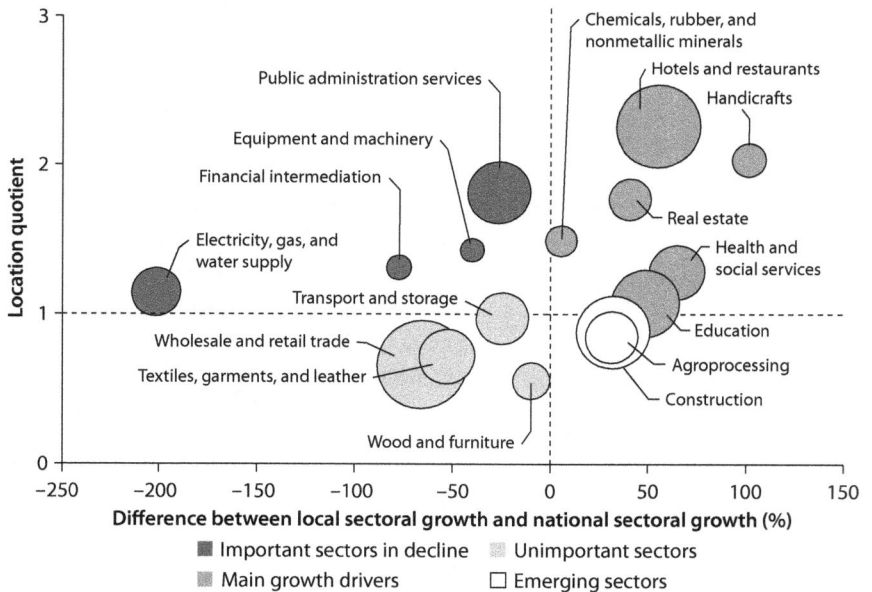

Sources: Based on CBS 1999, 2009.
Note: The analysis includes sectors with more than 1,000 employees in the region, Kathmandu Valley excluded.

Figure 4.3 Economic Base of Urban Areas in the Hill and Mountain Zones of West Nepal, 1998–2008

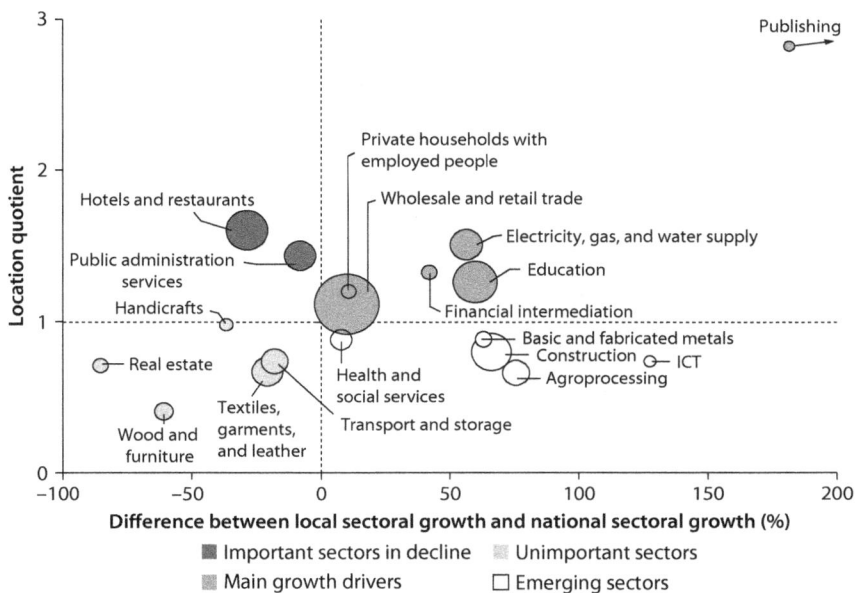

Sources: Based on CBS 1999, 2009.
Note: The analysis includes sectors with more than 1,000 employees in the region. West Nepal includes Western, Midwestern, and Far Western Regions. ICT = information and communication technology.

Figure 4.4 Economic Base of Urban Areas in the Tarai Zone of the Eastern Region, 1998–2008

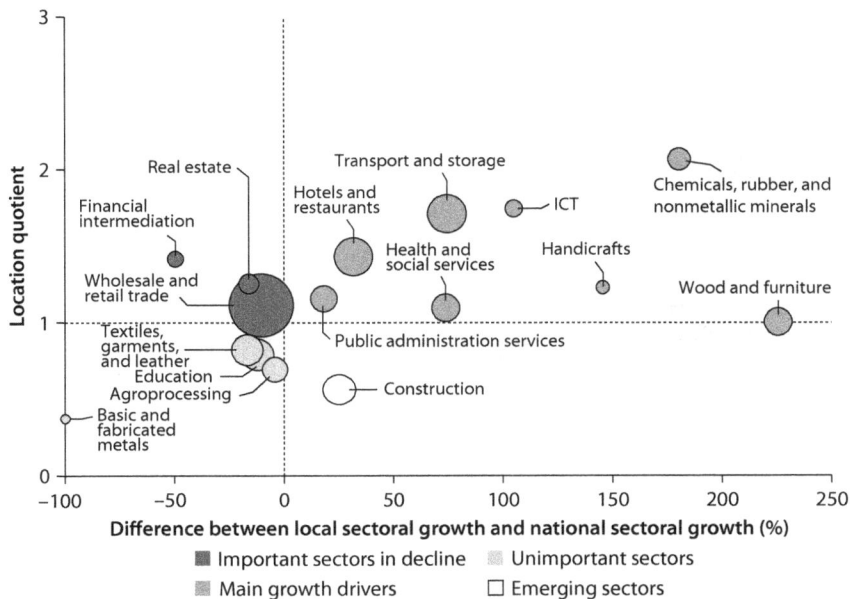

Sources: Based on CBS 1999, 2009.
Note: The analysis includes sectors with more than 1,000 employees in the region. ICT = information and communication technology.

Figure 4.5 Economic Base of Urban Areas in the Tarai Zone of the Central Region, 1998–2008

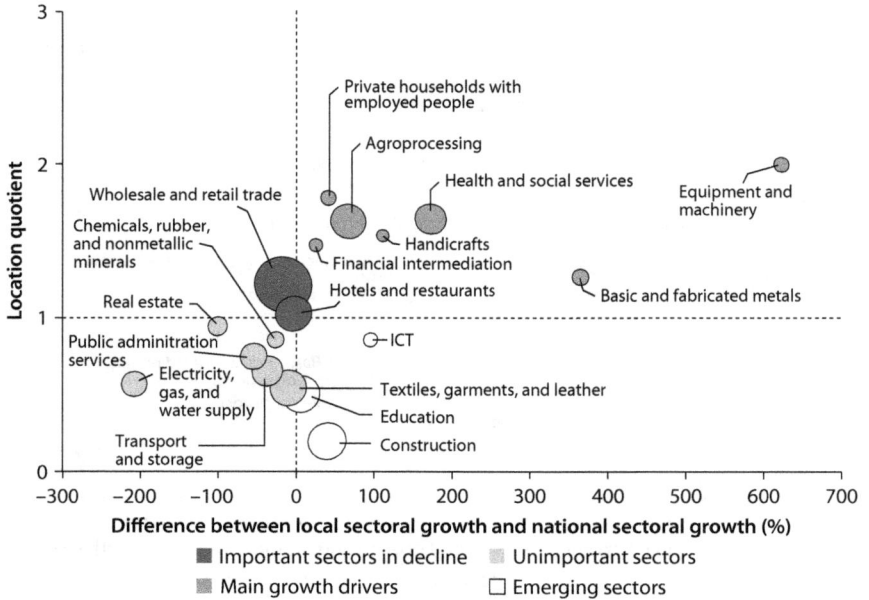

Sources: Based on CBS 1999, 2009.
Note: The analysis includes sectors with more than 1,000 employees in the region. ICT = information and communication technology.

Figure 4.6 Economic Base of Urban Areas in the Tarai Zone of the West Regions, 1998–2008

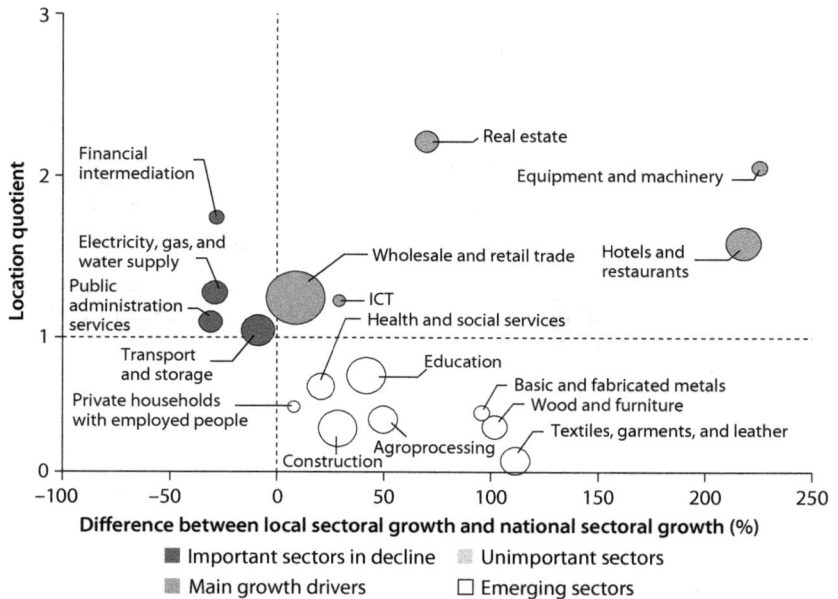

Sources: Based on CBS 1999, 2009.
Note: The analysis includes sectors with more than 1,000 employees in the region. ICT = information and communication technology.

Cultural Tourism: An Important Contributor to Job Creation

Tourism is an important source of income diversification and a contributor to poverty reduction through its economic, social, environmental, and cultural benefits. After a short presentation of tourism trends, the section focuses on cultural tourism in urban areas.

Tourism Trends

The government of Nepal considers tourism a driver of economic growth and plans to attain 2 million tourist arrivals by 2020. The government's commitment to tourism development rests on the awareness that, among all economic sectors, sustainable tourism development holds significant potential to generate income, create jobs, and provide foreign exchange (Government of Nepal 2010b). Tourism contributes 7.4 percent of Nepal's GDP—US$1 billion—including its wider economic impact. In 2011, tourism generated 726,000 jobs, including jobs indirectly supported by the industry, equivalent to 5.9 percent of total employment; 6.8 percent of total jobs will be in tourism by 2021 (World Travel and Tourism Council 2011). Tourism also has a ripple effect on the entire economy by sustaining the construction industry, fostering agricultural and handicraft production, and promoting the development of services. The Asian Development Bank estimates that 3.5 foreign tourists generate one direct job in the tourism industry, whereas 3.1 tourists generate one indirect job in the wider economy linked to the sector (ADB 2004). Finally, tourism positively affects the local population by promoting higher education and greater civic engagement.

As Nepal's political situation stabilizes, tourist arrivals are steadily increasing. The number of international tourists has resumed its preconflict level. From the conflict-influenced low of 275,468 tourists in 2002, the number of international tourists reached 602,000 in 2010 and 735,000 in 2011, registering an important 21 percent annual increase over the previous year, although falling short of the government's target of 1 million. In 2009, total tourism receipts in Nepal exceeded US$370 million. Nepal's principal tourist markets are India, China, the United States, Japan, the United Kingdom, Germany, France, Scandinavia, Spain, the Republic of Korea, and Thailand. Tourists from India are by far the largest group, with 154,000 arrivals in 2011, accounting for 21 percent of all international tourists. Tourists from China are the second-largest market, accounting for 10.3 percent of all tourists. They represent the fastest-growing segment, increasing by 63 percent, from 46,000 arrivals in 2010 to 75,000 in 2011. The markets of Europe and North America are important to Nepal because they are high-value (long-staying and high-spending) markets. The United Kingdom, Germany, and France are the largest sources of vacationers from Europe, with the United Kingdom accounting for more than 554,000 tourism days in Nepal in 2010. The United States has traditionally been an important source of tourism (currently ranking sixth in total days in Nepal, with 373,000 tourist days in 2011) and remains a strong market for tourism expenditure. Repeat visitors account for some 38 percent of total arrivals. Present hotel accommodation capacity in Nepal is about 66,000 beds, 25,000 of which are of international standard. The vast majority of international-standard beds are in the Kathmandu Valley (ETG 2012).[3]

Total tourism receipts in Nepal have grown at an average of 10.8 percent per year, owing to rising spending per tourist in the postconflict period, from US$592 per tourist in 2003 to US$727 in 2009. The visitors' average length of stay was 12.7 days in 2010, a figure consistent with the average length of stay registered during the last 20 years (ADB 2004). Seasonality tends to be consistent as well, with peaks from September to November and in February and March. In spite of the growth in tourism receipts, tourism expenditure averaged only US$40 per day in 2011, registering a drop from US$43 in 2010.[4] This recent drop in tourism daily expenditure was caused in large part by the increase in lower-spending pilgrimage tourists. The low expenditure also reflects the high percentage of young backpackers visiting on budgets of US$5–10 a day. Despite the lack of specific data, the average expenditure of cultural tourists is estimated to be around US$80 per day, nearly double the 2011 average.[5] Tourism expenditure per day is low in Nepal compared with other destinations: US$85 in the Arab Republic of Egypt, US$122 in Morocco, and nearly US$200 in Turkey (UNWTO 2007). Nepal's tourism expenditure is as low when international airfares are accounted for. A typical seven-day trip to Nepal from China or Japan costs US$2,000, half of which goes for the international airfare and another 10–15 percent for the international tour operator's overhead costs, leaving only 35–40 percent for tourism expenditure in the country. However, international experience shows that leakage of tourism expenditure tends to be lower for low-end tourism products, compared with high-end tourism products (ETG 2012).

Cultural Tourism and the Management of Cultural Heritage: A Focus on the Kathmandu Valley

Nepal's urban areas are home to a vast array of tangible and intangible cultural heritage, which has evolved over many centuries and maintains a considerable appeal and potential for expansion in cultural tourism. From the ancient hill towns in the west to the compact historic city cores of the Kathmandu Valley, distinct urban forms and architectural styles have evolved. Religious traditions are deeply held and are represented by such sites as Lumbini, the birthplace of Buddha in the Tarai, and a treasury of temples, *stupas*, and other religious sites throughout the country. With more than 100 ethnic and caste groups, Nepal is home to a wide variety of living cultures with intangible heritage in music and dance, art and handicrafts, festivals and celebrations, languages, and oral folklore. Much of the country's intangible heritage is still vibrant and evolving, although many traditional practices and skills are disappearing. Those that remain—celebrations in public squares, observances at religious sites, and production of traditional handicrafts—give vitality and meaning to the built heritage and urban fabric. Even more important, intangible cultural

Cities in Nepal are home to a variety of living cultures with their traditional festivals and celebrations.

© ECS Nepal. Used with permission. Permission required for further re-use.

heritage provides communities with a window to their history and accomplishments and supports a positive and strong "sense of place" and social cohesion. This section presents the specific challenges of cultural tourism facing the Kathmandu Valley.

The Kathmandu Valley is the most important heritage destination and the gateway for tourism in Nepal. The country's most widely recognized cultural asset is the UNESCO[6] Kathmandu Valley World Heritage site, which is composed of seven protected monument zones (PMZs). These zones include the three Durbar Squares of Bhaktapur municipality (hereafter, Bhaktapur), Kathmandu Metropolitan City (hereafter, Kathmandu), and Lalitpur Submetropolitan City (hereafter, Lalitpur).[7] The squares are important urban focal points, consisting of palaces, courtyards, temples, shrines, and monuments in the historic city cores of Bhaktapur, Kathmandu, and Lalitpur. The World Heritage designation also includes two highly significant Buddhist sites (Bauddhanath and Swayambhunath) and two Hindu centers of major importance (Pashupati and Changu Narayan). Great historic value and interest are also found in the valley's traditional neighborhoods, vernacular housing, ancient streets, and buildings inspired by 18th- and 19th-century European architecture. Together these heritage assets are the unique architectural expression of the social, political, religious, and cultural lifestyles of the Kathmandu Valley. Because of its landlocked and isolated geographical location, the Kathmandu Valley is also the main gateway for tourists in Nepal. Over 75 percent of

The conservation of traditional architecture is important for continued tourism development in Nepal.
© ECS Nepal. Used with permission. Permission required for further re-use.

tourists arrive in Nepal by air, and most visitors begin and end their travel to Nepal in the Kathmandu Valley. The valley serves as the hub for organizing trekking, leisure, and mountaineering trips to other regions of Nepal. The Kathmandu Valley also accounts for a high proportion of Nepal's total tourism income because the country's major tourism operators are based in the valley.

The evolution of tourism in the Kathmandu Valley over the last 30 years is characterized by an increasing number of tourists but a decreasing quality of the tourism experience. In the 1970s, the Kathmandu Valley—despite its rustic tourism hotels and infrastructure—was very attractive with its distinct and beautiful villages, separated by short distances from one another. Rice fields were scattered about, and vistas of the Himalayas were a common site. Reaching the main cultural sites from hotels was easy. Under the pressures of rapid urbanization, especially during the last 10 years, the tourism experience has been compromised. For example, inadequate and unreliable municipal and utility services (garbage collection, sewerage, water, power, and telecommunications) hamper hotel operations and often force hotel owners to resort to special service providers or establish backup utility systems with unwarranted additional costs. Although traffic is controlled in some areas, pedestrians are generally unsafe in the vicinity of the historic city center squares. Noise and air pollution undermine local residents' ability to relax and worship and tourists' enjoyment. The availability of land for hotels and new tourism complexes is highly constrained in the Kathmandu Valley. Moreover, it is often scattered in unsuitable urban areas that impede the

Swayambhunath is an ancient religious complex atop a hill in the Kathmandu Valley and an important destination for cultural tourism.
© ECS Nepal. Used with permission. Permission required for further re-use.

establishment of substantive hotel clusters with sufficient mass and variety of tourism facilities and services. To date, the local authorities of the Kathmandu Valley have been unable to come together to identify appropriate and adequate hotel development areas and to make them available to the tourism industry.

The public cultural and historic assets of the Kathmandu Valley have suffered considerable damage. Like the Kathmandu Valley at large, the World Heritage site and areas surrounding the site's monuments and complexes (buffer zones) suffer from deteriorating infrastructure, lack of basic urban services, traffic congestion, and intense population and commercial development. In the 1990s, UNESCO (World Heritage Center) was forced to list the Kathmandu Valley among the endangered heritage sites because of concerns about their protection and conservation. Recently, UNESCO has removed the Kathmandu Valley from that list, although after considerable damage had already occurred to the architectural integrity of the buffer zones. With the noticeable exception of Bhaktapur, the PMZs—originally surrounded by traditional Newar[8] buildings, with their elaborately carved wooden windows—are increasingly invaded by modern concrete structures that ring the squares and disrespect the original street alignments, building heights, and facade treatments. The Durbar Squares in Kathmandu and Lalitpur especially are losing cultural value, religious significance, and tourism potential because of inadequate development controls and management.

Overlapping authority and responsibilities and insufficient monitoring capacity prevent central and local agencies from fulfilling their responsibilities to protect

The condition of temples along the riverbanks in the Kathmandu Valley is deteriorating due to encroachment and inadequate solid waste management.

the country's cultural heritage. Responsibilities for the conservation of cultural heritage are institutionally highly fragmented among central and local agencies, which often results in little action being taken. (Institutional responsibilities for cultural heritage are outlined in box 4.1.) The more serious challenge for the protection of the tangible heritage, however, is enforcement. Local and national government authorities have been unable to enforce the policies established to protect

Box 4.1 Institutional Responsibilities for Cultural Heritage Conservation

At the central level of government, the responsibilities for cultural heritage conservation are shared among the Department of Archaeology (DoA), the Ministry of Urban Development (formerly the Ministry of Physical Planning and Works), and the Guthi Sansthan.

The DoA is responsible for conserving and protecting national monuments and World Heritage PMZs, preparing cultural heritage inventories, and prescribing building bylaws and approving building permits in the PMZs. The most recent and comprehensive initiative for heritage conservation is the development in 2007 of an integrated management framework and action plan for the seven PMZs based on a partnership among local authorities, UNESCO, and the DoA. The framework and action plan institutionalize strategies and actions to manage, monitor, and coordinate conservation of the seven PMZs. As part of the framework, the DoA has formed a working committee made up of members from each PMZ. The committee is tasked with coordinating and monitoring the integrated management plans. The DoA's purview covers monuments almost exclusively rather than broader conservation areas, such as the historic urban fabric or traditional streetscapes.

The Ministry of Urban Development carries out various development and infrastructure projects within the PMZs and other historic areas through its departments for urban infrastructure, water supply, and sewerage. The ministry is required to comply with DoA guidelines. In addition, the Special Physical Infrastructure Area Development Project within the ministry's Department of Urban Development and Building Construction is charged with conserving and developing areas with religious, cultural, and touristic importance (excluding monuments) and with undertaking work related to the conservation of the urban environment.

The Guthi Sansthan, under the Ministry of Land Reform and Management, is the legal owner of many monuments and historic and religious buildings and is responsible for their conservation. It also has responsibility for supporting religious rites and festivals, which private *guthis* performed before the 1964 land reforms. However, because of the lack of funds, the Guthi Sansthan performs very little conservation or maintenance of tangible heritage and makes only small contributions toward the performance of religious rites and festivals. Some private *guthis* still exist and, for the most part, are focused on maintaining community temples and the performance of rituals.

Urban local governments and village development committees (VDCs) in the valley are charged with managing the PMZ buffer zones and with recording, maintaining, and preserving the tangible and intangible heritage outside the PMZs. With respect to physical development, the local governments must prepare a land-use map and must approve building permits. In the case of PMZs, listed monuments, and historic buildings, building permits are approved through the DoA. However, contradicting bylaws are being implemented in the PMZs. For example, some major alterations to the DoA's 1991 building bylaws and guidelines were made in the municipal building bylaws for Bhaktapur, Kathmandu, and Lalitpur. One of the most drastic differences is the provision that allows reconstruction of private buildings with concrete frame structures and the use of inappropriate materials, such as galvanized sheet metal roofing.

box continues next page

Box 4.1 Institutional Responsibilities for Cultural Heritage Conservation *(continued)*

Wards and community members are responsible for the inventory and conservation of local monuments and the maintenance and cleanliness of these sites. Ward leaders are responsible for mobilizing community members (for example, individuals, *guthis*, nongovernmental organizations, and youth groups) for these activities.

Source: Ebbe 2012.

the monuments and historic homes in the buffer zones of the Durbar Squares because of inadequate monitoring capacity. Even when building plans meet regulatory requirements for design of traditional facades, roofs, and building heights, local permitting offices are unable to directly control illegal construction.

Community awareness and mobilization for the conservation of the country's heritage are weakening. Increasing urbanization and mobility and an escalating pace of life have reduced residents' awareness of the importance of cultural heritage as a strong and positive source of image and pride for their country. Moreover, the ability of communities to protect their heritage buildings, observe traditional practices, and participate in collective activities has been compromised. Fewer of the country's youth are being systematically introduced to and included in traditional cultural practices. The *guthis* of Nepal—one of the indigenous systems that traditionally played an important role in the conservation and perpetuation of cultural heritage—have been significantly weakened after the nationalization of *guthi* land in 1961 (see box 4.2). A lesson learned by conservationists around the world is that the strongest force for the protection of cultural resources is a community that understands and values its heritage. Consequently, community awareness campaigns to generate interest and involvement are a high priority. The country can build on lessons learned from Kathmandu, which has supported community awareness raising in the past and is mobilizing local communities at the ward level to contribute to heritage conservation in their immediate neighborhoods.

Most urban centers fail to capture the economic benefits of private heritage conservation. Many traditional buildings in the neighborhoods surrounding the Durbar Squares are disappearing because of lack of maintenance, especially private courtyard houses. Affluent families, for example, often leave their traditional homes to pursue more modern lifestyles, leaving their buildings vacant or renting to low-income families and neglecting maintenance. Another common problem is the demolition of traditional structures and their replacement with buildings of six- to eight-story reinforced concrete. These inappropriate modern buildings ring the historic squares and greatly diminish their visual appeal.[9] The practice of hereditary division of property is also a constraint to the conservation of private heritage. The historic buildings are divided vertically to allow all parties to own part of the land. Ownership and access to a top and ground floor are considered an asset because of the opportunity to conduct commercial activities (for example, restaurants at the top and shops at ground level). These

Box 4.2 Building on Local Communities for Cultural Heritage Conservation: The *Guthi* System

International experience indicates that the successful conservation of cultural heritage requires the active participation of local communities in the cultural heritage management process. Indigenous communities (for example, those in the Kathmandu Valley) have historically been the doyens of cultural traditions—from art, religious rituals, and architecture to handicrafts and handlooms. Fostering their vested interest in the cultural heritage management process is therefore vital to guaranteeing the sustainability of the cultural and historic endowment of the valley.

The *guthis* of Nepal, including the Newar *guthis* of the Kathmandu Valley, are one of the indigenous systems that traditionally played an important role in the conservation and perpetuation of cultural heritage.[a] The *guthi* is an association formed by groups of people on the basis of caste, patrilineal grouping, or territorial aspects. *Guthis* were originally set up to establish and maintain religious and charitable institutions. Before the land reforms of 1961, the Newar *guthis* enjoyed almost total autonomy in the operation and management of their affairs. The *guthiyars* (members of the *guthi* in charge of its management) were responsible for rent collection, sale of products, and purchase of materials required for religious ceremonies. The endowment of land made the *guthis* economically viable. The *guthis* generated financial and social capital from collective landownership, which financed regular maintenance of heritage items along with the observance of cultural rituals and festivals practiced by local people. Maintenance of local monuments, temples, and other culturally important edifices was carried out by local masons and carpenters using local materials and according to traditional craftsmanship, preserving the architecture of the region and perpetuating the unique set of local skills.

In 1961, drastic reforms set out to nationalize *guthi* land, effectively stripping local *guthi* leadership of its managerial responsibilities and replacing it with a centralized autonomous authority, known as the Guthi Sansthan.[b] The new centralized management, being unfamiliar with the local context, faced inefficiencies, such as the inability to collect rents and payments. Lower revenues and new administrative costs considerably reduced funds available for the maintenance of heritage buildings. The situation resulted in funds being prioritized and channeled to a few nationally significant monuments while smaller local edifices were left in disrepair.

Centralized authorities have much to gain by reconsidering the role of the local private *guthis* in the process of conserving cultural heritage. Today, even though the role of the *guthi* has been weakened, the local *guthis* remain involved in smaller-scale conservation of temples, water spouts, and *patis* (rest houses). Strengthening the *guthis* will allow them to do so with greater efficiency and at a lower cost. Empowering local *guthis* would also ensure that the restoration and conservation process remains true to the local architectural traditions and customs, while preserving the know-how of their craftsmanship for future generations. In addition, rehabilitated heritage buildings belonging to the *guthis* can be repurposed into income-generating touristic ventures, such as the homestay initiative championed by the government of Nepal. Other traditional *guthi* handicrafts, such as pottery, traditional

box continues next page

**Box 4.2 Building on Local Communities for Cultural Heritage Conservation:
The *Guthi* System** *(continued)*

hand-loomed garments, and wooden handicrafts, can also be marketed effectively to enable
indigenous art to become a means of livelihood.

Source: Pradhananga, Shrestha, and Dee 2009.
a. The socioeconomic functions of *guthis* are designed to uphold the religious and cultural heritage of their people, including
the careful upkeep of monuments and other culturally relevant legacies, such as temples and monasteries.
b. Guthi Sansthan Act of 1964.

divisions often lead to inefficient interior spaces and disfigurement of traditional
facades (Ebbe 2012). Conserving traditional buildings and adapting them for
new uses that generate income is a two-pronged strategy: it provides the funds
necessary for building maintenance and creates new economic activities and jobs.
Examples of the adaptation of traditional buildings for new commercial activities that generate income and provide funds for maintenance are the Garden of
Dreams in Kathmandu and the Newa Chen Hotel in Lalitpur. Rehabilitation has
been shown to be less expensive than new construction (approximately Nr 800
per square foot versus Nr 2,200–Nr 2,500 per square foot[10]).

Human resources in the tourism sector are lacking in quantity and quality, and
the tourism vocational training system is inadequate. Despite the availability of
abundant labor, the tourism sector has problems finding reliable staff with
proper training and professional experience. The problems created by the shortage of staff are compounded by strong labor unions and their inability to guide
a balanced dialogue between workers and their employers. These problems result
in unwarranted shortcomings in the services provided by tourism establishments
and in difficulty to predict and control additional costs in their operations. The
World Travel and Tourism Council (2011) ranks Nepal 131st in education and
training for tourism human resources and 129th in availability of qualified labor.
The vocational training system is inadequate, being divided between a few public
institutions (the Nepal Academy of Tourism and Hotel Management, universities
and affiliated colleges and schools, the Council for Technical Education and
Vocational Training) and about 300 private training institutions of which only 50
have been licensed by the World Travel and Tourism Council. The majority of
private training institutions operate informally and provide substandard training
services (ETG 2012).

With all its differences and specificities, the experience of Bhaktapur provides important lessons for the protection, conservation, and management of
tangible and intangible heritage. Bhaktapur is particularly renowned for its well-
preserved heritage buildings, colorful festivals, traditional dances, and indigenous Newar lifestyle. Bhaktapur has been effective in protecting its cultural
assets, in part because of its distance from Kathmandu and lesser urbanization
pressures. Bhaktapur's success in its conservation efforts can be traced to several
important factors, such as the ability to capture the socioeconomic benefits of
heritage conservation and the engagement of local communities (see box 4.3).

Box 4.3 Bhaktapur's Successful Efforts to Conserve Its Cultural Heritage

Bhaktapur, also known as Bhadgaon, lies in the Kathmandu Valley and is renowned for its well-preserved heritage buildings, colorful festivals, traditional dances, and indigenous Newar lifestyle. It is one of Nepal's most popular destinations, making tourism a key source of jobs, income, and foreign exchange. Since the end of the insurgency in 2006, tourist arrivals from both South Asian Association for Regional Cooperation (SAARC)[a] and non-SAARC countries have been on the rise. In 2009, Bhaktapur welcomed close to 150,000 visitors, indicating a steady return to preinsurgency levels of about 200,000 tourists per year. By fostering cultural tourism through renovations of cultural heritage buildings and reinforcing the niche market for traditional cultural products, Bhaktapur has been able to spur economic growth and provide jobs to the local community.

Bhaktapur's ability to weave cultural heritage conservation into its tourism strategy is central to ensuring its continued success. Bhaktapur's experience stands in contrast to that of most other historic sites in the Kathmandu Valley, whose heritage has been undermined by unplanned urban development. Underlying Bhaktapur's success is a strong, unified government with a commitment to an urban and economic development strategy that builds on the conservation of its cultural heritage. Several important elements have supported the city's conservation.

First, engaging the local community in the protection of cultural heritage helped embed conservation efforts in the sociocultural and economic fabric of Bhaktapur. For example, renovation projects are executed by local communities using traditional materials and techniques. In addition, authorities promote the production of traditional products as a specialized source of jobs for the local community.

Second, the municipality mobilizes resources for maintenance activities and infrastructure investment through tourist fees charged at the entrance to the city core (that is, Nr 100 or US$1.25 for SAARC-country visitors and Nr 1,100 or US$15 for non-SAARC visitors). Revenues serve to carry out renovation of traditional buildings as well as to finance the maintenance and improvement of local infrastructure (for example, street paving according to traditional patterns and drainage). The municipality estimates that up to 70 percent of its development budget is dedicated to the provision of urban services and the conservation of heritage buildings. In fiscal 2010,[b] 61 percent of the total revenues from tourism were spent on waste management.

Third, the municipality protects the traditional architectural landscape by providing subsidies to private homeowners to shield the additional costs of restoring original buildings or constructing new ones with traditional materials, such as *dachi apa* bricks, roof tiles, and local timber. The city also has a strong enforcement and inspection system focused on maintaining the traditional aspects of building facades.

Fourth, the local authority encourages repurposing traditional buildings into homestay residences. These residences generate additional revenues that can be channeled back into building conservation and maintenance, ensuring the long-term sustainability of such ventures and providing jobs and income to the local community.

box continues next page

Box 4.3 Bhaktapur's Successful Efforts to Preserve Its Cultural Heritage *(continued)*

Fifth, the municipality is involved in the development of cultural heritage training and education. For example, wood-carving workshops help maintain the skills to execute the elaborate architectural elements (such as, carved wooden window and door frames) that are basic to the local style. The Bhaktapur Tourism Development Committee has developed a training program for locals to become city tour guides for Bhaktapur. It has also established several schools to perpetuate traditional skills and knowledge among younger generations, such as the Khowpa Engineering College, which specializes in traditional Newar architecture.

Sixth, the municipality has engaged in important infrastructure investments to meet the needs of the growing tourism sector, as well as to support the rising demands from urbanization. Investments include renovating water wells and water spouts and paving the city core's lanes, streets, and courtyards—an estimated 74 percent of Bhaktapur's roads are paved, making all the cultural heritage sites readily accessible. The municipality's newly targeted projects include creating new bus terminals, designing pedestrian-only routes, and creating resting points at all tourist sites.

Sources: Byanju 2002; District Development Committee of Bhaktapur and Nepal Tourism Board 2010; and data made available by Bhaktapur.
a. SAARC includes Afghanistan, Bangladesh, Bhutan, India, Maldives, Nepal, Pakistan, and Sri Lanka.
b. A fiscal year is from July 1 through June 30 (for example, July 1, 2009, through June 30, 2010, constitutes fiscal 2010).

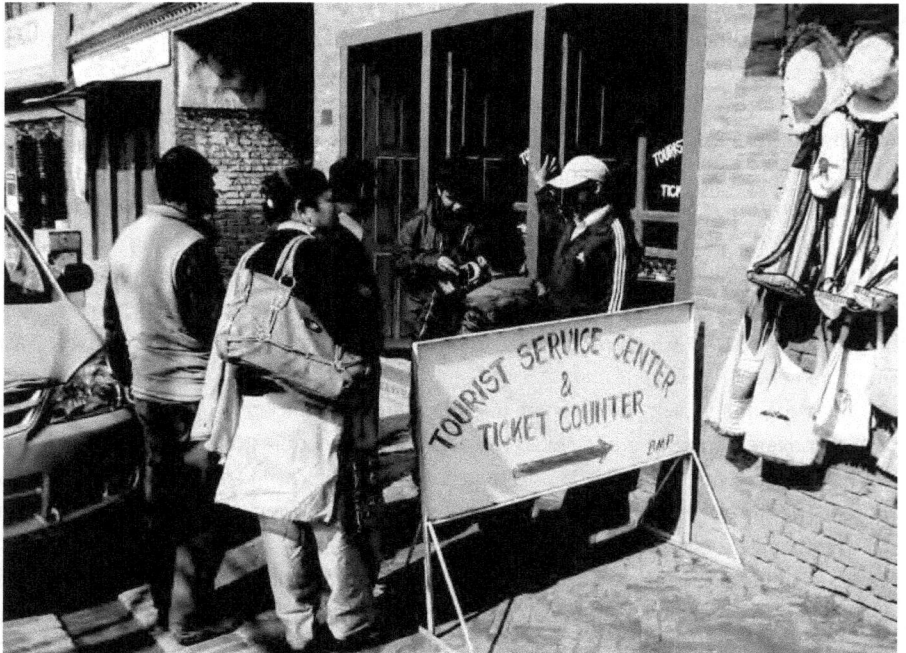

Tourist fees to enter Bhaktapur's city core are used for heritage conservation and infrastructure upgrading.

The conservation of historic buildings creates both skilled and unskilled jobs.

Other urban centers in the valley have recently taken some steps to manage and upgrade their historic environments. For example, Lalitpur has installed solar lighting, tourist information booths, and a public toilet in its PMZ, and Kathmandu has combined the cultural heritage division with the building division of its local government to better control building permits.

The Handicraft Industry: Dwindling Exports, but Strong Ties with Tourism

Nepal has a comparative advantage in the handicraft sector and the related craft industry. Handicraft products in Nepal have both a secular and religious history, and many traditional and new products are known and reputed internationally. For many years, the Nepalese government has recognized that, given the limitations imposed by the country's geography, handicraft manufacturing would necessarily be an integral part of the country's industrialization process. The handicraft industry—defined as the manufacture of products reflecting a country's traditions, art, and culture or using indigenous raw materials—engages a large number of employees, is a significant contributor to GDP, and is a major earner of foreign exchange.[11] The handicraft sector accounts for as much as 6.0 percent of Nepal's GDP, higher than in Tunisia (4.0 percent) but lower than in Morocco and Vietnam (11.0 percent).[12] The handicraft industry, broadly defined, contributes to about 60 percent of industrial

Urban Growth and Spatial Transition in Nepal • http://dx.doi.org/10.1596/978-0-8213-9659-9

production.[13] As of 2001, it accounted for 32 percent of nonfarm employment, and it engaged as many as 375,000 workers in the Central Region alone (see figures 4.7 and 4.8).

Handicrafts are labor-intensive manufactures that draw on Nepal's artistic traditions dating back centuries. Nepal's traditional handicraft products include leather goods, pottery, handmade paper and paper products, woodwork, metalwork, weaving, embroidery, basketry, garments and carpets, ceramics, beaded items, bamboo products, and stone crafts. In fiscal 2010, textiles dominated the handicraft markets and totaled Nr 1.5 billion in exports alone. In addition to pashmina, textile products include wool, felt, silk, cotton, *dhaka*, hemp, and allo (nettle fiber). Other handicraft products totaled Nr 1.3 billion in exports in fiscal 2010. The top five export contributors were pashmina (17.0 percent), woolen products (16.2 percent), silver jewelry (13.3 percent), metal craft

Figure 4.7 Handicraft Employees, by Region, 2001

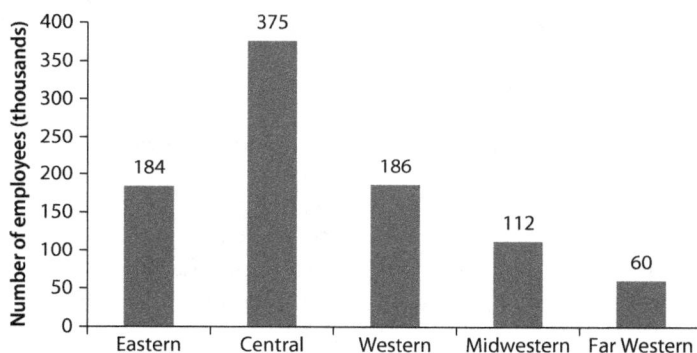

Source: CBS 2011.

Figure 4.8 Employment in the Handicraft Sector, by Region, 2001

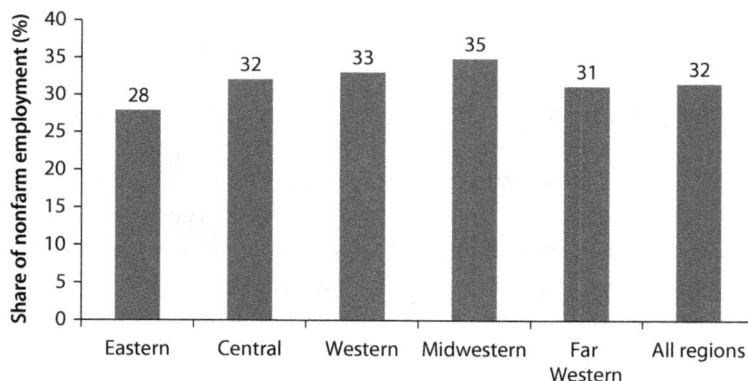

Source: CBS 2001.

Urban Growth and Spatial Transition in Nepal • http://dx.doi.org/10.1596/978-0-8213-9659-9

Artisans are often among the poorest and most vulnerable in the handicraft value chain.

(13.1 percent), and felt products (12.7 percent) (Pradhan 2011). Some of the main handicraft clusters in the Kathmandu Valley are described in box 4.4.

Urban local governments play a critical role in promoting the development of competitive handicraft clusters. Urban centers are not only the places where most artisans create and produce but also the natural locations of wholesalers and retailers. Although the handicraft industry was traditionally a rural-based activity, the number of artisans in urban areas has increased significantly over the last decade. Kathmandu and the urban centers in the Kathmandu Valley dominate the scene as market leaders and outlets. The number of handicraft workers in wood, textiles, leather, and related products increased at 7 percent per year in urban areas from 1999 to 2008, whereas it declined significantly countrywide, at an average of 3 percent per year (CBS 1999, 2009).

Nepal's domestic handicraft market is led by sales to tourists. Many handicraft products share backward and forward links with tourism, which indicates the complementarities between manufacturing and services (see box 4.4). The number of artisans in the Kathmandu Valley—the country's tourism hub—is increasing rapidly at 13 percent per year as the tourism sector recovers (CBS 1999, 2009).

In spite of the growth potential, handicraft exports are losing competitiveness; exports of most handicraft products show declining trends (Trade and Export Promotion Center 2011). One of the main reasons behind the decline in export competitiveness is the lack of effective marketing and branding and the

Box 4.4 A Snapshot of the Main Handicraft Products in the Kathmandu Valley

Wood Carving

Nepalese wood carving has been one of the country's primary art forms for over a millennium. Highly developed examples from as early as 1396 are still visible in the Kathmandu Valley (for example, at the Indresvara Mahadeva temple in Panauti). Even the word *Kathmandu* derives from the Sanskrit word for wood (*kashta*) and rest house (*mandapa*). Tourists who began flooding Nepal in the 1950s wanted souvenirs of their visits, which kick-started the industry of creating replicas of wooden temples and revived an ailing skill. Similarly, the recent architectural trend of constructing traditional buildings with modern conveniences has promoted the use of wood carvings for facades and interiors. Today, carvers use a very hard-wearing and difficult-to-handle timber known locally as sal (*Shorea robusta*) for structural elements, such as doors, pillars, and windows (because reputedly sal can survive up to 1,000 years submerged in water). The vast majority of this raw material is forested in the Southern Tarai. One of the major woodwork clusters is at Bungamati in Lalitpur.

Dhaka Cloth

Having earned an important place in the culture of the Kathmandu Valley, the textile known as *dhaka* cloth is now a symbol of Nepal. However, as its name suggests, the textile is not Nepalese in origin; it was brought from Bangladesh during the Rana period.

Tourist demand for handicrafts has created opportunities for small business development.

Box 4.4 A Snapshot of the Main Handicraft Products in the Kathmandu Valley *(continued)*

Although *dhaka* weaving used to be mastered all over Nepal, today craftspeople in Kathmandu are the main producers of the cloth. Predyed cotton bought from India is woven by Kathmandu's master craftspeople; using only a few colors, such as black, red, orange, and white, the creative weavers make a number of unique patterns. Although *dhaka* clothing no longer dominates Nepalese fashion, it remains an integral part of Nepalese society. For instance, *dhaka* hats (*topi*) are a popular sight in the streets of Kathmandu, and *dhaka* clothing still plays a role in rituals, such as weddings and funerals of many ethnic groups living in the valley.

Pottery

Bhaktapur is famous for its traditional pottery industry. In the vicinity of the square known as Potters' Square, streets are lined with small shops selling innumerable items produced in baked clay. Craftspeople have passed down the traditional pottery technique from generation to generation; even today, few have adopted a motorized wheel. Most craftspeople continue to turn the wheel with a large stick before kneeling to work the wet clay. In Potters' Square the most common clay item for sale is the piggy bank. However, in less visited areas, potters usually produce traditional bowls, small vessels for drinking local alcohol, and so forth. Although the availability of imported kitchenware has certainly harmed the pottery market, earthenware is still largely in use.

Metalwork

Cities in the Kathmandu Valley have rows of shops filled with metalware of copper, brass, and bronze. These shops are the continuation of generations of craftsmanship and trade in metal

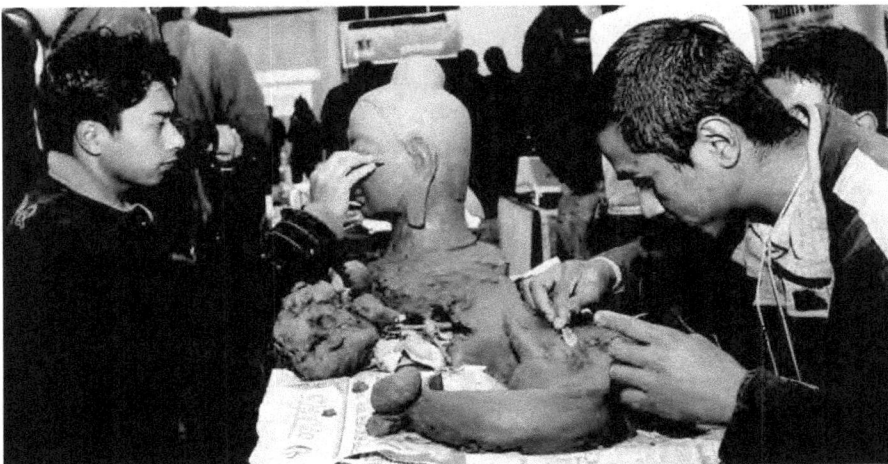

Artisans must deal with the tradeoffs between tradition and adapting their products for tourists and changes in local lifestyles.

box continues next page

Box 4.4 A Snapshot of the Main Handicraft Products in the Kathmandu Valley *(continued)*

objects. According to the Newar caste system, specific groups of the population are linked to distinct occupations. Members of the Tamrakar or Tamot caste were traditionally the metal-workers, and often the names of shops still refer to this caste. The main metalwork cluster is in Lalitpur.

Stone Carving

Although stone carving is an ancient craft in Nepal, it lost importance after the Malla period in the 18th century. Only recently has demand for stone carving increased in Nepal. The Shakyas are the traditional stone-carving caste, and knowledge is passed down from generation to generation. Granite, sandstone, and marble are transported from the Dakshinkali, Godavari, and Hattiban quarries and transformed into intricate works of art using only traditional tools. Numerous small stone-carving studios usually locate on the ground floor of traditional buildings in the backstreets of Bhaktapur, Lalitpur, and Kathmandu. Stone-carving clusters are also found at Sundhara and Bhinsebaal.

Source: UNESCO 2006.

Until recently, handicraft skills were closely guarded and passed down only among family and caste members.

© Kaushal Adhikari. Used with permission. Permission required for further re-use.

inability of the sector to modernize in response to international competition. Individual artisans note that they lack working capital, access to microcredit, bargaining power with retailers and exporters, and dependable power and water.[14] Artisans see their traditional skills and products as an important part of keeping Nepal's intangible heritage intact, but the younger generation is losing interest in learning those skills, mostly because incomes are low.

The pashmina industry is a case in point. The industry employed more than 50,000 people and made up at least 82 percent of all handicraft exports from Nepal in the 1990s. In 1997, Nepal exported Nr 3 million worth of the fabric, and by 2000 the figure had risen to more than Nr 5.6 billion. By fiscal 2010, pashmina exports plummeted to only Nr 474 million, and the industry's contribution to total handicraft exports declined to only 17 percent. The dramatic decline in exports is mostly caused by fierce competition from Indian and Chinese pashmina and the burgeoning market in "fake" pashmina as a result of the lack of public awareness and effective branding. The recent registration of Nepal's Chyangra Pashmina trademark is an important step in helping revive exports (Pradhan 2011).

Nepal's handicraft sector has the potential to rebound by building on the availability of skilled artisans and the expected growth in tourism. The handicraft sector is well organized with multiple specialty associations and a Federation of Handicraft Associations. These associations are committed to improving the products of their associates and to promote their sales on the export markets.

Agroprocessing: A Small but Strategic Industry Benefiting from Proximity to Urban Areas

Agroprocessing has the potential to become an important driver of economic growth and poverty alleviation in Nepal. Although the contribution of agroprocessing to economic growth is relatively modest, equivalent to less than 2 percent of the country's gross value added in 2006, agroprocessing plays an important role in generating jobs and earning foreign exchange. The agroprocessing sector accounts for 18 percent of total manufacturing jobs (2007 data) in firms with 10 or more employees, a marginal decline of 1 percent from 2002, and for 19 percent of all urban manufacturing jobs (CBS 2003, 2007, 2009). Agroprocessing products also represent 16 percent of total exports as of 2008.[15] Given the primacy of agriculture in Nepal's economy and its resource advantage, the creation of higher-productivity jobs in agroprocessing is an important part of Nepal's development strategy. Enhancing the competitiveness of the agroprocessing sector will enable Nepal to tap into higher-value-added production and to open up new export markets to stimulate the economy. International experience indicates that promoting agro-industrial links between urban and rural areas can be an important tool for economic growth and poverty alleviation at the early stage of a country's urban transition. It is also an important poverty reduction strategy. Measures to strengthen, grow, and promote the agroprocessing sector would help bring about increased economic security to vulnerable groups.[16] (See box 4.5 for international

Box 4.5   Agroprocessing and Poverty Alleviation in Developing Countries

The agroprocessing sector has the potential to play an important role in growth and poverty alleviation in developing countries. With abundant raw materials from agricultural production and a relatively low-cost labor force, developing countries lend themselves to the production of agroprocessing goods. These conditions—low-cost labor and abundance of raw materials—are conducive to efficient production, even in smaller-size plants. Developing a strategic agroprocessing sector is an important step in transitioning from a largely agricultural economy for several reasons:

- Many opportunities exist to develop forward linkages in the agroprocessing sector. Agroprocessing can start with relatively little initial capital and can provide the foundation for later developing more complex processed products. It also promotes the emergence of ancillary industries, such as packaging materials, and services, such as marketing and advertising. One of the most successful examples is that of Morocco. Its agro-industry characterizes well the potential for rural-urban links in the agroprocessing sector: strong, sophisticated agricultural activities are well integrated with a high-value-added food preservation industry, whose production ranges from juices to canned fruit.

- Strengthening the agricultural sector and its links to agro-industry plays an important role in increasing food security. It ensures that increased local production meets local demand. Such increased independence ensures greater access to food products by the most vulnerable groups. Chile, Morocco, and Turkey are examples of countries with well-developed agroprocessing sectors.

- Developing the agroprocessing sector requires a close integration of the raw material production and the processed product. The integration helps boost employment in the agricultural sectors as well as in agroprocessing and other manufacturing sectors.

The success of the agroprocessing industry in Nepal, as defined by its potential to drive growth and alleviate poverty, lies in its ability to develop strong urban, peri-urban, and rural links, most importantly through the creation of industrial corridors. The Asian Development Bank conducted a study of the impact of such links on development and poverty alleviation in the Greater Mekong Subregion, surveying seven areas of interest (ADB 2003). The three cases described below showcase the ability of agroprocessing to strengthen urban-rural linkages to foster economic activity and growth.

Case 1. Savannakhet Province, Lao People's Democratic Republic
Major infrastructure investments have been carried out in Savannakhet Province in the Lao PDR, most notably the construction of the east-west corridor (Route 9), which runs from northeastern Thailand across the Lao PDR to Vietnam. The new infrastructure investments have opened up opportunities for industrial development, such as the mining and agro-industries

box continues next page

Box 4.5 Agroprocessing and Poverty Alleviation in Developing Countries *(continued)*

along Route 9. In addition, new projects in the pipeline to create feeder roads off Route 9 into more remote areas of Savannakhet Province are thought to bring important development to agricultural production in this province (for example, cattle farming), while also boosting ancillary industries.

Case 2. "Boom Town" Suong, Cambodia
The town of Suong is relatively new in Cambodia and lies along Highway 7, which leads to the eastern border with Vietnam. Leveraging its proximity to Vietnam, Suong has transformed itself from a rural trading post into a medium-size market town with strong potential for commercial farming and trade with Vietnam.

Case 3. Northwestern Cambodian-Thai Border Area, Poipet and Kamrieng
The border towns of Poipet and Kamrieng in Cambodia and their hinterlands have experienced considerable growth since the opening of the border in 1994. These new access routes have fostered cross-border trade with Thailand. Demand for raw material from Cambodia has also boosted contract farming along the border. The increased trade in this region has created demand for ancillary facilities, such as storage.

Sources: ADB 2003; Pradhananga, Shrestha, and Dee 2009.

---

experience on the potential growth and poverty reduction impact of agroprocessing in developing countries.)

Nepal has a comparative advantage in the production of fresh and processed horticultural products and specialty agroproducts, including fruits, orthodox tea, coffee, honey, pulses (lentils), instant noodles, vegetable oils and fats (ghee), and medicinal and aromatic plants. About 20 enterprises in Nepal produce the finest orthodox tea in the world.[17] Orthodox tea accounts for 13 percent of Nepal's total tea production, which has grown at an annual rate of 4.3 percent. Nepal also has the opportunity to introduce its coffee production as specialty coffee in the international market because the demand for high-altitude specialty coffee is increasing. Nepal hosts five of the seven bee species in the world, and about 5,000 families are involved in commercial beekeeping. Approximately 1,500 plant species are used in the country for medicinal, aromatic, and religious purposes, and more than 140 species are commercially exported to the European Union (EU), Japan, and the United States. Herbs and spices and ghee accounted for 3 percent and 7 percent, respectively, of total exports in fiscal 2007. Export of herbs alone has recorded an increase of 36 percent, whereas pulses recorded an increase of 21 percent in 2008 (Nepal Rastra Bank 2009). Poultry production and cheese production are also growing fast, but they cater mostly to the domestic market (Government of Nepal 2011).

Chilli peppers and other spices are traded in market streets in urban areas.
© iStockphoto.com/Atid Kiattisaksiri.

The agroprocessing industry remains a relatively small-scale operation in Nepal, with limited investments. About 75 percent of agroprocessing firms operate with 20 or fewer employees; 18 percent employ fewer than 100 employees; and only 7 percent operate with over 100 employees. Most employees are in the food and beverage industry, where the number of establishments has increased by 19 percent, from 723 in fiscal 2002 to 863 in fiscal 2007 (Nepal Rastra Bank 2009). Production of pulses is mostly of a subsistence nature, and pulse cultivation is viewed as a small-scale activity rather than as a sector capable of generating economic returns.

Agroprocessing is clustered in the Tarai and Central Hills. Production is concentrated in three main regional clusters located in the Tarai, the Eastern Hills, and the Central Hills: the Kathmandu Valley (Bhaktapur, Kathmandu, and Kirtipur), the Birgunj conglomerate, and the Biratnagar conglomerate (see map 4.1). Together these three hubs, including their rural hinterland, account for 63 percent of total agroprocessing output. Other major urban agroprocessing hubs include Pokhara (Western Hills), Hetauda (Central Hills), Janakpur (Central Tarai), and Bhadrapur (Eastern Tarai). (See figures 4.9 and 4.10.) Together, they account for almost 10 percent of all agroprocessing output. These urban centers enjoy competitive advantages in the production of important agroproducts. For example, Biratnagar and Janakpur are competitive in the production of herbs and spices, whereas Bhadrapur and Pokhara have a competitive advantage in the production of cut flowers. Biratnagar and Ilam have the most potential for export growth in the production of herbs and spices, particularly, cardamom, tea, and ginger (ADB 2010).

Map 4.1 Agroprocessing Output Density, 2007

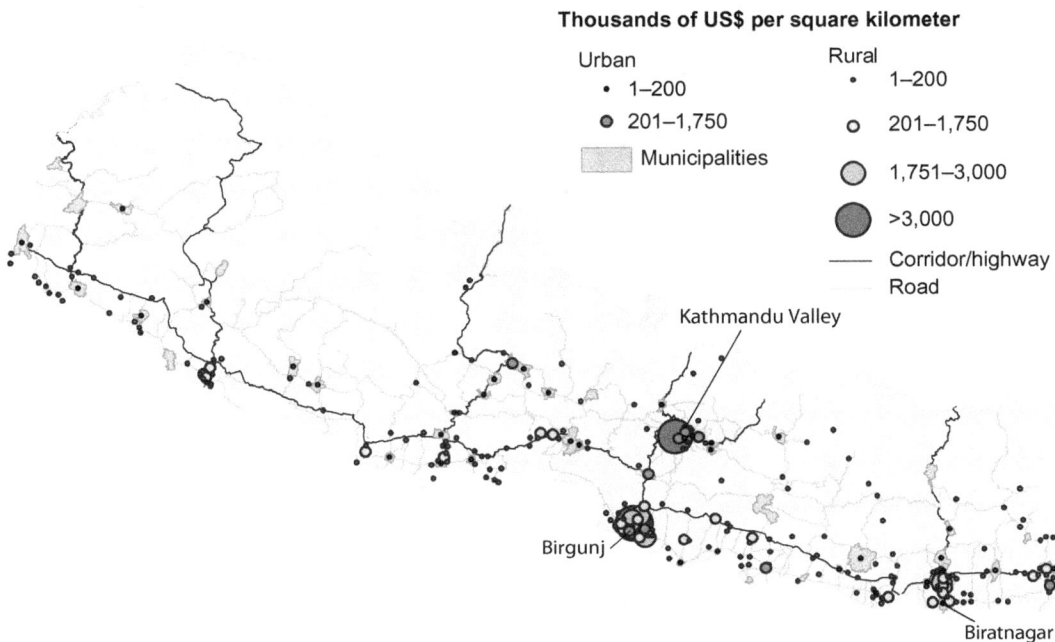

Thousands of US$ per square kilometer

Urban
- • 1–200
- ◉ 201–1,750
- ▨ Municipalities

Rural
- • 1–200
- ○ 201–1,750
- ◯ 1,751–3,000
- ● >3,000
- ── Corridor/highway
  Road

Kathmandu Valley

Birgunj

Biratnagar

Source: Based on Census of Manufacturing 2007 (CBS 2007).
Note: Biratnagar and Birgunj refer to the submetropolitan cities.

Figure 4.9 Agroprocessing Output Density of Urban Centers, 2007

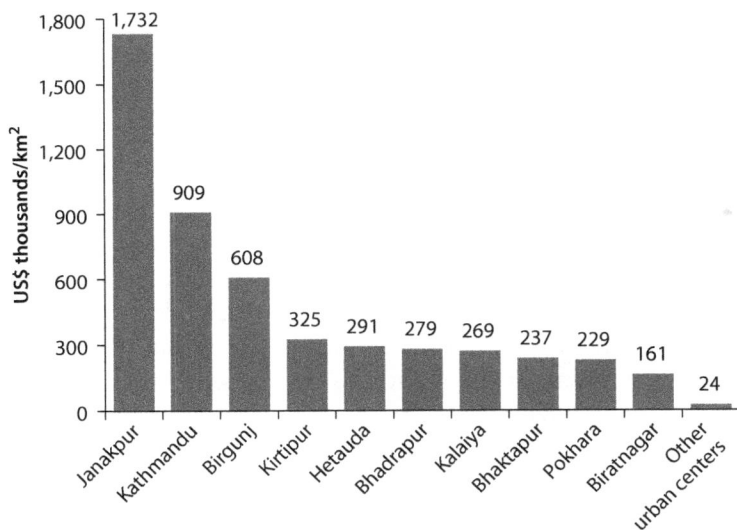

Source: Based on Census of Manufacturing 2007 (CBS 2007).
Note: Kathmandu refers to Kathmandu Metropolitan City; Birgunj, Pokhara, and Biratnagar refer to the submetropolitan cities; and all other locations are referred to as municipalities.

Urban Growth and Spatial Transition in Nepal • http://dx.doi.org/10.1596/978-0-8213-9659-9

Figure 4.10 Agroprocessing Employment Density of Urban Centers, 2007

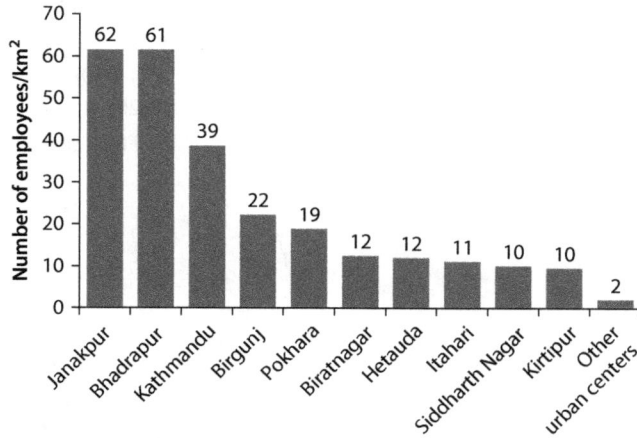

Source: Based on Census of Manufacturing 2007 (CBS 2007).
Note: Kathmandu refers to Kathmandu Metropolitan City; Birgunj, Pokhara, and Biratnagar refer to the submetropolitan cities; and all other locations are referred to as municipalities.

Figure 4.11 Agroprocessing Output Density, by Distance from Urban Centers, 2007

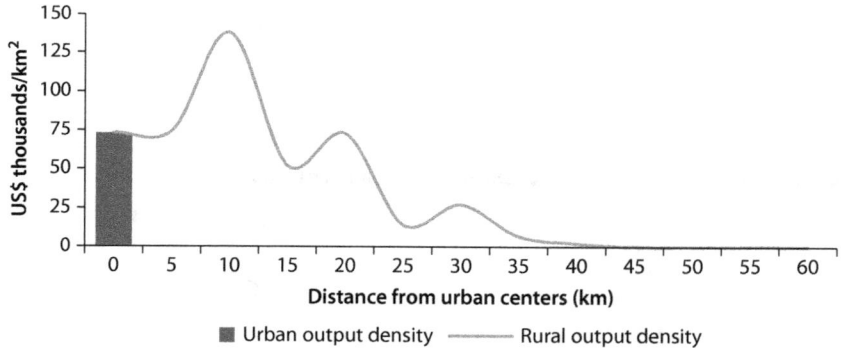

Source: Based on Census of Manufacturing 2007 (CBS 2007).

Agroprocessing firms benefit from proximity to urban centers. The geographic distribution of agroprocessing firms indicates that a strong potential exists for developing links between urban and rural economies through agroprocessing. Agroprocessing output density is highest at 10 kilometers from urban centers, with a second peak at 20 kilometers (see figure 4.11). This fact implies that even though more than half of the agroprocessing employment is located in rural areas, firms strongly depend on the proximity to urban centers. Urban areas play an important role in providing the necessary market infrastructure for trading agriculture commodities. Proximity to urban centers ensures access to larger local markets as well as export centers, especially in border towns. It also allows for economies of scale and more efficient use of infrastructure. Market infrastructure comprises collection centers linked to road heads (small towns located on main roads); *haat* bazaars (periodic markets operating with minimal facilities to allow for the trading of perishable commodities); *mandis* (wholesale marketplaces); and the major consumption markets and trading centers, such as Biratnagar, Birgunj, Butwal, Kathmandu, and Nepalgunj.

Nepal has been unable to transform its natural resource advantages into profitable trade because of inadequate infrastructure. Nepal's inadequate connective infrastructure is a major impediment to the expansion of agroprocessing operations because it limits access to markets. About 50 percent of the existing road network coverage is concentrated in the Tarai alone, servicing about 23 percent of the land area in Nepal (ADB 2010). The Central Region and Eastern Hills remain largely underserved. Losses from transportation are high, as much as 15–35 percent for perishable products. Poor road conditions result in higher repair costs for trucks and a much slower turnaround time (ADB 2010). Often, market infrastructure for processing and trading agricultural commodities is not strategically located and is unable to accommodate radical seasonal variation in the supply and demand of horticultural products. For example, many market yards provided by the government are of little use. Unstable provision of electricity and water is also an impediment to the further expansion of agroprocessing industries and remains an issue even for existing plants.

Lack of organized cluster support and market coordination has also impeded Nepal's ability to tap into its natural resource advantages. Market coordination is inadequate, and no organized cluster support and trading system exist for most agricultural commodities. Most herbs are traded to India unprocessed, resulting in no value added for Nepal. Standards and quality controls are often not enforced. For example, the EU banned the import of Nepal's honey in 2002 because the Department of Food Technology and Quality Control failed to submit the pesticide residue control plan that EU regulations require. Most of Nepal's agroproducts, such as tea and coffee, sell below value because of inadequate export marketing and lack of a branding strategy. For example, no clear vision exists of what tea varieties should be produced considering the market demand. Export of ginger is suffering because of a lack of certifying facilities. Because of the small and unorganized nature of the market, Nepalese growers and traders have no bargaining power with international buyers (Government of Nepal 2011).

Moreover, low productivity caused by substandard production technologies make agricultural trade unprofitable. The low productivity is partially the result of inadequate cluster support in the areas of farming technology, orchard management, and sustainable harvesting techniques. Many farmers, for example, are unaware of postharvest management practices for maintaining the quality of coffee. In addition, technological barriers interfere with the expansion of the agroprocessing industry. Organizations such as Practical Action[18] work on providing the agroprocessing sector in Nepal with access to information and technology, such as low-cost solar dryers, hydraulic oil presses, and herb distillation technologies. More complex technological processes, however, remain difficult to implement, thereby limiting the expansion of the value chain in the agro-industry.

Notes

1. Other studies of export competitiveness find that Nepal enjoys comparative advantages in handicrafts, leather products, oils, agroprocessing, carpets, textiles, wood products, paper, printing, and publishing. According to the revealed comparative advantage methodology—which measures a comparative advantage by the ratio of the country's share of world exports for a particular group to the country's share of total world exports of all commodities—Nepal's major manufacturing products are leather and leather products; wool carpets; jute and jute products; textiles and polyester yarn; pashmina mufflers, shawls, and other specific garments; and agroprocessing (see ADB 2010).

2. West Nepal includes the Western, Midwestern, and Far Western Regions.

3. Data are from the Ministry of Culture, Tourism and Civil Aviation website.

4. Data are from a 2012 preliminary study by the Ministry of Culture, Tourism and Civil Aviation, as reported in the *Kathmandu Post*, March 4, 2012.

5. Data are from team interviews with Nepal tour operators.

6. United Nations Educational, Scientific, and Cultural Organization.

7. Unless otherwise stated, Kathmandu refers to Kathmandu Metropolitan City; Biratnagar, Birgunj, Lalitpur, and Pokhara refer to the submetropolitan cities; and all other urban local governments are referred to as municipalities.

8. The Newar are the indigenous inhabitants of the Kathmandu Valley.

9. Inappropriate buildings are those that do not correspond in scale, height, or facade treatment (material, color, or decorative elements) with the surrounding historic buildings.

10. Estimate by a conservation architect based on 2005 prices.

11. See the statute of the Handicraft Association of Nepal, article 1.4.

12. Comparison data are from press and Internet search.

13. The prevalent Industrial Enterprises Act of 1992, amended in 1997, classifies industrial enterprises into four categories: (a) large industries, with a fixed-asset investment of more than Nr 100 million; (b) medium industries, with fixed assets between Nr 30 million and Nr 100 million; (c) small industries, with up to Nr 30 million in fixed assets; and (d) craft industries, defined as traditional industries using specific skills or local raw materials and resources, using electric motors of fewer than 5 kilowatts, and related to national tradition, art, and culture.

14. Artisans report that local retailers often keep 75 percent of the profit from the sale of their work.

15. Data are from the Trade and Export Promotion Centre (2011).

16. Data are from the International Labour Organization's LABORSTA database.

17. Orthodox tea refers to either hand-processed tea or tea that is rolled with machinery in a manner that mimics hand rolling.

18. This organization was formerly known as the Intermediate Technology Development Group.

References

ADB (Asian Development Bank). 2003. "Regional: Rural Urban and Sub-regional Linkages in the Mekong Region: A Holistic Approach to Development and Poverty Reduction." ADB, Manila.

———. 2004. *South Asia Subregional Economic Cooperation Tourism Development Plan.* Manila: ADB.

———. 2010. *Unleashing Economic Growth: Region-Based Urban Strategy for Nepal.* Manila: ADB.

Byanju, Ashok. 2002. "Urban Tourism and Poverty Reduction: A Case Study of Bhaktapur Municipality." Presented at the Regional Workshop on Urban Tourism and Poverty Reduction, November 20–22, Colombo.

CBS (Central Bureau of Statistics). 1999. *Report on the Nepal Labor Force Survey 1998/99.* Kathmandu: Government of Nepal.

———. 2001. *National Population Census 2001.* Kathmandu: Government of Nepal.

———. 2003. *Nepal—Census of Manufacturing Establishments 2001–2002.* Kathmandu: Government of Nepal.

———. 2007. *Nepal—Census of Manufacturing Establishments 2006–2007.* Kathmandu: Government of Nepal.

———. 2009. *Report on the Nepal Labor Force Survey 2008.* Kathmandu: Government of Nepal.

———. 2011. *Nepal Living Standards Survey 2010/11.* Kathmandu: Government of Nepal.

District Development Committee of Bhaktapur and Nepal Tourism Board. 2010. "Bhaktapur Tourism Development and Management Report 2010–2014." Nepal Tourism Board, Kathmandu.

ETG (Economic Transformations Group). 2012. "Kathmandu Valley Tourism Cluster Competitiveness Assessment and Action Plan." Background paper for this report, World Bank, Washington, DC.

Ebbe, Katrinka. 2012. "Kathmandu Valley Heritage Conservation and Local Economic Development—Assessment and Recommendations." Background paper for this report, World Bank, Washington, DC.

Government of Nepal, Ministry of Commerce and Supplies. 2010a. *Nepal Trade Integration Strategy 2010.* Kathmandu.

———, National Planning Commission. 2010b. "Three Year Plan Approach Paper 2010/11–2012/13." Kathmandu.

———, Ministry of Agriculture and Cooperatives. 2011. "Thematic Areas for Competitive Matching Grants." Project for Agriculture Commercialization and Trade, Ministry of Agriculture and Cooperatives, Kathmandu.

Karmacharya, Binod K. 2000. "Export Potentials of Nepal: Comparative and Competitive Advantage Analysis." Report prepared for the National Planning Commission and Asian Development Bank, Kathmandu.

LABORSTA (database). International Labour Organization, Geneva.

Nepal Rastra Bank. 2009. *Nepal Rastra Bank Economic Report, 2008/09.* Kathmandu: Nepal Rastra Bank.

Pradhan, Robin. 2011. "Regaining Lost Glory: Nepali Handicrafts." *ECS Nepal,* January.

Pradhananga, Neelam, Khrisna K. Shrestha, and John Dee. 2009. "Sustaining Indigenous Heritage: Learning from the Guthi System in Nepal." University of Newcastle, Australia.

Trade and Export Promotion Centre. 2011. "Trade Statistics." Ministry of Commerce and Supplies, Lalitpur.

UNESCO (United Nations Educational, Scientific, and Cultural Organization). 2006. *Cultural Portrait Handbook.* Vols. 1–7. Kathmandu: UNESCO.

UNWTO (United Nations World Tourism Organization). 2007. *Tourism Market Trends.* Madrid: UNWTO.

World Bank. 2003. *Nepal: Trade and Competitiveness Study.* Washington, DC: World Bank.

World Travel and Tourism Council. 2011. "Travel and Tourism Economic Impact 2011." World Travel and Tourism Council, London.

CHAPTER 5

Conclusions and Strategic Policy Directions

A predominantly rural country, Nepal is urbanizing rapidly, and urban areas are a major contributor to economic growth and poverty alleviation. The Kathmandu Valley constitutes the largest urban agglomeration and main cluster of economic activities in Nepal, and economic clusters have emerged in extended urban regions close to the border with India. But the spatial transformation that is associated with such a rapid urbanization poses several challenges. Urbanization is happening haphazardly, and under the radar in market and border towns, while the Kathmandu Valley faces institutional, planning, and infrastructure challenges that deserve urgent policy attention. In order to unlock growth and make the spatial transformation sustainable, Nepal needs to foster the growth and sustainability of its urban regions, promote the development and regeneration of the Kathmandu Valley, and enhance the competitiveness of strategic urban clusters. This chapter presents policy directions and actions for addressing the challenges associated with Nepal's urban transformation.

Even in a country like Nepal, at the initial phase of the urban transition, urban areas are major contributors to economic growth and poverty alleviation. Nepal is the fastest-urbanizing country in South Asia, and its urban areas have made a significant contribution to the growth of gross domestic product (GDP) and to poverty alleviation. Urban areas now generate about 62 percent of GDP, based on the latest available estimates, compared to only 28 percent of GDP in 1975 (World Bank 2011). The urban economy is growing significantly faster than the rural economy, and the incidence of poverty in urban areas declined from 22 percent to 15 percent from 1995/96 to 2010/11 (CBS 1996, 2011). Migration is a powerful force for urban change, and the contribution of migration to urbanization is important and increasing over time. Migrants who move for economic reasons are growing in number; they are willing to travel longer distances and tend to settle in urban areas. Nonfarm economic production is concentrated in three main clusters—in the Kathmandu Valley, the Central Tarai, and the Eastern Tarai—composing a core urban center surrounded by a hinterland of small towns and rural areas and functioning as extended urban economic regions. However, the study identifies several challenges associated with Nepal's spatial transformation.

As the largest urban agglomeration and main cluster of economic activities in Nepal, the Kathmandu Valley faces challenges that deserve urgent policy attention. Its important and growing economic role, as well as the sustainability of its urbanization, is threatened by the valley's large and growing environmental infrastructure deficits—for example, in water, sewerage, and solid waste. Unique and invaluable cultural assets that give the Kathmandu Valley a distinct comparative advantage as a tourist destination are at risk of becoming irreversibly compromised. The current public infrastructure expenditure bias against Kathmandu Metropolitan City (hereafter, Kathmandu),[1] if not timely reversed, will have high economic costs, not only for the residents of the Kathmandu Valley but also for the Nepalese population that directly and indirectly benefits from the growth of the valley.

Urbanization is happening under the radar in market and border towns. The spatial transformation that is under way in Nepal needs to be better understood and documented to inform evidence-based policy discussion. Developing a new urban classification that takes into account such criteria as population density, economic links, road access, and infrastructure would help provide a better understanding of urban growth patterns and the spatial transition. In particular, an economy-based classification of urban areas would allow the capture of the important demographic and economic transformation that is happening under the radar in strategically located settlements, such as market towns in proximity to the highways and border towns in proximity to India.

This chapter outlines strategic policy directions and actions for addressing the challenges associated with Nepal's spatial transformation. Strategic policy directions are grouped under three main objectives or pillars:

- To foster the growth and sustainability of the urban regions by (a) prioritizing the "where, what, and how" of public interventions in the urban regions based on development outcomes; (b) improving internal and external connectivity; and (c) creating the enabling environment for sustainable and inclusive urban development.
- To promote the development and regeneration of the Kathmandu Valley metropolitan region by (a) strengthening planning and its implementation in the valley, (b) developing an infrastructure financing policy and plan for the Kathmandu Valley, and (c) launching a regeneration plan for the valley's historic city centers.
- To enhance the competitiveness of strategic urban clusters by (a) promoting sustainable and responsible cultural tourism activities, (b) supporting the modernization of the handicraft sector, and (c) improving the competitiveness of the agroprocessing business.

Strategic policy directions and actions for the three pillars are summarized in table 5.1.

Table 5.1 Strategic Policy Directions and Actions for Fostering the Sustainable Growth of Nepal's Cities

Pillar 1: Foster the growth and sustainability of the urban regions	Pillar 2: Promote the development and regeneration of the Kathmandu Valley metropolitan region	Pillar 3: Enhance the competitiveness of strategic urban clusters
1.1 Prioritize the "where, what, and how" of public interventions in the urban regions based on development outcomes • Launch regional competitiveness strategies and develop action plans for the main urban clusters • Develop a countrywide infrastructure investment plan to prioritize investments • Design spatially targeted interventions, such as special economic zones, to unlock the economic potential of strategic manufacturing clusters	**2.1 Strengthen planning and its implementation in the valley** • Define the functional boundaries of the Kathmandu Valley metropolitan region • Develop customized institutional arrangements for metropolitan coordination • Promote integrated land-use and transport planning and mainstream the disaster risk management agenda at the metropolitan level	**3.1 Promote sustainable and responsible cultural tourism activities** • Improve and diversify tourism products in the Kathmandu Valley that respect local traditions • Develop tourism strategies and plans for heritage cities to enhance their market positioning • Improve human resource capacity in the tourism sector • Strengthen the municipal capacity to partner with the private sector to promote sustainable tourism activities
1.2 Improve internal and external connectivity • Prioritize strategic investments in transport corridors for improved market integration and trade facilitation • Upgrade and expand the international and domestic air transportation	**2.2 Develop an infrastructure financing policy and plan for the Kathmandu Valley** • Prioritize infrastructure investment needs at the metropolitan level • Develop a metropolitan infrastructure financing strategy and plan	**3.2 Support the modernization of the handicraft sector** • Promote market research for handicraft product innovation and commercialization • Develop a pilot public-private partnership program to support strategic handicraft product clusters • Promote initiatives in support of artisan communities to enhance their skills and facilitate access to the market
1.3 Create the enabling environment for sustainable and inclusive urban development • Strengthen municipalities' capacity to plan and provide basic services and connect all districts by all-season roads • Develop a coherent institutional framework for municipal capital financing • Facilitate the access of poor and disadvantaged local communities to markets	**2.3 Launch a regeneration program for the valley's historic city centers** • Realign the responsibilities for cultural heritage conservation among institutional actors • Promote integrated conservation and management of the built heritage • Raise community awareness and incentivize community mobilization for the sustainable conservation of cultural heritage	**3.3 Improve agroprocessing competitiveness** • Develop and upgrade market infrastructure in strategic locations • Strengthen agroprocessing cluster support through public-private partnership arrangements • Launch an action plan to improve production technology and commercialization to increase value addition

Pillar 1: Foster the Growth and Sustainability of the Urban Regions

Accelerating economic growth calls for unlocking the economic potential of the urban regions by facilitating the clustering of economic activities and enhancing the competitiveness of existing clusters in the Central Region and along the border with India. In parallel, appropriate redistributive policies need to be undertaken for balanced and equitable development. Nepal needs to pursue the following strategic policy directions and actions to foster the growth and sustainability of the urban regions.

Prioritize the "Where, What, and How" of Public Interventions in the Urban Regions Based on Development Outcomes

Prioritizing public interventions based on development outcomes would require developing a countrywide infrastructure investment plan based on regional competitiveness strategies. Given scarce financial resources, prioritizing strategic public investments based on economic returns is a positive-sum game for the country. Economic dividends of sustained growth can be redistributed to ensure that the benefits are spread equally across the entire population. Actions include the following:

- *Launch regional competitiveness strategies and develop action plans for the main urban clusters.* Cluster-based value chain analyses, strategies, and action plans need to be developed, starting with the most strategic clusters, identified by their potential for export growth, job creation, and poverty reduction. The first step is to define the economic area of influence for the extended economic regions, to identify the main regional growth drivers, and to develop public-private leadership-driven action plans to improve cluster competitiveness in each region. Competitiveness strategies and action plans for the main urban clusters should be developed by involving private and public leaders from the extended economic region, comprising both rural and urban space within the region, to better understand and exploit the links between urban areas and the hinterland. Because the Tarai clusters straddle India and Nepal, the economic and trade links between Nepalese border towns and the adjacent Indian settlements must also be taken into account in the formulation of the action plans.

- *Develop a countrywide infrastructure investment plan to prioritize investments.* Spreading investments thinly across many small towns has only a marginal effect, not only on economic development but also on improvements to basic services. Consequently, the urban areas selected for strategic investments should be prioritized according to their economic and industrial growth potential, not just their lack of basic infrastructure. Given the massive infrastructure requirements in urban areas, strategic investments made at the urban region scale based on competitiveness strategies would allow maximizing the socioeconomic impact of the investments by capturing economies of scale and spillover effects at the regional and country levels. In parallel, cost-recovery mechanisms need to be introduced (such as user fees and land-value capture instruments) to ensure the financial sustainability of infrastructure investments and to contribute to the costs of upgrading infrastructure in the lagging regions.

- *Design spatially targeted interventions, such as special economic zones (SEZs), to unlock the economic potential of strategic manufacturing clusters.* Firm-level monetary relocation incentives favoring lagging regions need to be replaced with spatial interventions, such as the establishment of SEZs in the strategic urban regions with the most potential for growth. This endeavor would require, as a first step, the enactment of the 2006 SEZ bill, which is awaiting approval by the Parliament. SEZs can be instrumental in improving the competitiveness of established and emerging manufacturing clusters. For example, developing a strategically located handicraft industrial zone could provide artisans with better working environments and infrastructure while benefiting from proximity to markets and tourist sites. SEZs could be established as "safe havens" to address in an integrated manner the main investment climate constraints that prevent manufacturing firms from growing their business and becoming internationally competitive, with a focus on infrastructure, connectivity, and labor market regulations. However, special care should be taken to avoid creating "firm enclaves" that exclude local communities from the economic development process.

Improve Internal and External Connectivity

The country's connective infrastructure has contributed to—and continues to affect—the shaping of the spatial transformation from both a demographic and economic perspective. Improving internal and external connectivity is therefore critical for reaping the full benefits of urbanization. Small growth centers are emerging on the main highways, and Nepal's low road density is a top obstacle to the growth of nonfarm economic activities. Improved connectivity is particularly important for the expansion of the agroprocessing sector, whereas external connectivity through air transportation is essential to accommodate the expected increase in tourists.

- *Prioritize strategic investments in transport corridors for improved market integration and trade facilitation.* Investments should focus on expanding, rehabilitating, and maintaining commercial corridors with potential high traffic for private sector investments. A fast-track route from the Kathmandu Valley to the Tarai may be an economically viable investment for substantially reducing the distance, time, and cost of transport between the valley and the Indian border. Available studies indicate that a new, more direct route, with tunnels, would reduce the road distance by over 100 kilometers to about 65 kilometers, could cut travel time by up to five hours, and may improve transport reliability. Main options include a Bagmati corridor route linking with the east-west highway or a tunnel route from Kathmandu to Hetauda (World Bank 2005; ADB 2010).

- *Upgrade and expand the international and domestic air transportation.* Nepal's accessibility by air is limited. Tribhuvan International Airport (TIA) in

Kathmandu constitutes a major impediment to tourism development. Upgrading and expanding the airport and improving the airport's management ability to handle more international flights is a necessity. Constraints can be reduced by relieving congestion in the existing terminal area and accommodating future international aircraft and passenger traffic. Similarly, the airport quality and experience of international travelers needs to be improved. Because of TIA's geographic limitations, priority should be given to the long-term solution of building the planned second, larger international airport in Nijgadh in the Bara District. In addition, domestic air transportation is limited and need to be expanded to effectively connect the Kathmandu Valley with the country's other cities and tourism destinations. Some of these destinations also require major improvements to their airport facilities.

Create the Enabling Environment for Sustainable and Inclusive Urban Development

A precondition for sustainable and inclusive urbanization is the local capacity to finance and provide basic services and to integrate the poor into local economic development. In countries at an incipient level of urbanization, such as Nepal, urban policy interventions should be directed at providing basic services across urban areas and ensuring sustainability of urban growth, while encouraging firms' efficient location decisions and the formation of clusters of economic activities. This would require the following actions:

- *Strengthen municipalities' capacity to plan and provide basic services and connect all districts by all-season roads.* Land-use planning, access, and quality of municipal services need to be improved across urban areas to enhance livability and to create a level playing field for private sector development. Improvements in water supply and environmental infrastructure, such as solid waste management, are particularly important to cope with increased urbanization. This effort would require (a) identifying and addressing the institutional bottlenecks that are at the root of the inefficiencies in land-use planning and the provision of basic services and (b) strengthening the capacity of municipal governments to deliver services to their constituencies. Improving accessibility is also essential for enhancing livability and access to markets, particularly in the remote areas of the country. Connecting all districts to all-season roads is also a priority to facilitate the transportation of agricultural commodities from the most remote locations to collection points.

- *Develop a coherent institutional framework for municipal capital financing.* Urban local governments are limited in their ability to mobilize local resources, and they are highly dependent on external sources of funding for capital expenditure. The multiple channels of investment funds from central to local governments do not, however, form part of a coherent strategy; as such, they do not provide urban local governments with adequate incentives to improve efficiency and maintain their assets. Even without increased spending, more resources could be directed to capital infrastructure investments by reducing inefficiencies in service provision. A new municipal finance strategy needs to be developed to streamline and harmonize mechanisms for capital financing and to move toward an integrated performance-based system. The objective of this strategy would be to ensure that all urban areas have the resources to provide basic services to their constituencies, while strengthening and rewarding local capacity to mobilize own-source funding and eventually enhancing municipal borrowing capacity as Nepal transitions to a federal state.

- *Facilitate the access of poor and disadvantaged local communities to markets.* A sustainable approach to local economic development aims at creating and strengthening links with local communities by integrating the poor into existing value chains. This endeavor would require, for example, (a) increasing local sourcing and developing the capacities of local producers in the agroprocessing sector, (b) facilitating the access of poor communities to the tourism value chain, and (c) providing incentives to firms for training members of poor artisan communities to enhance their skills and harness their entrepreneurial capacities. Local governments can, for instance, partner with grassroots organizations to develop initiatives to include the poor in local economic development, such as implementing a local sourcing strategy for agroproducts and creating local trademarks for inclusive and sustainable handicraft, agroprocessing, and tourism products that match international standards.

Pillar 2: Promote the Development and Regeneration of the Kathmandu Valley Metropolitan Region

The challenges of the Kathmandu Valley need to be addressed at the metropolitan level. The government needs to formulate and implement a Kathmandu Valley regeneration and development strategy and plan through a phased program of policy initiatives and priority investments. This program should address infrastructure, environmental improvements, cultural heritage conservation, transport, and land development. The interventions need to be done at the spatial scale of the valley to maximize effectiveness and economies of scale and to minimize costs and inequities. The following strategic policy directions and actions would contribute to addressing the challenges of the Kathmandu Valley.

Strengthen Planning and Its Implementation in the Valley

To manage rapid urbanization in the valley, the strengthening of planning and its implementation at the metropolitan level is urgently needed. The institutional mechanisms for metropolitan management and integrated planning should be designed keeping in mind the valley's unique social, cultural, and political conditions and lessons learned from international practices. Urgent actions are also needed to reduce vulnerability to seismic hazards in the Kathmandu Valley and to prevent potentially disastrous conditions, such as those in Haiti following the 2010 earthquakes. Priority interventions include the following:

- *Define the functional boundaries of the Kathmandu Valley metropolitan region.* Economically dynamic urban regions tend to outgrow subnational government boundaries. The Kathmandu Valley metropolitan region is a large agglomeration that links, through urban sprawl, various urban and rural local governments. As a first step, the economic boundaries of the metropolitan region need to be defined according to economic criteria, such as self-contained labor markets based on commuting flows, housing markets, and administrative or legal boundaries.

- *Develop customized institutional arrangements for metropolitan coordination.* Building on the recent establishment of the Kathmandu Valley Development Authority and the Ministry of Urban Development, the government has the opportunity to review and decide on the most effective and efficient allocations of metropolitan functional responsibilities across all levels of government. No universal model exists for effective metropolitan governance—institutions and management processes must be designed according to local social, cultural, and political conditions. A spectrum of governance models for metropolitan management ranges from relatively "heavy" to "light"—depending on the scope of the reforms. A governance model for metropolitan management is the creation of a formal metropolitan government with representation from the local authorities and legally defined functions, fiscal resource mobilization powers, and lines of accountability. Governance models also include "lighter" cooperative arrangements and voluntary coordination mechanisms. The choice of the optimal model will require careful analysis and extensive dialogue among local governments. This dialogue should recognize that local authorities can benefit from capacity building and technical assistance from metropolitan institutions and from the clear definition of local mandates and responsibilities. An important part of this dialogue should be the optimal assignment of revenue and expenditure responsibilities among tiers of governments. Once consensus has been reached on functional and fiscal responsibilities, they will need to be codified in law or regulation.

- *Promote integrated land-use and transport planning and mainstream the disaster risk management agenda at the metropolitan level.* The haphazard development characterizing the Kathmandu Valley calls for a metropolitan approach to land-use and transport planning to control urban sprawl and to limit uncontrolled development. Without improving the spatial distribution of housing and the transportation network, urban vulnerabilities, such as those to earthquakes, are likely to increase. Priority actions include (a) improving accessibility, (b) enforcing building codes and laws preventing land subdivisions and the building of substandard houses on open spaces, and (c) improving community preparedness and retrofitting public buildings (in particular, schools, health centers, public administration buildings, and others) that are designated as evacuation centers or treatment centers. Public awareness and community preparedness levels need to be improved by developing rescue and response plans and by educating and training the building industry. In particular, proper training of masons and supervising engineers is essential to ensure effective implementation of building codes and quality control on construction equipment and building materials for the safety and security of the valley residents. Responsible earthquake-resistant development techniques are better introduced and implemented through flexible means comprising incentives, consensus, and awareness programs rather than by rigid laws. For example, piloting the development of earthquake-resistant housing technologies that preserve the traditional architectural styles recognized by UNESCO (United Nations Educational, Scientific, and Cultural Organization) could have important demonstration effects and raise awareness at the household level.

Develop an Infrastructure Financing Policy and Plan for the Kathmandu Valley

The government needs to develop and implement a financing policy and plan for the Kathmandu Valley to address infrastructure backlogs and growing demand. The financing policy would comprise a number of interrelated policy reforms to develop the financing instruments for infrastructure investments supported by a portfolio of related investments targeted at remedying, in a phased manner, prioritized deficits in essential infrastructure and services. Priority actions include the following:

- *Prioritize infrastructure investment needs at the metropolitan level.* The core infrastructure investments to support the development and regeneration of the valley would involve (a) restoring the environment of the Bagmati River and its tributaries, including constructing main wastewater conveyor systems along the principal urban watercourses and intercepting and conveying all urban wastewater discharges to treatment outside the core areas; (b) upgrading and expanding water supply resources, treatment capacity, and distribution networks to address the growing water deficits in the valley and to ensure the sustainable management of local groundwater resources; (c) upgrading and channeling the principal river embankments adjacent to urban areas, providing for improved public access, community use, and green space to enhance local environmental well-being; (d) integral with the preceding efforts, enhancing the solid waste management systems, from collection and recycling to treatment and disposal, including behavior change and environmental advocacy; (e) improving the local street and sidewalk power and drainage in conjunction with the upgrading of water and sewerage infrastructure; and (f) modernizing information technology and communication systems in parallel with the services above to reap consequent economic and sociocultural gains.

- *Develop a metropolitan infrastructure financing strategy and plan.* The economic vibrancy of a metropolitan region ultimately depends on its fiscal vibrancy.

Urgent interventions are needed to develop adequate financing instruments to address the infrastructure needs of the metropolitan region. The priorities are (a) to enable the cost-effective provision of essential metropolitan infrastructure investments by strengthening cost recovery and capital efficiency and mobilizing local communities in the provision of infrastructure and services, while ensuring affordability for the poorest citizens; (b) to strengthen the revenue generation capacity and fiscal autonomy of the local governments in the valley; and (c) to "unlock" land value for infrastructure financing. Mobilizing private capital will likely be a critical element for financing large-scale capital expenditure, given the magnitude of the investment requirements. Attracting private capital would in turn require strengthening the regulatory framework for private sector participation and the capacities and skills of urban local governments to partner with the private sector.

Launch a Regeneration Program for the Valley's Historic City Centers

In addition to individual monuments, the urban fabric needs protection for all its historic, cultural, and architectural elements. When first initiated and practiced in Nepal, conservation was viewed as a means to protect important individual monuments, or groups of monuments, as in the case of the three Durbar Squares that are part of the UNESCO Kathmandu Valley World Heritage site. The danger of this narrow conservation approach is that eventually only isolated monuments will survive, surrounded by modern redevelopment. Deprived of their historic context, the monuments lose meaning and the ability to communicate their full cultural, historic, and artistic value to future generations. The ideal development outcome is that the urban areas continue to change and evolve but that change is managed to prevent the destruction of the historic environment, while improving the quality of life for the valley's citizens. Priority actions include the following:

- *Realign the responsibilities for cultural heritage conservation among institutional actors* by (a) creating clear lines of authority from central to local levels, and clarifying mandates for the conservation of cultural heritage; (b) addressing conflicting and inadequate laws and regulations; (c) strengthening enforcement capacity; (d) providing financing tools for the day-to-day management of the buffer zones and for the provision of local services around the sites; (e) strengthening cooperation and partnerships among agencies, local governments, and communities; and (f) establishing well-defined criteria and mechanisms to assess the effect of various development initiatives on tangible and intangible heritage.

- *Promote integrated conservation and management of the built heritage* by mainstreaming cultural heritage conservation into the planning process using a participatory approach. Future planning and development activities must be informed by the objective to protect not only the individual monuments but also the urban fabric. This endeavor would require (a) building on the

The protection of the historic, cultural, and architectural elements of the urban fabric is essential for the regeneration of the Kathmandu Valley.
© ECS Nepal. Used with permission. Permission required for further re-use.

UNESCO integrated management plans to establish a broad participatory stakeholder process and further integrate the protected monument zones (PMZs) into the Kathmandu Valley planning and management process; (b) creating an integrated information database using an updated and comprehensive geographic information system inventory and engaging local communities in the database's preparation and implementation; (c) prioritizing infrastructure improvements to open spaces in PMZs and buffer zones, including drainage, sewerage, stone paving, lighting, extension of pedestrian zones, overhead power line removal, and amenities (such as toilets, parking, and visitor drop-off areas); (d) enforcing existing regulations and updating norms and guidelines for evaluating the seismic stability of traditional buildings and for retrofitting them for seismic safety; and (e) supporting the adaptive reuse of traditional buildings (both residential and commercial) that can generate the income streams necessary for their continued viability and value in real estate markets.

- *Raise community awareness and incentivize community mobilization for the sustainable conservation of cultural heritage* by focusing especially on schools and youth. Central and local agencies also have much to gain by reconsidering and strengthening the traditional role of local communities, such as the *guthis*, in the process of cultural heritage conservation. Possible actions include (a) development of educational materials for teachers and use of social media;

(b) recognition and reward programs for "masters" in traditional skills (for example, handicrafts and music) and private owners who conserve historic buildings; (c) training, performances, and competitions in traditional performing arts and handicrafts; and (d) a participatory inventory of intangible heritage. Incentives for community mobilization for sustainable heritage conservation could include (a) creating a participatory monitoring and evaluation program for the integrated conservation and management of the built heritage (for example, evaluate progress and monitor illegal building activity) and (b) instituting a demand-driven and competitive matching grant for such activities as maintenance of heritage buildings and sites; neighborhood cleanup; adaptations of underused traditional buildings for community use; projects to meet community needs, such as water and disaster risk management; revitalization of traditional celebrations; and community-based cultural tourism initiatives.

Pillar 3: Enhance the Competitiveness of Strategic Urban Clusters

Sector-specific measures are required to enhance competitiveness and to accelerate growth and job creation in the cultural tourism, handicraft production, and agroprocessing clusters. Although adequate infrastructure and services are necessary for local economic development, in most cases they are insufficient and need to be complemented by sector-specific initiatives and interventions to strengthen cluster competitiveness. Interventions should be identified and prioritized through a coordinated effort among central agencies, local authorities, and the private sector. This section proposes a number of broad areas of strategic interventions for each cluster, with the objective of exemplifying how a successful partnership between the public and private sectors can be developed in support of local economic development and stimulating discussion on how to unlock the growth potential of urban clusters.

Promote Sustainable and Responsible Cultural Tourism Activities

Cultural tourism has great potential for driving economic growth and job creation in urban areas, but its growth needs to be sustainably managed. The sustainable and environmentally responsible development of cultural tourism rests on the effective conservation and valorization of cities' cultural assets, the capacity of local governments to plan and provide adequate infrastructure and services, and reliable connective infrastructure. In addition to these fundamental building blocks for tourism development, a number of sector-specific interventions are required to support private tourism initiatives and investments based on a partnership between private and public stakeholders. Priority actions include the following:

- *Improve and diversify tourism products in the Kathmandu Valley that respect local traditions.* The Kathmandu Valley's existing cultural tourism products need to be upgraded and better managed, and the flow of tourists to destinations within the UNESCO Kathmandu Valley World Heritage site needs to be coordinated to avoid overcrowding. This effort would require (a) expanding and diversifying the offer of tourism products to cater to a wider range of markets for cultural tourism in the valley—from potential high-end cultural heritage tourism (such as Bhaktapur and Lalitpur) to mass cultural tourism (such as Kathmandu's Durbar Square and pilgrimage sites); (b) increasing and focusing tourism product offerings around local festivals (for example, festival photography tours); and (c) developing innovative, environmentally sustainable tourism products in the outskirts of the Kathmandu Valley, such as hill station and village tourism (for example, the villages of Bungamati, Dhulikhel, Khokana, Panauti, and Sankhu) that feature nearby rural alternatives that are more peaceful than bustling Kathmandu, and developing experiential and spiritual tourism. In upgrading existing tourism products and developing new products, increasing the links between tourism and supplier industries (for example, agriculture and food, construction, and handicrafts) will support the development of the local economy and help alleviate poverty.

- *Develop tourism strategies and plans for heritage cities to enhance their market positioning.* The Kathmandu Valley and other heritage cities, such as Pokhara, must create a tourism brand whose value attracts a much wider clientele than at present. Although the Indian market will remain the most important numerical or volume market for Nepal, efforts must be made to genuinely research the needs of Nepal's other large neighbor, China, so that products can be developed to capitalize on the anticipated significant outbound tourism growth from that market. Selected long-haul markets must also be targeted; priority must be given to those segments that are likely to give the best returns in spending and length of stay, and thus added value and job creation for the economy. Telling the story of Nepalese culture serves both to attract international tourists and to reaffirm local values and identity.

- *Improve human resource capacity in the tourism sector.* Human resource skills for the tourism sector need improvement. This effort can be accomplished by (a) expanding and improving skill enhancement and vocational training programs for tourism workers and guides for the PMZs—especially in anticipation of the rapid growth of Chinese tourists and the need for language skills—and (b) developing alternative career paths in tourism that will provide a range of local employment and entrepreneurial opportunities and that will help reduce the exodus of Nepalese talent. Tourism training programs need to be innovative: on the one hand, helping tourism workers and guides better understand and relate to international visitors' needs and customs; and on the other hand, developing a sense of pride and value among Nepalese youth for their own unique culture. A systemic approach to training would aim at integrating private training institutions into the formal training system through the development of appropriate policies, curricula, examination and certification procedures, and so forth. By doing so, the number of available vocational training courses is expected to increase, as is their quality.

- *Strengthen the municipal capacity to partner with the private sector to promote sustainable tourism activities*, such as the adaptive reuse of heritage buildings. Local governments can promote a range of tourist activities and reinvest the revenue streams for heritage conservation. They can, for example, create heritage and special-interest walking trails (emphasizing both tangible and intangible heritage); promote museums as focal points for educational opportunities and tourist interests; develop maps, brochures, and historic building identification signs; support traditional homestay products; and promote performing arts events in traditional courtyards and buildings. Local governments should also encourage the use of traditional architectural design in any new buildings constructed in the buffer zones of the World Heritage site. Rehabilitated heritage buildings belonging to the private *guthis* can, for example, be repurposed into income-generating touristic ventures, such as homestay initiatives. Technical support and monetary incentives for adaptive reuse could include a demand-driven and competitive matching grant for adaptive reuse of traditional buildings, support for business planning for new commercial ventures, tool kits for planning and designing the retrofit of traditional buildings for modern use, and an architectural award program for best practice.

Support the Modernization of the Handicraft Sector

A market-led strategy needs to be developed to support the modernization of the handicraft industry, while preserving the industry's authenticity and links with local traditions. The growth of handicraft production and its contribution to the well-being of all social groups, including the most disadvantaged, will depend on the capacity of urban local governments to work with central agencies, local communities, and the private sector to modernize the sector. Urban local governments need to create a favorable and inclusive environment for artisans to carry out their activities and to pass on their skills and their businesses to future generations. Actions include the following:

- *Promote market research for handicraft product innovation and commercialization.* Central and local governments can play an important role in supporting the modernization of the sector by (a) strengthening the capacity of the Federation of Handicraft Associations to conduct market research and to innovate and identify new products that are strongly linked to demand in export and tourist markets, and (b) establishing a centrally located design bank with a pool of local and international designers with the objective of modernizing existing designs and increasing product quality in line with international demand, and making designs and new product ideas available to registered artisans and product clusters.

- *Develop a pilot public-private partnership program to support strategic handicraft product clusters.* The integrated cluster approach would strengthen the capacity of the local authorities to act as cluster facilitators, while addressing broken links along the value chain. As a first step, handicraft products for local and export markets need to be prioritized, based on their commercialization potential and Nepal's comparative advantage, including the availability of raw materials and the ability to scale up production. This step will allow the identification of a few strategic products for the pilot cluster support program. The program of support would cover the entire supply chain, from the raw materials to retail markets. Particular attention would need to be paid to (a) improving distribution channels by establishing a handicraft bazaar and handicraft outlets and by marketing them as tourist destinations; (b) preparing a marketing strategy for the development of high-value traditional products linked to specific places and production areas and creating a "network" of handicraft production centers for joint marketing and promotional events; and (c) developing a two-tiered production approach based on high quality and traditional methods for high-end products and industrial production for the export market.

- *Promote initiatives in support of artisan communities to enhance their skills and facilitate access to the market*, through training and microfinance programs. Individual artisans and communities need flexible and customized support to regularly enhance their skills, pass on their skills to new generations, and gain access to the distribution channels. A number of initiatives can be formulated to support artisan communities in these areas, such as (a) training to improve technical know-how and the use of modern tools and techniques, (b) the provision of attractive microfinance options, (c) programs to engage communities along the entire handicraft value chain (for example, raw material production, packaging, and marketing), and (d) the promotion of direct sales opportunities to visitors to limit leakages to middlemen.

Improve Agroprocessing Competitiveness

Urban local governments have an important role to play in improving the competitiveness of the agroprocessing sector. In coordination with business associations and central agencies, urban local governments can provide the market infrastructure together with the cluster support that is necessary to expand the agroprocessing sector from the current small-scale operation to industrial production and to support the growth of ancillary industries. Priority actions include the following:

- *Develop and upgrade market infrastructure in strategic locations.* Market yards need to provide physical facilities for trading and storing commodities. Because the location of market infrastructure is critical to success, local governments must set up market yards in close collaboration with the trading community. Traders should be incentivized to share the cost of establishing the market yards, including investing in the purchase of land. Agricultural production pocket areas need to be linked to the vehicle access road heads to reduce transportation costs and facilitate access to markets. The increasing production of high-value perishable commodities also requires a substantially different form of market infrastructure. The introduction of cold-storage technology is particularly important for perishable produce.

Urban Growth and Spatial Transition in Nepal • http://dx.doi.org/10.1596/978-0-8213-9659-9

• *Strengthen agroprocessing cluster support through public-private partnership arrangements.* Local governments can play a catalytic role in providing and coordinating cluster support to the currently highly fragmented agroprocessing business in partnership with business membership organizations. A number of initiatives can be promoted by business organizations, together with local governments, to improve productivity and competitiveness, such as (a) establishing cooperatives, (b) promoting and monitoring quality upgrades to international standards, (c) providing harvesting and packaging technological support, (d) enhancing information flows, and (e) developing training programs. In strategic sectors such as medicinal and aromatic plants, establishing and strengthening an apex body at the national level is also recommended to formulate policies for the overall development of the sector.

• *Launch an action plan to improve production technology and commercialization to increase value addition.* To increase value addition, agroproduction activities need to shift from small-scale operations to industrial production. Activities need to (a) strategically focus on products that are in high demand in international markets; (b) improve the survival of shipments, given Nepal's rugged terrain; and (c) capture seasonal market niches. This effort would require supporting market research and microcredit schemes to promote innovation and production technology upgrades (for example, the introduction of community-based microirrigation systems), while improving the marketing and branding strategy, expanding distribution channels, and building stronger ties with international buyers.

Note

1. Unless otherwise stated, Kathmandu refers to Kathmandu Metropolitan City; Biratnagar, Birgunj, Lalitpur, and Pokhara refer to the submetropolitan cities; and all other urban local governments are referred to as municipalities.

References

ADB (Asian Development Bank). 2010. "Nepal North South Fast Track Project. Review of Feasibility Study and Preliminary Engineering Reports." ADB, Manila.

CBS (Central Bureau of Statistics). 1996. *Nepal Living Standards Survey (1995/96).* Kathmandu: Government of Nepal.

———. 2011. *Nepal Living Standards Survey (2010/11).* Kathmandu: Government of Nepal.

World Bank. 2005. "Nepal: North-South Transport Corridor Options." Strategy Note, World Bank, Washington, DC.

———. 2011. *World Bank Indicators 2011.* Washington, DC: World Bank.

Population of Nepal's Urban Centers, 1991–2011

Urban center	Population			Population growth rate[a]	
	1991	2001	2011	1991–2001	2001–2011
Eastern Tarai					
Biratnagar	129,388	166,674	204,949	2.5	2.1
Dharan	66,457	95,332	119,915	3.6	2.3
Itahari[b]	26,824	41,210	76,869	4.3	6.2
Damak	41,321	35,009	75,743	−1.7	7.7
Mechinagar[b]	37,108	49,060	57,909	2.8	1.7
Rajbiraj	24,227	30,353	38,241	2.3	2.3
Lahan	19,018	27,654	33,927	3.7	2.0
Inaruwa	18,547	23,200	28,923	2.2	2.2
Siraha[b]	21,866	23,988	28,831	0.9	1.8
Bhadrapur	15,210	18,145	18,646	1.8	0.3
Eastern Hills					
Triyuga	37,512	55,291	71,405	3.9	2.6
Dhankuta	17,073	20,668	28,364	1.9	3.2
Ilam	13,197	16,237	19,427	2.1	1.8
Eastern Mountains					
Khandbari	18,756	21,789	26,658	1.5	2.0
Central Tarai					
Bharatpur	54,670	89,323	147,777	4.9	5.0
Birgunj	69,005	112,484	139,068	4.9	2.1
Janakpur	54,710	74,192	98,446	3.0	2.8
Ratnanagar[b]	25,118	37,791	46,607	4.1	2.1
Kalaiya	18,498	32,260	43,137	5.6	2.9
Gaur[b]	20,434	25,383	35,370	2.2	3.3
Malangawa	14,142	18,484	25,143	2.7	3.1
Jaleshwor	18,088	22,046	24,765	2.0	1.2

appendix continues next page

Appendix (continued)

Urban center	Population			Population growth rate[a]	
	1991	2001	2011	1991–2001	2001–2011
Central Hills					
Kathmandu	421,258	671,846	1,003,285	4.7	4.0
Lalitpur	115,865	162,991	226,728	3.4	3.3
Hetauda	53,836	68,482	85,653	2.4	2.2
Madhyapur Thimi[b]	31,970	47,751	84,142	4.0	5.7
Bhaktapur	61,405	72,543	83,658	1.7	1.4
Kirtipur[b]	31,338	40,835	67,171	2.6	5.0
Kamalamai[b]	24,368	32,838	41,117	3.0	2.2
Panauti[b]	20,467	25,563	28,312	2.2	1.0
Bidur	18,694	21,193	27,953	1.3	2.8
Banepa	12,537	15,822	24,894	2.3	4.5
Dhulikhel	9,812	11,521	16,263	1.6	3.4
Central Mountains					
Bhimeshwor[b]	19,261	21,916	23,337	1.3	0.6
Western Tarai					
Butwal	44,272	75,384	120,982	5.3	4.7
Siddarthnagar	39,473	52,569	64,566	2.9	2.1
Kapilvastu	17,126	27,170	30,890	4.6	1.3
Ramgram[b]	18,911	22,630	28,973	1.8	2.5
Western Hills					
Pokhara	95,286	156,312	264,991	4.9	5.3
Lekhnath[b]	30,107	41,369	59,498	3.2	3.6
Byas[b]	20,124	28,245	43,615	3.4	4.3
Gorkha[c]	20,633	25,783	33,865	2.2	2.7
Putalibazar[b]	25,870	29,667	31,338	1.4	0.5
Tansen	13,599	20,431	31,161	4.1	4.2
Baglung[b]	15,219	20,852	30,763	3.1	3.9
Waling[b]	16,712	20,414	24,199	2.0	1.7
Midwestern Tarai					
Nepalgunj	47,819	57,535	73,779	1.8	2.5
Ghorahi[d]	29,050	43,126	65,107	4.0	4.1
Gulariya[b]	30,631	46,011	57,232	4.1	2.2
Tulsipur[b]	22,654	33,876	52,224	4.0	4.3
Midwestern Hills					
Birendranagar	22,973	31,381	52,137	3.1	5.1
Narayan[b]	15,738	19,446	21,995	2.1	1.2
Far Western Tarai					
Bhimdatta[e]	62,050	80,839	106,666	2.6	2.8
Dhangadhi	44,753	67,447	104,047	4.1	4.3
Tikapur[b]	25,639	38,722	56,983	4.1	3.9

appendix continues next page

Appendix *(continued)*

Urban center	Population			Population growth rate[a]	
	1991	*2001*	*2011*	*1991–2001*	*2001–2011*
Far Western Hills					
Dipayal Silgadi	12,360	22,061	26,508	5.8	1.8
Amargadhi	16,454	18,390	22,241	1.1	1.9
Dasharathchanda[b]	18,054	18,345	17,427	0.2	−0.5
Total	1,695,719	3,227,879	4,523,820	6.4	3.4

Sources: CBS 1991, 2001, and 2012.
Note: Kathmandu refers to Kathmandu Metropolitan City; Biratnagar, Birgunj, Lalitpur, and Pokhara refer to the submetropolitan cities; and all other urban local governments are municipalities.
a. Annual exponential growth rates. Reclassification (conversion of rural areas into urban areas) included.
b. Municipalities declared after the 1991 census.
c. Prithbinarayan.
d. Tribhuwannagar.
e. Mahandranagar.

References

CBS (Central Bureau of Statistics). 1991. *National Population Census 1991.* Kathmandu: Government of Nepal.

———. 2001. *National Population Census 2001.* Kathmandu: Government of Nepal.

———. 2012. *National Population and Housing Census 2011.* Kathmandu: Government of Nepal.

Environmental Benefits Statement

The World Bank is committed to reducing its environmental footprint. In support of this commitment, the Office of the Publisher leverages electronic publishing options and print-on-demand technology, which is located in regional hubs worldwide. Together, these initiatives enable print runs to be lowered and shipping distances decreased, resulting in reduced paper consumption, chemical use, greenhouse gas emissions, and waste.

The Office of the Publisher follows the recommended standards for paper use set by the Green Press Initiative. Whenever possible, books are printed on 50% to 100% postconsumer recycled paper, and at least 50% of the fiber in our book paper is either unbleached or bleached using Totally Chlorine Free (TCF), Processed Chlorine Free (PCF), or Enhanced Elemental Chlorine Free (EECF) processes.

More information about the Bank's environmental philosophy can be found at http://crinfo.worldbank.org/crinfo/environmental_responsibility/index.html.

green press
INITIATIVE

www.ingramcontent.com/pod-product-compliance
Lightning Source LLC
Chambersburg PA
CBHW080614270326
41928CB00016B/3062